I0822215

TRAGEDY AND COMEDY FROM DANTE TO PSEUDO-DANTE

By the Same Author

The Devil, Demonology, and Witchcraft
Doubleday 1968; ed. 2, 1974 (repr. Wipf and Stock 2004)
Divine Providence in the England of Shakespeare's Histories
Harvard, 1970 (repr. Wipf and Stock, 2004)
Love and Marriage in the Age of Chaucer
Cornell, 1975 (repr. Wipf and Stock, 2004)
"Aristotle-Averroes-Alemannus on Tragedy: The Influence of the *Poetics* on the Latin Middle Ages"
Viator 10 (1979) 161-209
"The Varieties of Love in Medieval Literature According to Gaston Paris"
Romance Philology 40 (1986-87) 301-27
Ideas and Forms of Tragedy from Aristotle to the Middle Ages
Cambridge, 1993
"*Cangrande* and the Ortho-Dantists"
Lectura Dantis nos. 14-15 (1994) 61-95
"Reply to Robert Hollander"
Lectura Dantis no. 14-15 (1994) 111-15.
Chaucerian Tragedy
Brewer, 1997 (paperback 2000)

Tragedy and Comedy from Dante to Pseudo-Dante

Henry Ansgar Kelly

Wipf and Stock Publishers
199 West 8th Avenue, Suite 3
Eugene, Oregon 97401

Tragedy and Comedy from Dante to Pseudo-Dante
By Kelly, Henry A.

ISBN: 1-59244-521-7
Publication date 1/30/2004
Previously published by University of California Press, 1989

Addenda:

For a summary of the conclusions in this book, see my *Ideas and Forms of Tragedy from Aristotle to the Middle Ages* (Cambridge University Press, 1993), pp. 144-57: "Dante and His Commentators." On pp. 145-46, I analyze Dante's lyric poem, *Donne ch'avete intelletto d'amore*, as a tragedy (see below, p. 3 nn. 11-12).

In "*Cangrande* and the Ortho-Dantists," *Lectura Dantis* 14-15 (1994), 61-95, I address Robert Hollander's reactions to *Tragedy and Comedy* in his book, *Dante's Epistle to Cangrande* (University of Michigan, 1993). Hollander responds on pp. 97-110, and my reply is on pp. 111-15.

p. 48 n. 20: Add: Cf. 3 Benvenuto 1:16, where he objects to people saying that the matter of Vergil is tragedy, the matter of Horace is satire, and the matter of Ovid is comedy: "Nec dicas, ut aliqui dixerunt, quod materia libri sit comedia; nam comedia est stylus, non materia. Unde sicut inconvenienter dicitur, materia Vergilii est tragedia, Horatii satyra, et Ovidii comedia, ita est in proposito."

p. 79: For a clearer method of analyzing cadences, see my article, "*Cangrande* and the Ortho-Dantists," *Lectura Dantis* 14-15 (1994) 61-95, p. 67. Here are the seven authentic "Dantean cadences":

Velox:

V^1 ...óoo ooóo (e.g., *dénique recomméndo*)

V^2 ...óoo o oóo (e.g., *doctíssimum et amícum*)

V^3 ...óoo òo óo (e.g., *magnália vèstra vídi*)

Planus:

P^1 ...óo oóo (e.g., *fuísse constábit*)

P^2 ...óo o óo (e.g., *sectári non décet*)

Tardus:

T^1 ...óo oóoo (e.g., *segregáta percénsui*)

T^2 ...óo o óoo (e.g., *símul et tétigi*)

p. 103 par. [4]: Enzo Cecchini's edition of the *Epistola a Cangrande* (Florence 1995) modifies the text of paragraph 4. I analyze these modifications in my "Reply to Robert Hollander," *Lectura Dantis* 14-15 (1994) 113.

Corrigenda:

p. 1 n. 2 line 2 up (and p. 113): for "G. V. Alessio" read "G. C. Alessio"
p. 7 n. 27 line 5 up: for "uiatrious" read "uiatorius"
p. 24 n. 24 line 2 up: for "cioè" read "cioè che è"
p. 36 line 2: for "finen" read "finem"
p. 38 n. 10: for "22.64-65" read "22.62, 23.64-65"
p. 40 n. 18 line 6: for "his est" read "hic est"
p. 48 par. 2 line 4: for "notes of" read "notes recopied a century later by"
p. 54 par. 2 line 1: for "Ricaldone" read "the student whom Ricaldone copied"
p. 55 par. 2 line 1: for "Ricaldone" read "the Ricaldone text"
p. 57 n. 55 line 1: for "interpretarsi" read "interpetrasi"
p. 64 n. 16: the quoted statement is found only in Toynbee's Appendix C, not in his 1918 article.
p. 103 par. [4] line 2: for "pius" read "plus"
p. 104 par. [6] line 4: for "premittendium" read "premittendum"

In memoriam
Morton W. Bloomfield
praeceptoris et amici

Et signifer sanctus Michael repraesentet eum
in lucem sanctam, quam olim Abrahae
promisisti et semini eius

Contents

Abbreviations

DVE	Dante, *De vulgari eloquentia*
ED	*Enciclopedia dantesca*, 6 vols. (Rome 1970–78)
GSLI	*Giornale storico della letteratura italiana*
IMU	*Italia medioevale e umanistica*
PL	Patrologia latina
SD	*Studi danteschi*

Preface

The focal point of this study is Dante's characterization of his great poem as a comedy and the puzzlement that this designation caused his admirers in the fourteenth century. I have come to this subject through my researches into the various meanings of *tragedia* in the Middle Ages, which are often linked to understandings of *comedia*. I believe that Dante and his commentators deserve a separate study because of the quantity of primary sources and the complexity of the questions involved, and I have turned away from my general history to undertake the task.

My object is to set out Dante's own ideas about tragedy and comedy, so far as they can be gathered from his authentic writings, and then to give a chronological survey of the ideas of each of the commentators. To accomplish this object, it is necessary to decide whether the *Epistle to Cangrande* is an authentic work of Dante and, if it is not, to date it and deal with it in its proper chronological sequence.

The earliest reference to *Cangrande* as a letter by Dante occurs in Filippo Villani's commentary at the end of the fourteenth century. Its authenticity has frequently been questioned on grounds of content and style. I find most of the arguments against Dante's authorship to be convincing and in keeping with my own conclusions about the differences between Dante's recognized writings and *Cangrande* on the specific questions of tragedy and comedy. But since the primary purpose of this study is not to reargue the case for or against the spuriousness of *Cangrande*, I will simply refer to the arguments made by other scholars against Dante's authorship; they are well summed up, along with arguments for Dante as author, by Giorgio Brugnoli in his recent edition of *Cangrande* (Dante, *Opere minori*, vol. 2 [Milan: Ricciardi, 1979], pp. 512–21, 598–643); and I will exclude *Cangrande* from consideration in my first chapter, where I deal with Dante's genuine ideas.

In my second chapter, however, when I come to the question of dating *Cangrande* as a non-Dantean commentary, I will give further arguments of my own for its spuriousness, since I place part of it at mid-century and attribute the assemblage of the work in its final form to a "Compiler," designated also as "Pseudo-Dante," at the end of the century.

I trust that even those who are not convinced by any arguments against Dante's authorship of *Cangrande* will be able to gather some fruit from my analyses of the doctrines of all of the commentaries, including *Cangrande*, while reattributing *Cangrande*'s positions to Dante.

Let me say a word about the Latin texts that I cite in the course of my discussions. I give all manuscript texts exactly as they appear, except for silently expanding standard contractions and abbreviations. I give texts from medieval-spelling editions as they are to be found there, except that where necessary I regularize *u* and *v* to modern usage and change *j* to *i*. I also change scribal *ct* to *tt* and *x* to *s* when appropriate. For texts taken from classicized editions, I use the medieval spelling of *e* for the archaic diphthongs *ae* and *oe*. When referring to Dante's works, I use the medieval Italian or Latin titles or modern English equivalents rather than modern Italian forms: thus, *Comedia* or *Comedy* rather than *Commedia*, *Vita nova* rather than *Vita nuova*.

I have been assisted by the advice of many colleagues, especially Giuseppe Billanovich, Giorgio Brugnoli, Dennis Dutschke, Ricardo Quinones, Giorgio Varanini, Giuseppe Velli, and Tibor Wlassics; the last-named, as editor of *Lectura Dantis*, arranged for the preprinting of Chapter 2 in the second number (Spring 1988) of that journal. Though not all of these scholars agree with my major conclusions about authorship, chronology, and interpretation, they have all given most generously of their help, and I am very grateful. I also wish to thank the Friends of English (UCLA) and the UCLA Center for Medieval and Renaissance Studies for supporting the publication of this study.

1

The Authentic Dante

Dante clearly considered the ideas of tragedy and comedy to be very important. Tragedy is the main focus of the finished portion of the *De vulgari eloquentia*, and comedy was to be the subject of the fourth book of that work. Furthermore, he endowed his poetic masterwork with the title of *Comedy*, or at least considered it to be a comedy. It is essential, then, that we look systematically at the evidence to see what meanings he attached to the terms.

Dante was a man of great learning, but his learning had certain limitations. He largely missed out on the beginnings of the Florentine classical revival; and there is little evidence that he benefited from the learning of the Paduan prehumanists (though many scholars feel that there is no reason why he should *not* have so benefited). When Dante speaks in the *Convivio* of "the ancient writing of Latin comedies and tragedies that cannot change,"[1] he does not seem to be referring to the comedies of Terence or Plautus and the tragedies of Seneca. In the case of Terence, Dante would not have had to wait for a classical renascence, for the text was readily available in his day; but there is no indication that Dante knew him more than by name.[2] As for Seneca, Giorgio Brugnoli has thrown into

1. Dante, *Convivio* 1.5.8, ed. G. Busnelli and G. Vandelli, 2d ed.: ed. Antonio Enzo Quaglio, 2 vols. (Florence 1964), 1:33: "Onde vedemo ne le scritture antiche de le comedie e tragedie latine, che non si possono transmutare, quello medesimo che oggi avemo; che non avviene del volgare, lo quale a piacimento artificiato si transmuta."

2. Giorgio Brugnoli, notes to his edition of *Cangrande*, in *Opere minori*, vol. 2, ed. P.V. Mengaldo et al. (Florence 1979), pp. 512–21, 598–643, esp. 618. (This edition was obviously much delayed: Brugnoli's preface is dated 1973, and he refers to no work dated later than 1969.) Claudia Villa, *La lectura Terentii*, vol. 1: *Da Ildemaro a Francesco Petrarca*, Studi sul Petrarca 17 (Padua 1984), notes that out of the seven hundred glossed Terence manuscripts she has studied, more than one hundred antedate the fourteenth century (p. 171). In chapter 5, "La tradizione toscana da Dante al Petrarca" (pp. 137–89), which is an expanded version of "Un'ipotesi per l'*Epistola a Cangrande*," *IMU* 24 (1981) 18–63, Villa assumes that Dante wrote *Cangrande* (see p. 140 n. 6), and suggests that some of its doctrines may have come from a Terence commentary (pp. 186–87). But the parallels that she adduces between the commentaries and *Cangrande*, and especially between the commentaries and Dante's undisputed works, are not convincing. For instance, on pp. 152–53, she cites the accessus *Novem requiruntur*, ed. G.V. Alessio, "Hec Franciscus de Buiti," *IMU* 24 (1981) 64–122, pp. 94–101, on the Donatian aspects of comedy: "in primis

doubt all the evidence put forward for Dante's use of the tragedies.[3] Rather, to judge from the *De vulgari eloquentia*, Dante takes "comedies" and "tragedies" to mean nondramatic works written in certain styles about appropriate subjects.

Dante followed a stylistic paradigm named after three related types of literature. The most common such paradigm was that of tragedy, satire, and comedy, which is found in an early form in a twelfth-century commentary on the *Rhetorica ad Herennium*.[4] In addition to later authors who adopted it (including Benvenuto da Imola), the Paduan scholar Guizzardo da Bologna, who wrote the commentary on Albertino Mussato's tragedy *Ecerinis*, used it in his commentary on the *Poetria nova* of Geoffrey of Vinsauf.[5] Dante, however, used the triad of tragedy, comedy, and elegy.

The immediate source of Dante's paradigm is not known. That it was not his own invention is indicated by its appearance in another author unconnected with Dante—namely, the priest Jean de Herent, writing in 1349. Herent gives this gloss to a line in Everard Alemannus's *Laborynthus*:

> Elegy is the description [composition] of poems dealing with miseries, and it is written in pentameters and hexameters. Comedy is a second manner of writing, and it is the description of poems about banquets. Tragedy is the third manner, it being the description of poems about the deeds of kings, like Alexander.[6]

Dante's explanation is much different and runs as follows: "By tragedy we mean a superior style, by comedy an inferior, and by elegy we understand the style of

---

pericula, in fine vero leti exitus actionum" (p. 99, no. 54), which she compares with Huguccio's "Comedia a tristibus incipit sed cum letis desinit," *Cangrande*'s "Comedia vero inchoat asperitatem alicuius rei, sed eius materia prospere terminatur" (10.29), and Dante's "selva selvaggia e aspra e forte" (*Inferno* 1.5). In light of the explanation that I give below, I speculate instead that Dante's "aspra" inspired Guido da Pisa's "asperitas," which in turn was taken over by *Cangrande*.

3. Brugnoli, *Cangrande*, pp. 617–19; idem, "Ut patet per Senecam in suis tragediis," *Rivista di cultura classica e medioevale* 5 (1963) 146–63; idem, "Dante *Inf.* 30.13 sgg.," *L'Alighieri* 7 (1966) 98–99; idem, *Per suo richiamo* (Pisa 1981), pp. 90–94.

4. See Harry Caplan, "A Mediaeval Commentary on the *Rhetorica ad Herennium*," in Caplan's *Of Eloquence*, ed. Anne King and Helen North (Ithaca, N.Y., 1970), pp. 247–70. The relevant passage is given by Franz Quadlbauer, *Die antike Theorie der Genera dicendi im lateinischen Mittelalter* (Vienna 1962), pp. 150–51, 172–74; by Pier Vincenzo Mengaldo, "L'elegia 'umile' (*DVE* 2,4,5–6)," a 1966 essay, revised for Mengaldo's collection, *Linguistica e retorica di Dante* (Pisa 1978), pp. 200–22, esp. 206–7; and by Luis Jenaro-MacLennan, " 'Remissus est modus et humilis' (*Epistle to Cangrande*, § 10)," *Lettere italiane* 31 (1979) 406–18, esp. 411–12.

5. Guizzardo da Bologna, *Recollecte super Poetria magistri Gualfredi*, Vatican MS Ottob. lat. 3291, fols. 1–17, esp. 15v; text quoted in H.A. Kelly, "Aristotle-Averroes-Alemannus on Tragedy: The Influence of the *Poetics* on the Latin Middle Ages," *Viator* 10 (1979) 161–209, on p. 195 n. 155: tragedy and satire are higher, graver, and serious styles, comedy light. On Guizzardo as the sole author of the accessus to the commentary on *Ecerinis*, see ibid., p. 193 n. 150.

6. Jean de Herent, gloss to *Laborintus*, line 5, ed. Edmond Faral, *Les arts poétiques du xiie et du xiiie siècles* (Paris 1924), p. 337: "Elegia est descriptio carminum tractantium de miseriis, et versu pentametro et exametro scribitur. Comedia est secundus modus scribendi, et est descriptio carminum de conviviis. Tragedia est tertius modus, et est descriptio carminum de gestibus regum, ut in Alexandro." For Herent, see Faral, p. 39.

the miserable."[7] In the vernacular, he says, one writes tragically by using the *vulgaris illustris*; comically by using now the *mediocris*, now the *humilis*; and elegiacally by using only the *humilis*.[8] Tragic style is attained when the most superb verse forms, elevated construction, and excellence of vocabulary are joined harmoniously with gravity of substance (*sententia*).[9] Thus, only the highest subjects—love, virtue, and self-defense (or the proper use of arms)—are appropriate for the tragic style, and these subjects must not be demeaned by any additional element (*accidens*).[10]

When the hendecasyllabic meter is used in a tragic combination, the poem is called a *cantio*, whereas when it is used in a comic combination it is a *cantilena*.[11] When one tries to write tragically, the hendecasyllabic line is the best.[12] Heptasyllabic lines are also allowable for the tragic, so long as the hendecasyllabic lines dominate and begin the stanzas, though Dante has noticed that some poets have written tragically when beginning with a heptasyllabic; however, he adds, if one wishes to assess the sense of these pieces carefully, it will be apparent that the tragedy here has progressed not without a shade of elegy.[13] As for

7. Dante, *DVE* 2.4.5: "Per tragediam superiorem stilum inducimus, per comediam inferiorem; per elegiam stilum intelligimus miserorum." I use P. V. Mengaldo's edition in *Opere minori* 2 (Milan 1979), pp. 1–237, this passage being on p. 164. Mengaldo's introductory matter is dated 1973 (p. 25).

8. *DVE* 2.4.6: "Si tragice canenda videntur, tunc assumendum est vulgare illustre, et per consequens cantionem ligare. Si vero comice, tunc quandoque mediocre, quandoque humile vulgare sumatur: et huius discretionem in quarto huius reservamus ostendere. Si autem elegiace, solum humile oportet nos sumere."

9. *DVE* 2.4.7: "Sed ommittamus alios, et nunc, ut conveniens est, de stilo tragico pertractemus. Stilo equidem tragico tunc uti videmur quando cum gravitate sententie tam superbia carminum quam constructionis elatio et excellentia vocabulorum concordat."

10. *DVE* 2.4.8: "Quare, si bene recolimus summa summis esse digna iam fuisse probatum, et iste quem tragicum appellamus summus videtur esse stilorum, illa que summe canenda distinximus isto solo sunt stilo canenda: videlicet salus, amor, et virtus, et que propter ea concipimus, dum nullo accidente vilescant." Cf. 2.2.6–8 for the three great subjects.

11. *DVE* 2.8.8: "Dicimus ergo quod cantio, in quantum per superexcellentiam dicitur, ut et nos querimus, est equalium stantiarum sine responsorio ad unam sententiam tragica coniugatio, ut nos ostendimus cum dicimus *Donne che avete intelletto d'amore* [*Vita nova* 19]. Quod autem dicimus 'tragica coniugatio' est quia, cum comice fiat hec coniugatio, cantilenam vocamus per diminutionem: de qua in quarto huius tractare intendimus." The second sentence is thought to have been added later by Dante, since it appears out of place (at the end of the chapter) in the manuscripts. See Mengaldo, "L'elegia," pp. 221–22 n. 48, for a discussion of Dante's meaning in this passage.

12. *DVE* 2.12.3: "Horum prorsus, cum tragice poetari conamur, endecasillabum propter quandam excellentiam in contextu vincendi privilegium promeretur." He goes on to cite his *Donne ch'avete* again.

13. *DVE* 2.12.5–6: "Et sicut quedam stantia est uno solo eptasillabo conformata, sic duobus, tribus, quatuor, quinque videtur posse contexi, dummodo in tragico vincat endecasillabum et principiet. Verumtamen quosdam ab eptasillabo tragice principiasse invenimus, videlicet [Guidonem Guinizelli], Guidonem de Ghisileriis, et Fabrutium bononienses: *Di fermo sofferire*, et *Donna, lo fermo core*, et *Lo meo lontano gire*, et quosdam alios. Sed si ad eorum sensum subtiliter intrare velimus, non sine quodam elegie umbraculo hec tragedia processisse videbitur."

pentasyllabic lines, one or at most two per stanza are allowable in great writing (*magnum dictamen*).[14] A self-standing trisyllabic line, it seems, cannot be used for the tragic.[15] Finally, tragedy uses a mixture of rough and smooth rhyme.[16]

Perhaps the most puzzling point of this strange discussion of literary genres is Dante's remark about the tragic poems whose *sensus* reveals that they have been somewhat overshadowed by elegy. The statement has been interpreted to mean that Dante is referring to content. If so, since elegy is the style of the miserable, he would seem to be excluding love laments from the tragic style.[17] But such a reading does not fit the context, which is one of form, not content. Dante is speaking of poets who have used a stanza form that is just on the borderline of acceptability for tragic writing. He can hardly mean that the poets who take such a risk always slightly debase their subject matter, as if bad form invariably stimulates bad content. Rather, he must mean that the form itself shades into the form appropriate for elegy.

As far as content is concerned, Dante is clear about the noble subjects of tragedy, and we can infer that the subject of elegy concerns lamentation. On the subject matter of comedy, however, we must draw our own conclusions from the vast panorama of the work that he later called a comedy. Dante twice refers to the *Inferno* as a comedy,[18] and in the second case it is in obvious contrast to the *Aeneid*, which Vergil designates as an *alta tragedia*.[19] In using these terms here, it may be that Dante was reflecting the doctrine of the *De vulgari eloquentia* only to the extent of considering comedy a style inferior to that of tragedy, and that he was humbly classifying his poem as such in comparison to Vergil's great work. He offers no more on the nature of comedy or tragedy in the *Purgatorio*, but in the *Paradiso* he confesses at one point that he is defeated more than any other comic or tragedic poet.[20] This would seem to indicate that both kinds of

---

14. *DVE* 2.12.7: "De pentasillabo quoque non sic concedimus: in dictamine magno sufficit enim unicum pentasillabum in tota stantia conseri, vel duo ad plus [in pedibus]—et dico 'pedibus' propter necessitatem qua pedibus, versibusque, cantatur."

15. *DVE* 2.12.8: "Minime autem trisillabum in tragico videtur esse sumendum per se subsistens."

16. *DVE* 2.13.13: "Lenium asperorumque rithimorum mixtura ipsa tragedia nitescit."

17. So Enrico Fenzi, "Boezio e Jean de Meun, Filosofia e Ragione nelle rime allegoriche di Dante," *Studi di filologia e letteratura* 2-3 (Genoa 1975) 9-69, esp. 63-68.

18. *Inferno* 16.127-28:

> Ma qui tacer nol posso, e per le note
> di questa comedia, lettor, ti giuro . . .

and 21.1-2:

> Così di ponte in ponte altro parlando
> che la mia comedia cantar non cura . . .

19. *Inferno* 20.112-13:

> Euripilo ebbe nome, e così 'l canta
> l'alta mia tragedia in alcun loco.

20. *Paradiso* 30.22-24:

> Da questo passo vinto me concedo
> più che già mai da punto di suo tema
> soprato fosse comico o tragedo.

poets can deal with sublime subjects, and, of course, this conclusion is borne out by the content of *Paradiso*.

Dante touches on the question of genre in only one other place, when putting into the mouth of Giovanni del Vergilio the supercilious characterization of the language of Dante's masterwork as *comica verba*, the speech of women.[21] The fact that the *Epistle to Cangrande* makes this point seriously, saying that the style of the *Comedy* is lowly and humble because it is in the vernacular tongue of women, has been taken as evidence that the author did not know the *De vulgari eloquentia*.[22]

P. V. Mengaldo has revived A. Marigo's theory that Dante's threefold paradigm was based on John of Garland's *Parisiana poetria*. Garland defines elegy as dealing with the misery of love and as sometimes being joined with the

---

21. *Eclogue* 1.52–54:

Comica nonne vides ipsum reprehendere verba,
tum quia femineo resonant ut trita labello,
tum quia Castalias pudet acceptare sorores?

The text of the *Eclogues* was transmitted by Boccaccio, who glosses *comica* as "vulgaria" (see below, p. 47). See the edition, *Le egloghe*, by Giorgio Brugnoli and Riccardo Scarcia (Milan 1980) and Brugnoli's discussion on pp. 44–45.

22. *Cangrande* 10.31: "Ad modum loquendi, remissus est modus et humilis, quia locutio vulgaris in qua et muliercule comunicant." See Brugnoli's commentary, pp. 620–22. One line of defense taken by those who defend Dante's authorship of *Cangrande* is to deny that the letter identifies the vernacular with low style. See Amilcare A. Iannucci, "Dante's Theory of Genres and the *Divina commedia*," *Dante Studies* 91 (1973) 1–25, esp. 4 and 22–23 n. 9. Often the denial is entirely tacit, as with Rocco Montano, *Lo spirito e le lettere: Disegno storico della letteratura italiana* (Milan 1970), 1: 174: Dante had to use the *stilo comico* rather than the *stilo tragico* or *volgare illustre* for *Inferno*; but when he wrote *Paradiso* (which Montano presumably believes to be in the *stilo tragico*), he continued to call the poem a comedy because of its happy end (as specified in *Cangrande*).

Other defenders of Dante's authorship of *Cangrande* accept the identification of the vernacular with low style: for instance, Natalino Sapegno, *Storia letteraria del Trecento* (Milan 1963), p. 139 n. 1, and, in more detail, Robert Hollander, "Tragedia nella *Commedia*" (TC), in *Il Virgilio dantesco* (Florence 1983), pp. 117–54. The text of Hollander's essay, somewhat shortened and without the notes, appears in English as "Tragedy in Dante's *Comedy*" (TDC), *Sewanee Review* 91 (1983) 240–60. His arguments are given in briefer form in "The Tragedy of Divination in *Inferno* 20" (TDI) in his *Studies in Dante* (Ravenna 1980), pp. 131–218, esp. 214–17. To sum up, Hollander believes that when Dante turned from lyric to narrative poetry, his priorities changed from style to plot. Since the plot of the *Comedy* is comic, it may *properly* employ only the low style (TC 118, TDC 241), or, as he puts it, "Given the poem's comic plot, Dante's choice of vernacular over Latin makes the style of the *Comedy* 'low' " (TDC 243, cf. TC 121). He believes that "Dante is revenging himself upon the younger and more proudly classicizing self who found true poetic value limited to the high style" (TDI 215). But Dante also allowed himself occasional use of the high style in the *Comedy*, as licensed by Horace (TC 120, TDC 242). "Thus the words and phrases of the *Comedy* may be sublime or humble on an ad hoc basis, but the use of the vernacular is itself generically defended as being comic, in keeping with the subject of the poem" (TDC 244, TC 121). (Note that Hollander here identifies "subject" with "plot" rather than with "subject matter.") Dante believed that the *Aeneid* was a tragedy not only because of its high style but also because of its tragic plot, since it ends with the death of Turnus (TDI 215–17, TC 130–31, TDC 251–52). I quote Hollander's views at length because they illustrate the kind of difficulties one encounters in trying to reconcile Dante's authentic views with *Cangrande*.

bucolic, which uses the low style (as opposed to the middle style or the grave style).[23] But Garland contradicts Dante at so many points that Dante would hardly have taken him seriously. He says, for instance, that both tragedy and comedy deal with sorrow (in reverse order, of course: joy to sorrow for tragedy, and sorrow to joy for comedy), and that "every comedy is an elegy." (Garland's hodgepodge of ideas was in fact an incoherent cribbing from the longer version of Geoffrey of Vinsauf's *Documentum de arte versificandi.*)[24] Furthermore, the influence of Garland's work was almost nonexistent.[25]

Other works, I believe, were much more likely to serve as sources, whether direct or indirect, of Dante's ideas of the three genres he singles out. I propose specifically certain entries in the three standard Latin dictionaries of his time, those of Papias, Huguccio, and John Balbus.

Scholars have often assumed that Huguccio's *Magne derivationes* was the only dictionary that Dante consulted, because it is the only one that he mentions by name (in the *Convivio*) and because it contains definitions corresponding to those in the *Epistle to Cangrande.*[26] But I will suggest that even the *Epistle to Cangrande* does not get its doctrine on tragedy and comedy directly from Huguccio.

Huguccio's explanation of tragedy and comedy, which is buried in his entry on *oda*, is obviously foreign to the *De vulgari eloquentia*. Huguccio makes four main points: (1) tragedy deals with great crimes; (2) tragedy moves from joy to sorrow, whereas comedy goes from sorrow to joy; (3) tragedy deals with great characters, whereas comedy treats of private persons; and (4) tragedy is written in high style, whereas comedy is in low style. He adds that one often hears persons wishing each other a tragic beginning and a comic end.[27]

---

23. Mengaldo, *DVE*, p. 166; idem, "L'elegia," pp. 212–22. Cf. Fenzi, "Boezio e Jean de Meun," p. 64. See the edition by Traugott Lawler, *The Parisiana poetria of John of Garland*, Yale Studies in English 182 (New Haven 1974), pp. 24, 102.

24. See Lawler, ibid., pp. 327–32.

25. Only six manuscripts of Garland's work are extant; see Lawler, ibid., and Susan Gallick, "Medieval Rhetorical Arts in England and the Manuscript Traditions," *Manuscripta* 18 (1974) 67–95, esp. 71–72.

26. See Paget Toynbee, "Dante's Latin Dictionary," in his *Dante Studies and Researches* (London 1902), pp. 97–114.

27. The entry is given in part by Toynbee, ibid., pp. 103–4. I use Oxford Bodleian MS Laud Misc. 626, where the whole entry (on fol. 124r–v) reads: "*Oda* grece, latine dicitur laus, et *oda* cantus, et *oda* finis, et *oda* uia; hinc quidam liber Oracij intitulatur *Liber odarum*, id est cantuum uel laudum, quia ibi laudare intendit, et quelibet eius distinctio est cantabilis. Vnde et quelibet eius distinctio oda dicitur, quod est laus uel cantus. Et ab *oda* quod est cantus, et *pros-* quod est ad, dicitur *hec prosodia*, id est accentus. Item ab *oda* quod est cantus, et ab *ex*, componitur *exodium*, *-ij*, primus cantus, inicium cantilene; Ivenalis: 'tandemque redit ad pulpita nonum exodium.' Et hinc *exodiarius*, *-rij*, id est, precentor, qui cantum incipit ante alios, et *exodiarius*, *-a*, *-um*, ad exodium uel exodiarium pertinens. Item *oda* quod est cantus uel laus componitur cum *comos* quod est uilla, et dicitur *hec comedia*, *-e*, id est uillanus cantus, uel uillana laus, quia tractat de rebus uillanis, rusticanis, et affinis est cottidiane locucioni; uel quia circa uillas fiebat et recitabatur; uel *comedia* a commessacione: solebant enim post cibum homines ad audiendum eam uenire; et hinc

Quite clearly, both Vergil's *Aeneid* and Dante's *Comedy* are misfits in this system. Huguccio's twofold paradigm of tragedy and comedy coincides with Dante's threefold schema of tragedy, comedy, and elegy only in the points concerning the high style and (by inference) the great characters of tragedy and the low style of comedy. But, according to Dante, the low style is only one of two options for comedy.

I will not dismiss Huguccio's work entirely, but I wish to look first at the earliest of the dictionaries, Papias's *Elementarium doctrinae rudimentum*.[28] Papias's treatment of tragedy under *tragoedi* gives the standard Isidorian definition about the deeds and crimes of wicked kings,[29] which is not relevant to

---

comedus, *-a*, *-um*, qui comediam describit; et hinc *comedicus*, *-a*, *-um*, ad comediam uel ad comedum pertinens, uel delectabilis. Vnde *comedice*, id est delectabiliter; Plautus: 'Heus astitisti et dulce et comedice.' Item a comedia *comicus*, *-a*, *-um*, id est, comedus uel ad comediam pertinens, uel facetus. Item *oda* in eodem sensu componitur cum *tragos* quod est hircus, et dicitur *hec tragedia*, *-e*, id est, hircina laus, uel hircinus cantus, id est fetidus; est enim de crudelissimis rebus, sicut qui patrem uel matrem interfecit et comedit filium, uel e contrario, et huiusmodi. Vnde et tragedo dabatur hircus, scilicet animal fetidum, non quod non haberet aliud dignum premium, sed ad fetorem materie designandum. Et inde *tragedus*, *-a*, *-um*, et *hic tragedus*, *-di*, tragedie scriptor, et hinc *tragedicus*, *-a*, *-um*. Item a tragedia *tragicus*, *-a*, *-um*, tragedus uel ad tragedum pertinens. Et differunt tragedia et comedia, quia comedia priuatorum hominum continet acta, tragedia regum et magnatum. Item comedia [124v] humili stilo scribitur, traged[i]a alto. Item comedia a tristibus incipit sed in letis desinit, tragedia e contrario. Vnde in salutacione solemus mittere et optare amicis tragicum principium et comicum finem, id est, principium bonum et letum et bonum et letum finem. Item *oda*, id est uia uel finis, componitur cum *peri-*, quod est circum, et dicitur *hic periodus*, *-i*, circuitus uel ambitus uel quod est circa finem, et accipitur in tribus significacionibus sicut superius exposuimus. Item *oda* quod est uia componitur cum *ex* et dicitur *hic exodus*, *-di*, quod est itus, uiacio extra, et hinc quidam liber dictus est Exodus, qui continet exitum uel egressum populi Israhel de Egypto. Item componitur *odeporicus*, *-a*, *-um*, tanetorius, uiatrious, sed *odeporium* dicitur laus cantilene. Item *oda* quod est uia componitur cum *sin-* quod est *con-* et dicitur *hic sinodus*, *-di*, id est cetus, conuentus, comitatus, congregatio, et proprie senum siue presbyterorum, quem solent facere episcopi, quia ibi simul conueniunt et coeunt. Vnde *hic* et *hoc synodalis*, *-le*, quod ad synodum pertinet."

28. Bonino Mombrizio's fourth edition of *Papias vocabulista* (Venice 1496) was reprinted in Turin in 1966, with a supplement later added from the first edition (Milan 1476) for the missing section *pecus-placidus*. Mombrizio used the defective alpha tradition, and some of the entries are garbled. For my main text I use instead a manuscript of the beta tradition, Vatican Ottob. lat. 2231, named by Violetta De Angelis as MS V[1] (first half of the twelfth century); see her edition of Papias, *Elementarium*, vols. 1-3: *Littera A*, Testi e documenti per lo studio dell' antichità 58.1-3 (Milan 1977-80), esp. 1:xlv. She gives the terminus ante quem of Papias's work as A.D. 1045 (1:ii). See also her "Indagine sulle fonti dell'*Elementarium* di Papias, lettera A," *Scripta philologica* 1 (Milan 1977) 117-34.

29. Papias, *Elementarium*, fol. 262: "*Tragoedi* sunt qui antiqua gesta et facinora sceleratorum regum concinebant, populo spectante," drawing on Isidore, *Etymologiae* 18.45, who in turn is drawing on Lactantius, *Divinae institutiones* 6.20.27-28. See Kelly, "Aristotle," p. 171 n. 41. for other elements behind Isidore's treatments, see H. A. Kelly, "Tragedy and the Performance of Tragedy in Late Roman Antiquity," *Traditio* 35 (1979) 21-44. In the rest of this entry, Papias uses *Etym.* 8.7.5 as well as 18.45; Papias's words are: "Dicti tragedi quia in initio canentibus premium erat hircus, quem greci *tragos* uocant. Sequentes uero tragici multum honorem adepti sunt, excellentes in argumento fabularum" (fol. 2624-v). There follows another entry: "*Tragoedia*

Dante's schema. The definition of *comedi* is closer: they were so called because men used to come to hear them before meals; but later the term referred to those who "in the scene" exposed and rebuked the deeds and sins of all people.[30] In his first entry under *comedia*, he gives Placidus's characterization of it as dealing with humble persons, not in a high style like tragedy but in a middling and sweet style. Then he adds a statement based on a distortion of Donatus, in which he attributes to comedy what Donatus attributes to tragedy: comedy also often deals with historical facts and important persons.[31] This description of comedy would account at least for the middle style specified by the *De vulgari eloquentia* and also for the fact that the *Comedy* deals with historical persons of all classes and rebukes their vices. Papias defines *elegi* as *versus miserorum* and *elegiacum* as referring to a poem that befits the miserable (Isidore's definition); he describes the elegiac distich and cites as an example the opening lines of Boethius's *Consolation of Philosophy*.[32] Huguccio's entries are independent of Papias's but similarly deal with misery.[33]

Balbus combines what both of his predecessors have to say on elegy. In his treatment of comedy, he begins with Huguccio's characterization of comedy as

---

quicquid luctuosis carminibus describebant [cf. Isidore, 18.45]. *Tragoedus* uero tragediarum genus describentium erat, qui coturnis utebantur." Note that the classical *oe* is preserved in the tragedy entries but not in the comedy entries (see next notes).

30. Papias, fol. 40v: "*Comedi* dicti quia prius pre commessatione ad eos audiendos uenire solebant homines. sed postea aggressi gesta uniuersorum et delicta corripientes in scena [proferebant]." I add the last word from Mombrizio's text (p. 71), since it corresponds to the statement in Papias's source, the *Liber glossarum*, ed. Georg Goetz, *Corpus glossariorum latinorum* 5 (Leipzig 1894) 181; cf. 6 (1899) 241.

31. Papias, fol. 40v: "*Comedia* est que res priuatorum et humilium personarum comprehendit, non tam alto stilo ut tragedia sed mediocri et dulci, que sepe etiam de historica fide et de grauibus personis tractat." Cf. Placidus, *Glossae*, S 21 *scaena*, ed. J. W. Pirie and W. M. Lindsay, *Glossaria latina* 4 (Paris 1930, repr. 1965), p. 34; Donatus, *Commentum Terentii* 4.2, ed. Paulus Wessner, vol. 1 (Leipzig 1902, repr. Stuttgart 1962), p. 21 = Evanthius, *De fabula* 4.2, ed. Giovanni Cupaiuolo (Naples 1979), pp. 146–47. Papias has further entries under *comedia* (the Vatican MS has a hole at this point, so that I must partially rely on Mombrizio); he etymologizes it and explains it as *uillanus cantus*, and he gives the Donatus-Evanthius division into prologue, protasis (or protesis; Mom. prothesis), epitasis (Mom. epithesis), and catastrophe. In due alphabetical course come the entries: "*Comici* res letas, traici [Mom. tragici] argumenta ex rebus luctuosis describunt. Duo sunt genera comicorum, ueteres qui ioculatores [Mom. ioculares] extiterunt, ut Terentius; noui, qui et satirici, quibus generaliter uitia carpuntur, ut Persius, Iuuenalis. Et nudi pinguntur, quia uitia denudent. *Comicus*: qui comedias describit." Cf. Isidore 8.7.6–7.

32. Papias, fol. 60v: "*Eligiacum* dictum quia modulatio eiusdem carminis miseris conueniat [Isidore, *Etym.* 1.39.14], quod metrum constat primo uersu heroico, secundo prima pentimereri heroica, secunda dictilica, vt

Carmina que quondam studio florente peregi
Flebilis heu mestos cogor inire modos."

For others who associate elegy with misery, see Mengaldo, "L'elegia," pp. 214–15 n. 36, and his article, "Stili," *ED* 5:435–38, pp. 436–37.

33. Huguccio, fol. 50: "*Elegus*, *-a*, *-um*, id est miser, -a, -um. Vnde versus facti de miseria dicantur *eligi*; vnde *hec elegia*, *-e*, id est miseria; et hinc *elegiacus*, *-a*, *-um*, id est, miser uel de miseria compositus."

a "farmerish song" that deals with rustic affairs and is close to daily speech. For the differences between comedy and tragedy, he refers the reader to his entry on tragedy (which follows Huguccio's *oda* account). Then he gives Papias's entry on comedy, with its designation of middle style and wide allowance of subject matter.[34]

I hypothesize that Dante (or perhaps Dante's immediate source) found most of the elements of his tragedy-comedy-elegy triad from consulting Balbus's new *Catholicon*, which was first published in 1286, on comedy and elegy. From this triad, thus understood, Dante could have arrived at a rationale for calling his great poem a comedy. For comedy according to Balbus uses common speech and deals with common persons and things, but it also uses a middling and sweet style and deals with historical matters and persons of great importance. Therefore, comedy is a form of writing that is unrestricted in subject matter and can take in the whole of humanity, and it also has a wide stylistic range.

If Dante knew the *Ars poetica*, as has been argued,[35] he could have had his humble opinion of elegy reinforced by Horace's statement that *querimonia* is expressed by *exigui elegi*.[36] He may also have drawn on Horace for the stylistic contrast between tragedy and comedy and for permission to use the grand style of tragedy in comedy when called for: "Interdum tamen et vocem Comedia tollit."[37] We shall see Pietro Alighieri drawing the latter conclusion: he adds Horace's high style to Huguccio's low style and Papias's middle style. The stylistic contrast between tragedy and elegy is also brought out by Ovid in the *Amores*, but it is questionable whether Dante had direct knowledge of the *Amores*.[38] One might also object that Dante could not have been well acquainted with the *Ars poetica*, or at least the passages where Horace treats of comedy and tragedy. The quoted line from Horace shows clearly that *comedia* is proparoxytone (*comédia*), whereas Dante in *Inferno* treats it as paroxytone (*comedía*), and presumably he did the

---

34. Iohannes Balbus, *Catholicon* (Mainz 1460, repr. Farnborough 1971), s.v. *comedia, elegus, tragedia*. I have also consulted the Lyons 1494 edition.

35. See Giorgio Brugnoli, "Orazio," *ED* 4:173–77, esp. 174.

36. Horace, *Ars poetica* 75–77. I medievalize Horace's spelling in subsequent citations.

37. Ibid., 93.

38. Ovid, *Amores* 3.1. See Kelly, "Aristotle," p. 186, where I offer the *Amores* as a more likely source for Dante than Herman Alemannus's translation of Averroes's commentary on the *Poetics* (where tragedy is restricted to the praise of virtue). I should mention that Giorgio Agamben, "Comedìa: La svolta comica di Dante e la concezione della colpa," *Paragone* 29, no. 346 (December 1978) 3–27, who accepts Dante's authorship of *Cangrande*, believes that Dante drew on Alemannus's translation for his idea of comedy (p. 11). But Alemannus does not use the word *comedia*; Agamben mistakenly uses a later Latin translation of the medieval Hebrew translation of Averroes (see Kelly, "Aristotle," p. 209). Agamben's idea that Dante also drew on William of Moerbeke's translation of the *Poetics* is very unlikely. Moerbeke was, however, used by Mussato (see p. 22 below), and, I should add, by Petrarch, *Invective contra medicum*, bk. 3, ed. Pier Giorgio Ricci, in *Prose*, ed. Guido Martellotti et al. (Milan 1955), p. 656: "nescire te quid sit tragedia, aut quid de tetrametris in iambicos transisse" (cf. *Poetics*, end of Chap. 4). Cf. Renate Haas, "Chaucer's *Monk's Tale*: An Ingenious Criticism of Early Humanist Conceptions of Tragedy," *Humanistica lovaniensia* 36 (1987) 44–70, esp. 48–49.

same in his Latin prose. As we will see in Chapter 7 and Appendix 2, Dante was alert to word stress because of his practice of the rhythmical *cursus*. Is it conceivable that he would deliberately go against classical norms? The answer may well be yes. We have John Balbus's testimony in his treatise on stress at the beginning of the *Catholicon* that the penultimate vowel in Greek words like *sophia* and *comedia*, though not long by nature, was pronounced long by custom.[39]

In trying to determine why Dante called his long poem a comedy, we have the advantage of consulting his generic comments in the *De vulgari eloquentia*. It was an advantage denied, I believe, to the fourteenth-century commentators who tried to understand his choice of title. I am firmly of the opinion that none of them, even Boccaccio, had access to the treatise. Even though Boccaccio mentions it and may have drawn on it at one stage, I maintain that when he came to deal with Dante's poem he did not have the text at hand and did not remember what Dante had said about comedy (if he had read it in the first place).[40] It follows that everyone, including the author or authors of the *Epistle to Cangrande*, was speculating on his own.

---

39. Balbus, *Catholicon*, ed. 1460, fol. [9ra–b]: "Si nomen terminetur in *a*, aut est proprium aut attributivum, aut commune. Si proprium, producitur penultima, non tamen natura sed usu, vel dicitur sine causa, ut *Catilina*, *Maria*, *Stephania*. Si sit commune, aut grecum aut latinum. Si grecum, producitur penultima, ut *yconia*, *sophia*; et hec adhuc nomina non producuntur natura sed usu, cum sint aliena vocabula." Later (fol. [15rb]) he indicates his mistaken belief that words like *comedia* have an interchangeable long and short penultimate syllable, viz. *ei* and *i*, therefore either *comede͞ia* or *comedĭa*. He says: "Usus eciam acuit penultimam quorundam nominum latinorum, ut *Lombardia*, *rectoria*, *Papia*, quamvis ipsa sit brevia; sed dicimus quod hoc contingit causa mutacionis; immutantur enim greca desinentia in *a* que habent penultimam acutam, ut *comedia*, *tragedia*, *elegia*, *abbatia*, *theologia*, et hiis similia. Et sciendum quod huiusmodi greca possunt corripere subtracta una vocali de dyptongo que ibi est, sc. *ei*, et possunt eandem producere. Sed in communi sermone semper retinemus accentum acutum vel circumflexum et numquam gravem, ut *Maria*, quamvis possit corripi." A fourteenth-century Italian treatise, *Metricam siquidem artem*, Paris, Bibl. Nat. MS lat. 8175, fols. 1–35, has a similar doctrine: "Si penultima acuitur sive circumflectitur, longa est, . . . preter . . . greca vel a grecis exorta, ut *comedia*, *tragedia*, *Maria*, *chorea*, *platea*, et preter latina imitantia grecismum, ut *rectoria*, *cancelleria*, *Lombardia*, in quibus omnibus, quamvis penultima acuatur, tamen brevis est. Sed greca possunt penultimam tam producere quam corripere, ut *Maria*, *chorea*, *platea*" (fol. 34). Quoted by Charles Thurot, *Notices et extraits de divers manuscrits latins pour servir à l'histoire des doctrines grammaticales au moyen âge*, Notices et extraits des manuscrits de la Bibliothèque Impériale et autres bibliothèques 22.2 (Paris 1868), p. 406 (cf. p. 50). In a twelfth-century treatise from Cîteaux, *Opusculum de accentibus*, there is a long list of such *-ia* words (Montpellier, MS 322, fol. 55v) and an even longer list in a thirteenth-century copy, Paris, Bibl. Nat. lat. 5102.2, fol. 155), but many of them are listed as proparoxytone. Of the fifty-four words in the later copy, thirty are given as paroxytone (e.g., *monarchía*, *theología*), the others as proparoxytone, including *comédia* and *tragédia*. In some cases, the two copies differ: the Montpellier version gives *astronomía*, *cyrúrgia*, and *tropológia*, whereas the Paris text has *astronómia*, *cyrurgía*, and *tropología* (Thurot, p. 406; cf. p. 25). Another twelfth-century French prosody, Paris, Bibl. Nat. 14193, fol. 108v, gives a short list, including *tragedía* (Thurot, p. 406), which goes contrary to the Cistercian usage.

40. For a general discussion of the *fortuna* of the *DVE*, see P. V. Mengaldo's introduction to his 1968 edition, as updated in his 1978 book (n. 4 above), pp. 11–123, esp. 23–24.

2

The Chronology of the Proto-Accessus

The *Epistle to Cangrande* is clearly divided by its final author into two main parts, the opening epistle and the concluding introduction to the *Paradiso*.[1] The second part in turn is subdivided into a preliminary discussion of the whole *Comedia* and the discussion proper of *Paradiso*.[2] I call the epistolary section (paragraphs 1–4) the Dedication, the discussion of the whole work (paragraphs 5–16) the Accessus, and the *Paradiso* discussion (paragraphs 17–33) the Exposition. I call the resulting composite the Compilation and the person responsible for it the Compiler—a designation for the most part interchangeable with "Pseudo-Dante." In this chapter I am particularly concerned with the Accessus, and insofar as it is thought of as antedating Pseudo-Dante's Compilation I refer to it as the Proto-Accessus and its original author as the Accessor.

Among the scholars who have questioned the authenticity of the *Epistle to Cangrande*, one school, led by Augusto Mancini and Bruno Nardi, impugns the Dantean character only of the Accessus and the Exposition, while accepting the Dedication as a letter that Dante actually wrote to Cangrande. Others, including Giorgio Brugnoli, reject the Dedication as well.[3] I will consider this matter

1. This division is set forth in *Cangrande* 4.13: "Itaque, formula consumata epistoli, ad introductionem oblati operis aliquid sub lectoris officio compendiose aggrediar." For the text of *Cangrande* I generally follow Giorgio Brugnoli's edition; the original manuscripts are given in Friedrich Schneider's facsimile edition, *Die Handschriften des Briefes Dantes an Can Grande della Scala* (Zwickau 1933), and the text of an additional MS of the Dedication, *B*, is given by Augusto Mancini, "Un nuovo codice dell'*Epistola a Can Grande*," *SD* 24 (1939) 111–22. I have also consulted the editions of Giuseppe Boffito, *L'Epistola di Dante Alighieri a Cangrande della Scala* (Turin 1907), and Paget Toynbee, *Dantis Alagherii Epistolae* (Oxford 1920; repr. with preface and additional bibliography by Colin Hardie, Oxford 1966), pp. 166–211. Toynbee's variants are not based on the manuscripts but on Boffito's edition, which is not reliable.

2. This subdivision is explained in *Cangrande* 6.17: "Volentes igitur aliqualem introductionem tradere de parte operis alicuius, oportet aliquam notitiam tradere de toto cuius est pars. Quapropter et ego, volens de parte supra nominata totius *Comedie* aliquid tradere per modum introductionis, aliquid de toto opere premittendum existimavi, ut facilior et perfectior sit ad partem introitus." The transition to the *Paradiso* discussion comes at 17.42: "Hiis itaque premissis, ad expositionem littere secundum quandam prelibationem accedendum est."

3. See Brugnoli's introduction to his edition of *Cangrande* in Dante, *Opere minori*, vol.

in Chapter 7. Here I only note my agreement that the Accessus and the Exposition are not by Dante. I maintain further that the Accessus in its original form was not by the Compiler posing as Dante. The main reason for this last point is that Giuseppe Vandelli in 1901 presented conclusive evidence that Boccaccio, in one sentence of his Italian commentary, was drawing on the corresponding Latin sentence of the Accessus; that is, he demonstrated that the Italian must derive from the Latin, and not vice versa.[4] Since it is unthinkable that Boccaccio knew the *Epistle to Cangrande* in its present form as the words of the venerated Dante himself, he must have seen it in another form.

It is possible that the entire *Epistle to Cangrande* was in existence by Boccaccio's time and that Boccaccio saw only an excerpt of it containing all or some of the Accessus. But I consider it very unlikely that a portion of such an astoundingly revelatory letter by Dante could have been circulated without word of the whole letter getting around. Therefore, I postulate that an earlier version of the Accessus was written before Boccaccio's time and used by him, and that it was later taken up by the Compiler and incorporated into his *Epistle to Cangrande.*

I assume as a working hypothesis that it was the Compiler rather than the Accessor who was responsible for the Exposition, and that the Proto-Accessus was substantially the same as the Accessus that now appears in *Cangrande*, except for adjustments made by the Compiler in adapting it to his context of an introduction to *Paradiso* (see Appendix 3 below, pp. 104–6).

To determine the terminus post quem of the Proto-Accessus, we must look at the material held in common by it and the commentaries written before Boccaccio's time. This material has been most thoroughly studied by Luis Jenaro-MacLennan. Jenaro deliberately sets aside the question of whether *Cangrande* was by Dante. Yet his analysis seems designed to make such a conclusion plausible, primarily because of his claim that *Cangrande* antedates Guido da Pisa's long commentary on the *Inferno* and was drawn upon by Guido. I hold that the influence is in the opposite direction.

Jenaro proceeds by isolating passages common to Guido, Jacopo della Lana, and the second and third versions of the *Ottimo commento*, and he designates

---

2, ed. P.V. Mengaldo et al. (Florence 1979), pp. 517–19. A skeptic not mentioned by him is Allan H. Gilbert, "Did Dante Dedicate the *Paradiso* to Can Grande della Scala?" *Italica* 43 (1966) 100–24.

4. Giuseppe Vandelli, review article in the *Bullettino della Società Dantesca Italiana* n.s. 8 (1900–01) 137–64, esp. 156 n. 2. He cites a line from *Cangrande* 7.22, which reads in Brugnoli's edition: "Et quanquam isti sensus mistici variis appellentur nominibus, generaliter omnes dici possunt allegorici." Boccaccio read the *generaliter* as going with the first part of the sentence: "Et quanquam isti sensus mistici variis appellentur nominibus generaliter," etc., with the following result: "E così come questi sensi mistici sono generalmente per vari nomi appellati, tutti nondimeno si possono appellare allegorici." Cited from his *Esposizioni sopra la Comedia di Dante* 1.2.21, ed. Giorgio Padoan, *Tutte le opere* 6 (Milan 1965), p. 58. Vandelli's argument is accepted by Luis Jenaro-MacLennan, *The Trecento Commentaries on the Divina commedia and the Epistle to Cangrande* (Oxford 1974), p. 105 (he mistakenly cites the argument as appearing on p. 165 rather than 156).

these passages collectively as *N*. The passages common to *Cangrande* and Guido are labeled *E*[1]. Jenaro says[5] that Guido must have taken E[1] from *Cangrande*, since *Cangrande* could not have taken *E*[1] from Guido without its being contaminated by N and by Guido's intercalations in *E*[1]. But since Jenaro is the one who is assigning the labels, he has seen to it that there is no contamination; he has simply designated only unconnected (or "uncontaminated") sections as *N*. Jenaro's basic objection would seem to be that he finds it implausible that *Cangrande*, if it were posterior to Guido, would have made such a selective use of Guido; but he does not seem to find it puzzling that Guido should have made such a selective use of *Cangrande*. Why, for instance, would Guido say that there are only four kinds of literature when *Cangrande* says that there are six?[6] Furthermore, Jenaro has begged the crucial question by calling the extra material in Guido's *E*[1] sections "intercalations." In my view, it is much more probable on the face of it that the material was original to Guido and was accidentally or deliberately dropped by the Accessor or by the Compiler.

There seems to be a likelihood of accidental omission by reason of homoeoteleuton in *Cangrande*'s statement of Dante's literal subject. Here is Guido's commentary on the point, with the passage omitted by *Cangrande* in brackets (I have italicized the long identical phrases that would have given rise to the scribal "eyeskip"):

> Si enim accipiatur litteraliter, dico quod *subiectum huius operis est status animarum post mortem simpliciter sumptus*: [qui quidem status dividitur in tres partes, prout conditio animarum est triplex. Primus status sive conditio est illarum animarum que eternaliter sunt damnate, et que in penis habitant sine spe aliqua evadendi ex illis; et ista pars appellatur *Infernus*. Secundus status sive conditio est illarum animarum que voluntarie stant in penis, ut Deo satisfaciant de commissis, et sunt in ipsis penis cum spe ad gloriam ascendendi; et ista pars *Purgatorium* appellatur. Tertius status sive conditio est illarum animarum que sunt in beata gloria, ipsi summo et eterno bono eternaliter (hoc est, sine fine) coniuncte; et ista pars appellatur *Paradisus*. Et sic patet quomodo *subiectum huius operis est status animarum post mortem simpliciter sumptus*]. Nam de illo et circa illum totius huius operis versatur processus.[7]

The text of *Cangrande* is as follows:

> Est ergo subiectum totius operis, litteraliter tantum accepti, status animarum post mortem simpliciter sumptus. Nam de illo et circa illum totius operis versatur processus.[8]

---

5. Jenaro, *Trecento*, pp. 60–61, 67, 75.

6. Guido names lyric, satiric, tragic, and comic poets. *Cangrande* speaks of poetic narrations and names comedy, tragedy, bucolic verse, elegy, satire, and votive sentence. See below, p. 38.

7. Guido da Pisa, *Expositiones et glose super Comediam Dantis; or, Commentary on Dante's Inferno*, ed. Vincenzo Cioffari (Albany, N.Y., 1974), Prologue, pp. 2–3.

8. *Cangrande* 8.24.

In this case, according to my hypothesis, it must have been the Accessor and not the Compiler who made the omission, since it is reflected in Boccaccio's commentary:

> È adunque il suggetto, secondo il senso litterale, lo stato dell'anime dopo la morte de' corpi semplicemente preso; per ciò che di quello e intorno a quello tutto il processo della presente opera intende.[9]

Guido's authoritative *dico* in his version of the passage is also an indication of priority.[10]

In another passage, where the topic under discussion is the final cause or purpose of Dante's poem, the likelihood is that the *Cangrande* text represents a deliberate truncation of Guido's lengthy discourse. I give Guido's text and bracket the material not in *Cangrande*:

> Circa quartam, id est circa causam finalem, nota quod autor istud opus composuit ad hunc finem principaliter, licet et multi alii possint assignari fines. Est autem principalis eius intentio removere viventes a statu miserie, [relinquendo peccata, et sic composuit *Infernum*; reducere ad virtutes, et sic composuit *Purgatorium*,] ut sic eos perducat ad gloriam, [et sic composuit *Paradisum*. Fines vero alii qui possunt assignari in hoc opere sunt tres: primus, ut discant homines polite et ordinate loqui. . . . Secundus finis est ut libros poetarum . . . renovaret. . . . Tertius finis est ut vitam . . . malorum . . . condemnaret, bonorum autem . . . commendaret. Et sic patet que est causa finalis in hoc opere].[11]

I have omitted a good deal of the last part, but one can see the sort of expansiveness in which Guido indulges. *Cangrande*, in contrast, has an air of cutting through garrulity. The text reads:

> Finis totius et partis esse posset et multiplex, scilicet propinquus et remotus. Sed, omissa subtili investigatione, dicendum est breviter quod finis totius et partis est removere viventes in hac vita de statu miserie et perducere ad statum felicitatis.[12]

I assume that the cut was made by the Accessor, but that it was the Compiler, drawing on scholastic tradition for his terminology of proximate and remote ends, who added the *totius et partis* phrases when he adjusted the Proto-Accessus to his discussion of the *Paradiso*. Boccaccio's commentary must preserve something of the original form of the Proto-Accessus passage:

> La causa finale della presente opera è remuovere quegli che nella presente vita vivono dallo stato della miseria allo stato della felicità.[13]

---

9. Boccaccio, *Esposizioni*, Accessus 8. Boccaccio's "tutto il processo della presente opera" does not correspond to Guido's "totius huius operis versatur processus" or *Cangrande*'s "totius operis versatur processus"; but rather it agrees with the Laurentian version of Guido's prologue given by Vandelli (see n. 4 above), p. 151: "totus huius operis versatur processus" (for a discussion of the Laurentian text, see Chapter 3). I can only explain the similarity as a coincidence. Cf. n. 15 below.

10. This point is disputed by Jenaro, *Trecento*, pp. 82–83.

11. Guido, *Expositiones*, p. 4.

12. *Cangrande* 15.39.

13. Boccaccio, Accessus 12.

But Boccaccio dropped the phrase, *omissa subtili investigatione*, which I presume was in the Accessor's original text.

However, one reference to the "whole and part" appears in Guido's commentary: "Non ad speculandum sed ad opus inventum et fictum est *totum et pars*." This statement is repeated in *Cangrande*, except that "et fictum" is omitted.[14] Defenders of Dante's authorship of *Cangrande*, or defenders of the priority of *Cangrande*, have alleged this passage as proof that Guido must be drawing on *Cangrande*, since Guido would have had no reason to contrast one of the parts of the *Comedy* with the whole. The same would be true, I must add, if there was indeed a Proto-Accessus of the sort that I have postulated: the Accessor would be speaking of all three parts of the *Comedy*, and not of one in particular. Nevertheless, I consider it plausible that the expression was in fact original to Guido, for two reasons. First, Guido goes on to contrast whole with parts by referring to occasional speculative passages within the *Comedy* as possible exceptions to his general statement: "Nam etsi *in aliquo loco vel passu* pertractatur ad modum speculativi negotii, hoc non est gratia speculativi negotii principaliter, sed operis."[15] The second reason is suggested by Giuseppe Boffito, who points out that *totum* and *pars* are often coupled together without evident reason.[16] I prefer to say that the reason for such couplings is obvious but unstated: the expression *totum et pars* is an elliptical-pleonastic way of emphasizing completeness, short for *totum et omnis pars* or *in toto et in omni parte*.[17]

The Guido/Accessus passage goes on to cite Aristotle: "quia, ut ait Philosophus, secundo *Methaphysice*, 'Ad aliquid et nunc speculantur practici,' aliquando."[18] One might be inclined to think it too much of a coincidence that the Compiler also quotes from the same paragraph of the *Metaphysics* when introducing the Accessus, to justify his dealing with the whole *Comedy* before considering *Paradiso*. He says, "Sicut dicit Phylosophus in secundo *Metaphysice*,

---

14. Guido, *Expositiones*, pp. 4–5; *Cangrande* 16.40. Boccaccio, Accessus 42, omits the whole explanatory clause.

15. Guido, *Expositiones*, p. 5; *Cangrande* 16.41 omits *principaliter* and puts a second *gratia* before *operis*. *Me* and *M*[1] have *pertractatur*, *R* has *passim pertratatur*, *M*[2] has *pertractat*, *V* has *pertractamus*, and *M*[3] has *tractamus*. The Laurentian Guido has *tractatur*, and puts *si* for *etsi* (for *Cangrande* on *etsi*, see below). Cf. Boccaccio, Accessus 42: "per ciò che, quantunque in alcun passo si tratti per modo speculativo, non è perciò per cagione di speculazione ciò posto, ma per cagione dell'opera, la quale quivi ha quel modo richesto di trattare." Here Boccaccio's *quantunque* agrees with the *etsi* of the cited text rather than with the *si* of the Laurentian Guido (see n. 9 above). As for *Cangrande*, *V*, *M*[1], and *M*[2] have *si et*, *Me* and *R* have *si*, and *M*[3] has *et si*.

16. Boffito, *L'Epistola*, p. 28.

17. Cf. the somewhat similar English expressions, "whole and some," "all and some," "all and sundry," "one and all," and so on. See the *Oxford English Dictionary* s.v. "All" A.12; "One" B.29, "Whole" A.7b. Legal documents are particularly rich in such tautological expressions; a good example is "all and every," translating the Latin "universi et singuli"; see ibid., s.v. "Every" 7b.

18. This is the reading of Guido's text. As for *Cangrande* 16.41, Brugnoli puts *Metaphysicorum*, but *V* has *metaphysice*, *M*[3] has *Methaphysice*, and the other MSS abbreviate the title. Five of the MSS cite the text as in Guido, including the *aliquando* at the end, but *V* substitutes "aliquando etiam speculantur practici" for the whole quotation.

'sicut res se habet ad esse, sic se habet ad veritatem.' "[19] But if one accepts my hypothesis that the Compiler is making use of a preexisting Accessus, there is no coincidence at all: the Compiler did not independently think of drawing on the Aristotle passage; rather, he would have been inspired by the Accessor's use of it. (The Exposition also refers to this part of the *Metaphysics*; I will discuss the implications of this point in Chapter 7.)

This explanation is verified by the circumstance that the translation used by the Compiler is different from that used in the Guido/Accessus passage. Guido employs the twelfth-century Anonymous translation, whether in its original form or in the revision made by William of Moerbeke in the 1260s. Moerbeke's was the fifth version of the *Metaphysics* to be produced in less than a century. The version used by the Compiler was the oldest of the translations, that made by James of Venice (Iacobus Veneticus Grecus). The Anonymous/Moerbeke version of the first passage is, "ad aliquid et nunc speculantur practici," and of the second, "sicut habet esse, ita et veritatem" (Anonymous) or "sicut se habet ut sit, ita et ad veritatem" (Moerbeke).[20] James gives the first as, "ad aliquid et nunc considerant practici," and the second as, "sicut se habet ad esse, sic et ad veritatem" (or, as one manuscript has it, "sicut se habet ad esse, ita se habet ad veritatem").[21]

We know that Dante himself had some familiarity with the *Metaphysics*. In the *Convivio* and the *De monarchia*, he drew on the first part of Thomas Aquinas's prologue to his commentary on the *Metaphysics*;[22] and in the *De monarchia* he quotes from Moerbeke's translation at the point where Thomas's copy ended.[23]

19. *Cangrande* 5.14. Brugnoli again has *Metaphysicorum*, but all of the MSS except *V* abbreviate it, and *V* has *metaphysice*. The same is true of 20.56 (see below, Chapter 7, n. 29). As for the text of the citation from Aristotle, only *M*[1] gives it as I cite it above (where I follow Brugnoli's edition). *V*, *Me*, and *M*[3] invert the second *se habet* and read *habet se*, and for the first *se habet M*[3] has *sese habet*. For the second *se habet R* has *habet* with *et se* careted in after it.

20. Aristotle, *Metaphysica* 2.1 (993b22–23): *Translatio Anonyma sive "Media,"* ed. Gudrun Vuillemin-Diem, Aristoteles latinus 25.2 (Leiden 1976), p. 37; *Translatio Guillelmi de Moerbeka*, as given in Thomas Aquinas, *In duodecim libros Metaphysicorum Aristotelis expositio*, ed. Raimundo M. Spiazzi (Turin: Marietti, 1950), p. 84. Dr. Vuillemin is preparing an edition of Moerbeke, to appear as Aristoteles latinus 25.3. See her "Untersuchungen zu Wilhelm von Moerbekes Metaphysikübersetzung," in *Studien zur mittelalterlichen Geistesgeschichte und ihren Quellen*, ed. Albert Zimmermann and Gudrun Vuillemin-Diem, Miscellanea mediaevalia 15 (Berlin 1982), pp. 102–208.

21. Aristotle, *Metaphysica* 2.1, *Translatio Iacobi*, ed. G. Vuillemin-Diem, Aristoteles latinus 25.1 (Brussels 1970), p. 37. For details of these and the other translations, see the Praefatio, pp. xi–xii, and see my Appendix 1. In a personal communication, Dr. Vuillemin tells me that she knows of no manuscript (or *florilegium*) that mixes translations in this passage.

22. Dante, *Convivio* 4.4.4–5; *De monarchia* 1.3.10. See Lorenzo Minio-Paluello, "Dante's Reading of Aristotle," in *The World of Dante*, ed. Cecil Grayson (Oxford 1980), pp. 61–80, esp. 74–76.

23. Dante, *De monarchia* 1.10.6, ed. Pier Giorgio Ricci (Milan 1965), p. 153: "Et hanc rationem videbat Phylosophus cum dicebat: 'Entia nolunt male disponi; malum autem pluralitas principatuum. Unus ergo princeps.' " Moerbeke's translation reads: "Entia vero nolunt disponi male, nec bonum pluralitas principatuum. Unus ergo princeps" (Thomas Aquinas, *In Meta.*, p. 611;

If he was using the whole work and not simply repeating an excerpt cited by some other author, he may have been using the text of the translation accompanying Aquinas's commentary. In any case, it does not seem likely that Dante as author of the *Epistle to Cangrande* would be drawing on two different translations of the *Metaphysics* (or excerpts from two different translations) to cite portions of the same paragraph.

The same unlikelihood does not apply to a later Compiler, for the Anonymous/Moerbeke text would simply have been swept in with the block of material taken from Guido da Pisa—or rather taken over by the Accessor from Guido. The Compiler, then, would be drawing directly only on the James of Venice translation.

If the Compiler himself was the author of the Accessus, we would have to postulate that the Accessus had somehow become separated from the Dedication (and, probably, from the Exposition as well) before it was consulted by Boccaccio. If the Compiler was not the author of the Accessus (the hypothesis I favor), we must date the Accessus in its original form (before the Compiler adapted it) to a time after Guido's commentary and before Boccaccio's. We can say nothing more about the Accessor's sources until we deal further with Guido and examine what some of the other commentators have to say. But since it is certain that Boccaccio used the Accessus in some form at the time of his lectures on Dante in the 1370s, we must ask whether there are any signs of his earlier acquaintance with the work.

In the first version of his *Trattatello in laude di Dante*, which is now dated 1350–55,[24] Boccaccio's statement of Dante's intention in the *Comedy*, "cioè a volere secondo i meriti e mordere e premiare, secondo la sua diversità, la vita degli uomini,"[25] may have been influenced by the Accessor's characterization of the subject of the poem as "homo prout merendo et demerendo per arbitrii libertatem iustitie premiandi et puniendi obnoxius est."[26] Furthermore, the Accessor's account of the *Comedy*'s divisions ("quelibet cantica dividitur in cantus . . . quilibet cantus dividitur in rithimos")[27] is suggestive of Boccaccio's formulation: "De' quali tre libri egli ciascuno distinse per canti e i canti per rittimi."[28] Boccaccio speaks of Dante's title as referring to the poem's humble style: "L'andar quieto significa l'umilità dello stilo, il quale nelle comedie di necessità

Aristotle, *Meta.* 12.10, Bekker 1076a3–4). The James of Venice and Composite translations of this portion of the *Metaphysics* do not survive (or did not extend this far); the Anonymous version reads as follows (p. 224): "Entia vero nolunt tractari male. Nec bonum plures dominatus. Unus ergo dominatus" (some texts read *princeps* for the last *dominatus*).

24. See Pier Giorgio Ricci's introduction to his edition of Boccaccio's *Trattatello*, *Tutte le opere* 3 (Milan 1974), pp. 426–27.

25. Boccaccio, *1 Trattatello* 177 (Ricci, p. 481).

26. *Cangrande* 8.25. This and the other similarities noted in the text above between *Cangrande* and the *Trattatello* were pointed out to me by Professor Giuseppe Velli.

27. *Cangrande* 9.26., ed. Brugnoli. As I note below (p. 63), the MSS have *rhythmos* or other disyllabic forms.

28. Boccaccio, *1 Trattatello* 177 (Ricci, p. 482).

si richiede, come color sanno che intendono che vuole dire 'comedia.' "[29] In so doing he accepts a reason that he will reject in his *Esposizioni*, where he is clearly drawing on the Accessor.[30] The conclusion that he was also drawing on the Accessor in the earlier work is strengthened by the fact that he uses the word *quieto*. As we will see, *quieta* was the Accessor's substitution for Guido's *grata* in his description of the first part of tragedy.[31]

---

29. Ibid. 226 (p. 494).
30. See below, pp. 45–46.
31. See below, pp. 35, 38.

3

Guido da Pisa, Jacopo della Lana, and Jacopo Alighieri

Until recently, the learned Carmelite friar Guido da Pisa was considered to be a "second-generation" commentator on Dante's *Comedy*, but he is now generally regarded as the most important of the earliest students of Dante's poem. Jenaro-MacLennan has convincingly argued against a late date for Guido's long commentary on the *Inferno* and assigned it a terminus ante quem of 16 August 1328.[1] A present-day Carmelite, Antonio Canal, has claimed to have identified an earlier form of his commentary, or at least excerpts from it, that covers not only the *Inferno* but the *Purgatorio* and *Paradiso* as well. He dates Guido's literary interest in Dante to about 1318, when he was working on his *Fiore d'Italia* and citing passages from the *Comedy*.[2]

Canal believes that the Guidonian elements in the Laurentian Codex XL.2, which have been taken to be dependent on his *Inferno* commentary, are derived from his earlier glosses on the entire *Comedy*. The Laurentian version of the Prologue, published by Vandelli,[3] is almost identical with that of the version in the Chantilly manuscript, except that it lacks the dedicatory references to Lucano Spinola and the epitaph that Guido says he wrote to commemorate Dante. Canal dates the epitaph to 1321, the year of Dante's death, and thus it would stand as the first extant commentary on the literary form of the *Comedy*:

> Hic iacet excelsus poeta comicus Dantes,
> Necnon et satirus et liricus atque tragedus.[4]

Guido knows Dante's work by the title *Profundissima et altissima comedia Dantis excellentissimi poete*,[5] unless the superlatives are his own addition. The full title in fact sums up or parallels Guido's notion of the genre, or at least his

1. Luis Jenaro-MacLennan, *The Trecento Commentaries on the Divina commedia and the Epistle to Cangrande* (Oxford 1974), pp. 22–58.

2. Antonio Canal, *Il mondo morale di Guido da Pisa interprete di Dante*, Il mondo medievale 8 (Bologna 1981). See p. 12 for a statement of his main conclusions.

3. Giuseppe Vandelli, review article in the *Bulletino della Società Dantesca Italiana* n.s. 8 (1900–01) 150–57.

4. Guido, *Expositiones*, ed. Vincenzo Cioffari (Albany, N.Y., 1974), p. 6. See Canal, *Il mondo*, p. 62.

5. Guido, *Expositiones*, p. 5.

notion of Dante's exemplification of comedy. It is deep because it deals with hell and high because it deals with heaven. It is a comedy because it is horrible in the beginning but delectable in the end.

Guido divides poetry into the four genres of lyric, satiric, "tragedic," and comic, a schema that he may have derived from Isidore of Seville.[6] Guido cites Isidore by name for his discussion of tragedy:

> Certain poets are called tragedic, and their science is called tragedy. Now tragedy is a kind of poetic narration which in the beginning is admirable and pleasing, but in the end or outcome is fetid and horrible; and because of this it is named from *tragos*, goat, and *oda*, song; hence tragedy is a "goatish song," that is, fetid like a goat, as appears in Seneca's tragedies. Or, as St. Isidore says in the eighth book of his *Etymologies*, "Tragedies are so called because at the beginning the prize for the singers was a goat. Whence too Horace: 'Who competed for a vile goat with a tragic poem.' "[7]

His treatment of comedy is much briefer than his discussions of the other genres. "Certain other poets," he says, "are called comic, and their science is comedy. Now comedy is a kind of poetic narration that has the harshness of some misery in the beginning, but its matter is prosperously terminated, as is apparent in the comedies of Terence."[8] He applies this to Dante's poem: "In the beginning of its narration or description, it has hardship and horribleness, because it deals with the pains of hell, but in the end jocundity and delectation, because it deals with the joys of Paradise."[9]

We note that in characterizing comedy in general and as illustrated in Terence's comedies, Guido does not speak of *horribilitas* but only *asperitas*. The reason may be that Terence's plays clearly do not begin in horror. But is *asperitas alicuius miserie*, in the absence of any reference to the humorous aspect of comedy, an accurate characterization of the amusing predicaments and complications that precede the happy resolutions of Terence's plays? Guido's tragic scheme is even more inappropriate for Seneca's plays. How could any of Seneca's tragedies strike a reader as *admirabilis et grata* at the beginning? A better characterization of them would be that they begin in asperity or misery and end in horror

---

6. Isidore, *Etymologiae* 8.7.4–8. See Jenaro, *Trecento*, p. 30.

7. Guido, *Expositiones*, 5–6: "Quidam dicuntur tragedi, et eorum scientia dicitur tragedia. Est autem tragedia quedam poetica narratio que in principio est admirabilis et grata, in fine vero sive exitu est fetida et horribilis. Et propter hoc dicitur a *tragos*, quod est hircus, et *oda*, quod est cantus; inde *tragedia* quasi cantus hircinus, id est, fetidus ad modum hirci, ut patet per Senecam in suis tragediis. Vel, ut dicit beatus Isidorus octavo libro *Etymologiarum*: 'Tragedi dicuntur eo quod initia [*lege* initio, *as in Vandelli, p. 155*] canentibus premium erat hircus, quem Greci *tragos* uocant; unde et Horatius: "Carmine qui tragico vilem certavit ob hircum." ' "

8. Guido, *Expositiones*, p. 6: "Quidam vero dicuntur comici, et eorum scientia comedia. Est autem comedia quedam narratio poetica que in principio habet asperitatem alicuius miserie, sed eius materia prospere terminatur, ut patet per Terentium in suis comediis."

9. Ibid.: "Dicitur autem iste liber *Comedia* quia in prinicipio suae narrationis sive descriptionis habet asperitatem et horribilitatem, quia tractat de penis inferni, in fine vero continet iocunditatem et delectationem, quia tractat de gaudiis paradisi."

(we can except the upbeat coda of *Hercules Oetaeus*, but not Medea's terrible triumph).

Perhaps Guido was simply carried along by the weight of traditional definitions, and did not notice that the classical examples of the genres failed to bear them out. Alternatively, it is possible that he was not familiar with the works of Terence and Seneca, or at least not familiar with the overall structure the plays. Despite the availability of the comedies of Terence in Guido's time, Guido himself never quotes from any of them in the course of his long commentary. He does give frequent quotations from the much rarer Senecan corpus, but perhaps he was drawing on a collection of passages (although his quotations, which come from all ten of the plays, correspond to no known *florilegium*).[10]

The idea of tragedy or comedy as *narratio*, which Guido defines as *descriptio*, may derive from Horace: "Indignatur . . . *narrari* cena Thyeste."[11] But Guido probably did not know Horace at first hand.[12] The citation from the *Ars poetica* in his explanation of tragedy clearly comes from Isidore, as I indicate in my use of quotation marks.[13] The terms "prosperity" and "adversity" were introduced into discussions of tragedy and comedy by William of Conches in his commentary on Boethius's *Consolation of Philosophy*, and were repeated by Nicholas Trevet.[14] But unlike Conches and Trevet, Guido does not characterize the bad outcome of tragedy as consequent on great iniquities. It is not so much the fetor of vice as the fetor of horror that Guido seems to have in mind.

The best lyric poets, Guido says, are Boethius and Simonides; Horace and Persius are the best satirists; Homer and Vergil are the best in tragedy; and the best comics are Plautus and Terence.[15] Guido shares with Mussato the idea that heroic poets as well as Seneca wrote tragedies; moreover, if like Mussato he knew

10. For the Senecan citations, see Guido, *Expositiones*, pp. 26, 28, 62, 121, 144, 182, 186, 227, 250, 271, 273–74, 277, 283, 395, 617, 653–54, 672. See Saverio Bellomo, "Tradizione manoscritta e tradizione culturale delle *Expositiones* di Guido da Pisa (prime note e appunti)," *Lettere italiane* 31 (1979) 153–75, esp. 164, and Anna Maria Caglio, "Materiali enciclopedici nelle *Expositiones* di Guido da Pisa," *IMU* 24 (1981) 213–56, esp. 250–53. For Senecan *florilegia*, see Giorgio Brugnoli, "La tradizione manoscritta di Seneca tragico alla luce delle testimonianze medioevali" (1957), *Atti della Accademia Nazionale dei Lincei: Memorie, classe di scienze morali, storiche, e filologiche* 8.8 (Rome 1959) 199–289; but Brugnoli gives the wrong citations for two of the most important collections, namely those of Vincent of Beauvais, *Speculum historiale* book 8 (*not* book 9), chaps. 113–14, and the *Anecdoton lugdunense*, ed. Friedrich Leo, *Commentationes (not Festschrift) in honorem Francisci Buecheleri, Hermanni Useneri* (Bonn 1873), pp. 29–60.

11. Horace, *Ars poetica* 90–91.

12. See Caglio, "Materiali enciclopedici," pp. 245–46.

13. He cites the *Ars poetica* by name once when quoting lines 394–95 (p. 672). Elsewhere, he quotes Horace's *Epistle* 1.1.45–46 but attributes it to Lucan (p. 153), and then he attributes a line to Horace that is not his (p. 155). On p. 314, he gives two lines from an unnamed *poeta*, the first of which is Horace, *Epistle* 1.1.33, and the second an adaptation of *Ars poetica* 170.

14. For the texts of Conches and Trevet, see Alastair Minnis, "Aspects of the Medieval French and English Traditions of the *De consolatione Philosophiae*," in *Boethius*, ed. Margaret Gibson (Oxford 1981), pp. 312–61, esp. 336–37, 359 n. 82.

15. Guido, *Expositiones*, p. 6; Vergil is not named in the British Library MS.

the entire text of Seneca's plays, he was also like him in knowing nothing of the acted nature of tragedy. One might wish to conclude from this that Guido did not know Book 18 of the *Etymologies*, where Isidore discusses the pantomimic acting out of tragedy, or Trevet's commentary on Seneca, which repeats what Isidore says. But Mussato was able to remain in the dark on the subject even though he had Aristotle's *Poetics* at hand in the Latin translation of William of Moerbeke.[16]

Mussato sees tragedy as dealing primarily with important persons and events, whereas Guido, like Trevet in commenting on Boethius, regards it above all as a story with a certain sequence of events. However, when Guido sums up his discussion, he says that Dante is a tragic poet because of the grandeur of his subject matter, not because of plot considerations. Dante's *Comedy*, he says, makes him not only a comic poet, but also a lyric poet because of the diversity of his rhythms or rhymes and the sweet and mellifluous sounds they produce; a satiric poet because of his reprehension of vice and commendation of virtue; and a tragedic poet because of the great deeds of sublime persons that he narrates.[17]

Guido has no comment on the passage in the *Inferno* where Dante has Vergil call the *Aeneid* a high tragedy,[18] perhaps because Vergil's poem completely violates the genre's requirement of a fetid or horrible ending. Are we then to take the Laurentian and Chantilly versions of his commentary as less authentic than the British Library copy when they include Vergil as a leading tragedian? We can at least say that, if the *Aeneid* does not fulfill Guido's definition of tragedy, the work could still be considered to be as tragedic as Dante's poem, in that it deals with great characters and events.

Guido is less reticent on the subject of comedy in the body of his commentary than he is on tragedy. When dealing with canto 1, he says that Dante speaks poetically and fictively, "and therefore this book is called a comedy, which is a certain species of poetry that involves cloaking truth in poetic garb and prophetic ambiguities."[19] At the point in canto 16 where Dante refers to his work as a comedy, Guido simply refers to the explanation he gave in the Prologue.[20] But he gives a bizarre new explanation of the plot movement of comedy when he comes to canto 21:

> This book is called a comedy because, as we said above in the Prologue, it is a certain kind of poetic writing. And the word comedy comes from *comos*, that is, vil-

---

16. See H.A. Kelly, "Aristotle-Averroes-Alemannus on Tragedy," *Viator* 10 (1979) 188–91.

17. Guido, *Expositiones*, p. 6: "Dantes autem potest dici non solum comicus propter suam *Comediam*, sed etiam poeta liricus, propter diversitatem rithimorum et propter dulcissimum et mellifluum que reddant sonum; et satyricus, propter reprehensionem vitiorum et commendationem virtutum quas facit; et tragedus, propter magnalia gesta que narrat sublimium personarum."

18. Ibid., p. 395.

19. Ibid., p. 31: "Et ideo iste liber dicitur comedia, que est quoddam genus poesie ad quem spectat vera in tegumentis poeticis et propheticis ambagibus nubilare."

20. Ibid., p. 304.

> lage, and *oda*, song; hence comedy is "village song," because it begins in misery and ends in felicity, just as villagers who live in the village or country, when they become city-dwellers, move from rustic work to urban employment. Just so, comic poets begin their works with vile matter and terminate them in noble matter, that is, they begin in misery and adversity and end in prosperity and felicity.[21]

Given this point of view, Guido should have had no hesitation in associating fetor with the first part of comedies—if not the metaphorical fetor of horror, then at least the filth and stink of goats.

Let us now consider the commentators who seem to have been the first to draw on Guido's commentary, namely, Jacopo della Lana and Jacopo Alighieri. Lana, who composed a commentary on the entire *Comedy*, must have written his comment on *Inferno* 20 before 16 August 1328, when Passerino Bonacolsi was assassinated, since he speaks of the victim as still living. Nevertheless, Jenaro-MacLennan believes that Lana's prologue and some of his glosses on the first part of the *Inferno* are dependent on Guido's commentary.[22] If 1328 is thought to be too early for such dependence on Guido's final *Inferno* commentary, it may give support to Canal's theory of an earlier set of Guidonian glosses.

When Lana discusses comedy in his prologue, he says that it is a fictive poetic form that deals with "positive" exempla. Then he seems to say that, of the various kinds of poetry, most of them are called comedies: they begin in a bad state and end in a perfect condition.[23] Perhaps his statement is a garbled attempt to abridge Guido's classification. Doubtless it has the intended meaning, "Of the various kinds of poetry, those that end happily are called comedies."

This interpretation is borne out by Lana's account of the passage in which Vergil refers to his high tragedy. He says that tragedy is poetry that is the opposite of comedy, since comedy treats of the "novels" (events in the lives) of those who in the beginning are small and feeble and of little fortune and in the end are great, strong, and well favored. Tragedy does the reverse: it deals with the lives of those who in the beginning are grand and splendid but in the end are reduced to low estate and no esteem. When Vergil treats of Troy, which was great and victorious and exalted and then was brought to destruction, his treatment was

21. Ibid., p. 404: "Iste autem liber ideo dicitur comedia quia, ut dictum est supra in Prologo, est quoddam genus poetice descriptionis. Et dicitur comedia a *comos*, quod est villa, et *oda*, quod est cantus; inde comedia quasi villanus cantus: quia incipit a miseria et finit in felicitatem, sicut villani qui in villa vel comitatu habitantes, dum efficiuntur cives, de rustico opere ad civile negotium transeunt. Ita poete comici sua opera incipiunt a vili materia et terminant ipsam [*lege* ipsa] in nobilem, id est, incipiunt a miseria et adversitate et finiunt in prosperitatem et felicitatem."

22. Jenaro, *Trecento*, pp. 7–8.

23. Jacopo della Lana, *Commento*, ed. Luciano Scarabelli, *Comedia di Dante*, 2d ed. (Bologna 1866), 1:104: "L'altro modo è la forma poetica, la quale è fittiva e di esempli positivi, dalla qual forma ello tolle lo nome overo titulo, cioè *Comedia*, che è quasi a dire villano dittato, cioè che anticamente le villani sonnando sue sestole overo pive si ritimavano. Ed è da sapere che le più specie di poetiche dittazioni frall'altre—quelle che cominciano [da] stato fatigoso et arduo e vanno, migliorando stato, insino in perfetto essere—hanno nome comedie."

necessarily a tragedy. He calls it a high tragedy because of its high style and diction.[24] We can deduce from this statement that Lana did not consider the whole of the *Aeneid* to be a tragedy, but only that part of it that dealt with Troy.[25] We can note too that a work is a tragedy because of the turn of events it describes, not because of style. Vergil's tragedy of Troy was a high tragedy, because it was written in an elevated style; but presumably another author could have produced a low tragedy, one written in a humble style.

Jacopo Alighieri's commentary is definitely dependent on Guido, as Jenaro shows.[26] But rather than following Guido in dividing poetry into the four styles of tragedy, comedy, satire, and lyric, Jacopo speaks of the four styles of tragedy, comedy, satire, and elegy, a grouping found in Matthew of Vendôme's *Ars versificatoria* (in the order of tragedy, satire, comedy, and elegy) and in the commentary on Geoffrey of Vinsauf's *Poetria nova* by the Paduan scholar Pace of Ferrara (in the order of elegy, comedy, tragedy, and satire).[27]

Jacopo says that the first of the styles, tragedy, deals with "architectonic magnificences," as illustrated by Lucan and by Vergil in the *Aeneid*. The second style, comedy, deals with every subject, and that is why Dante's work is called a comedy. The third style, satire, uses the mode of reprehension, and Horace's poetry is an example. The fourth is elegy, which treats of misery in one form or another, as can be seen in Boethius.[28] Whether his formulation of the nature of tragedy and satire was affected by Guido's discussion is not clear. But his notion of comedy seems far removed from anything that Guido says.

---

24. Ibid., 1:350: "Tragedia è una poetria opposita alla comedia, imperocchè la comedia tratta novelle di quelli che nel principio sono stati piccoli e fievoli e da poca fortuna, e nella fine grandi, forti, e graziosi; la tragedia è l'opposito, chè tratta novelle di quelle di quelli che nel principio sono stati grandi ed eccellenti, nel fine piccioli e di nessuno valore. Or trattando di Troia Virgilio, che fu grande, vittoriosa, ed eccelsa, e poi fu condotta a destruzione, fu necessario che tal trattato fosse tragedia, e perchè nelli affari di Troia fu necessario nomar Euripilo, sì come auguro de'Greci, però dice che così lo chiama l'alta sua tragedia; e nota che dice 'alta,' cioè d'alto stile e dittato."

25. Hollander (see above, p. 5 n. 22) is mistaken, I think, when he assumes that Lana considered the whole *Aeneid* to be a tragedy (TDI 216, TC 130, TDC 251–52).

26. Jenaro, *Trecento*, pp. 132–37.

27. For Matthew, see P.V. Mengaldo, "L'elegia 'umile' (DVE 2.4.5–6)," in *Linguistica e retorica di Dante* (Pisa 1978), p. 204; for Pace, see Kelly, "Aristotle," pp. 197–98; Pace at one point cites Matthew's work.

28. Jacopo Alighieri, *Chiose alla cantica dell'Inferno*, ed. Jarro, a.k.a. G. Piccini (Florence 1915), pp. 43–44: "Il cui ordine brievemente così comincio che, secondo quello che ciertamente appare, in quattro stili ogni autentico parlare si conchiude, de' quali il primo tragedia è chiamato, sotto 'l quale, particularmente d'architettoniche magnificenze si tratta, si come Lucano, e Vergilio nell'*Eneidos*; il secondo, commedia, sotto il quale generalmente e universalmente si tratta di tutte le cose, e quindi il titol del presente volume procede; il terzo, satira, sotto il quale si tratta in modo di riprensione, siccome Orazio; il quarto e ultimo, elegia, sotto il quale d'alcuna miseria si tratta, si come Boezio."

4

Andrea Lancia, Pietro Alighieri, and Alberigo da Rosciate

The so-called *Ottimo commento* is now firmly assigned to the Florentine notary Andrea Lancia.[1] The early Palatine manuscript of the commentary, which we can call *0 Ottimo*, was composed between 1331 and 1334, and it draws upon an Italian epitome of Guido da Pisa's *Expositiones*.[2] But neither this version (it seems) nor *1 Ottimo*, which was finished around 1334,[3] has anything to say about tragedy and comedy. The next version, *2 Ottimo*, finished before the death of Giotto in 1337, does take up these forms, but instead of following Guido's series of lyric, satire, tragedy and comedy, it uses Jacopo Alighieri's classification of tragedy, comedy, satire, and elegy.[4]

For Lancia, tragedy either deals with great things, as in Lucan and in Vergil's *Aeneid*, or else it begins in felicity and ends in misery.[5] This distinction corresponds somewhat to Mussato's two kinds of tragedy (tragedy is a high style that deals with either great triumphs or great disasters).[6] It would enable one to explain how the *Aeneid* could be an *alta tragedia* without having a disastrous plot. Lancia also has a double definition of comedy: it is a style that treats equally (or commonly) of things low, middling, and high, or else it begins in misery and ends in felicity. He cites Ovid's *Metamorphoses* (presumably as an example of the first

1. Saverio Bellomo, "Primi appunti sull'*Ottimo commento* dantesco," *GSLI* 157 (1980) 368–82 (part 1: "Andrea Lancia, 'ottimo' commentatore trecentesco della *Commedia*") and 532–40 (part 2: "Il codice Palatino 313, primo abbozzo dell'*Ottimo commento*"). See also Giuliana De Medici, "Le fonti dell' *Ottimo commento* alla *Divina commedia*," *IMU* 26 (1983) 71–123, esp. 71 n. 4.

2. Bellomo, "Primi appunti," pp. 538-39.

3. A. Torri, ed., *L'Ottimo commento della Divina commedia*, 3 vols. (Pisa 1827–29).

4. The Proemio of *2 Ottimo* was edited by Luciano Scarabelli, *Comedia di Dante*, 2d ed., (Bologna 1866), 1:95–98 but attributed to Lana. See Luis Jenaro-MacLennan, *The Trecento Commentaries on the Divina commedia and the Epistle to Cangrande* (Oxford 1974), p. 18.

5. *2 Ottimo* 97: "Tragedia si è lo stile nel quale si tratta magnifiche cose, siccome è Lucano, Vergilio nell'*Eneida*; o vero tragedia è lo stile che comincia da felicitade e finische in miseria."

6. Mussato, *Lucii Annei Senece cordubensis vita et mores*, ed. Anastasios Megas, *'O προουμανιστικὸς κύκλος τῆς Πάδουας (Lovato Lovati—Albertino Mussato) καὶ οἱ τραγῳδίες τοῦ L. S. Seneca* (Salonica 1967), pp. 154–61. See H. A. Kelly, "Aristotle-Averroes-Alemannus on Tragedy," *Viator* 10 (1979) 192–93.

kind of comedy) and Dante's present poem (which would seem to fit both definitions). Then Lancia explains, perhaps drawing on one of the Latin dictionaries, how the style took its name from a rustic type of song.[7] Finally, he notes that satire is a style involving reprehension and garrulity, as in Horace, whereas elegy is a style dealing with misery, as in Boethius.

In the last version of Lancia's commentary (*3 Ottimo*),[8] produced after Giotto's death,[9] Lancia, or a reviser other than Lancia, repeats the idea that there are four styles of poetic speech; but this time the reviser begins with comedy and takes his doctrine straight from Papias. Comedy, he says, deals with private and low persons in a middling style, and sometimes treats of history and authoritative persons; the word comes from the Greek for *villa* and *canto*; and comedies are divided into four parts, namely, prologue, "prothesis," epitasis, and catastrophe.[10]

As for tragedy, the reviser keeps the first definition of *2 Ottimo*: it deals with great things, as in Lucan and Vergil. But then he gives Papias's Isidorian mixture (combining Book 18 with Book 8 of the *Etymologies*): the ancient deeds and felonies of scelerate kings are written in this style; tragedies used to be rewarded with a goat, which the Greeks call *trages*. The reviser then adds that tragedies were written with tearful verses, which he illustrates by giving the incipits of the *Pharsalia*, *Thebaid*, and *Aeneid*.[11] His treatment of satire and elegy simply expands upon *2 Ottimo*.

The first version of Pietro Alighieri's commentary on his father's great work seems to have been finished in 1340 or 1341. Two other versions are contained in two manuscripts, of which the Ashburnham is usually called the second and the Ottoboni the third. Often these versions seem to be not so much revisions

7. *2 Ottimo* 97: "Comedia è uno stile che tratta comunemente di cose basse, mezzane, e alte, o vero che comincia in miseria e termina a la felicitade, come Ovidio nel *Metamorphoseos*, e qui l'Autore; ed è detto comedia da *comos* greco che è in latino *villa*; usavano li villani quando avevano piena la casa de' beni temporali darsi al ventre, e far loro canzoni, e metterle in nota coi loro otricelli e simili strumenti, e dicevano comedia [*lege* comedi]; poi li poeti tolsero quello nome, e puoderlo [*lege* puoserlo] al detto stile."

8. The proem is edited by Giuseppe Vandelli in the course of his study, "Una nuova redazione dell'*Ottimo*," *SD* 14 (1930) 93–174.

9. Bellomo, "Primi appunti," pp. 368–69 n. 4, puts *3 Ottimo* between 1337 and 1350, but probably before 1340, since it does not draw on Pietro Alighieri's commentary.

10. *3 Ottimo*, p. 144: "Comedia è uno stile quando il poeta scrive cose di private e basse persone con stile mezzano, e alcuna volta tratta ystoria e di persone autorevoli; ed è così chiamata da *comos*, che è la villa, e *odos*, che viene a dire canto; e dividesi in quattro parti: in prologo, protesi, epytasi, e ca[ta]strofen." Vandelli, pp. 145–46, refers to Balbus, but the reviser used Papias rather than Balbus, for the latter does not give the four parts of comedy.

11. Ibid. (p. 144): "Tragedia è uno stile poetico nel quale si trattano magnifiche cose, sì come fa Lucano e Virgilio ne l'*Eneyda*; scrivensi in questo stile le antiche opere e le fellonie delli scelerati re. E a li scrittori delle tragedie si dava per merito il becco, lo quale li Greci chiamano *trages*; scriveansi con versi piangnevoli. Onde dice Lucano: 'Bella per emathios plus quam civilia campos / Jusque datum sceleri,' etc. E Stazio nel *Thebaidos* comincia: 'Fraternas acies alternaque regna profanis / Decertata odiis,' etc. E Virgilio: 'Arma virumque cano Troie qui primus ab horis,' etc."

of the original commentary as supplements to it. They can be tentatively dated as having been finished by 1350.[12]

Pietro is the first of the commentators to connect comedy and tragedy with the ancient theater, since, as we saw, Guido da Pisa showed no sign of knowing about the acting out of the works of Terence and Seneca. His understanding of the ancient theater may have come from Nicholas Trevet's commentary on Seneca's tragedies. Pietro begins by explaining that the scene, which was in the middle of the semicircular theater, was a little house with a pulpit. Then, however, he seems to identify the scene with the pulpit, for he says that the poet ascended "upon it" (*super id*), while "outside" mimes went through motions in keeping with the sense of the poems he recited. Pietro probably had in mind nothing other than the sort of freestanding medieval pulpit with stairs and roof. He says that the poet ascended the pulpit as a singer and recited his poems in the way in which one performs songs; and if he sang in rustic fashion, his song was called a comedy.[13] But it becomes clear that by song he simply means poem.

Pietro etymologizes comedy as *villanus cantus* and says that its style consisted of matter beginning with a sad recitation and ending in a joyful one, whence even now writers sometimes say in place of a salutation, "Tragic beginning and happy end!" It was for this reason, Pietro says, that Dante called his work a comedy, since he intended to begin in hell and end in paradise.[14] Another reason was that the poet in comedy is meant to speak in a low rather than high manner (*remisse et non alte*), as Terence did in his comedies. Dante therefore used

12. See the discussion by Jenaro, *Trecento*, pp. 19–20. I will call the original version 1 Pietro, the Ashburnham text 2 Pietro, and the Ottoboni version 3 Pietro. The *Inferno* portions of all three texts have been provided, but with egregious errors, in *Il "Commentarium" di Pietro Alighieri nelle redazioni ashburnhamiana e ottoboniana*, transcribed by Roberto Della Vedova and Maria Teresa Silvotti, introduction by Egidio Guidubaldi (Florence 1978). 1 Pietro appears on the bottom of the pages, taken from the edition by Vincenzo Nannucci, 2 Pietro at the upper left, and 3 Pietro at the upper right. For 1 Pietro, I follow Nannucci's text, *Petri Allegherii super Dantis ipsius genitoris Comoediam commentarium, nunc primum in lucem editum, consilio et sumtibus G. I. Bar. Vernon*, which appears in identical form in two imprints, "Apud Guilielmum Piatti" (Florence 1845) and "Apud Angelum Garinei" (Florence 1846).

13. 1 Pietro (Nannucci, p. 9): "Antiquitus in theatro, quod erat area semicircularis, et in eius medio erat domuncula que *scena* dicebatur, in qua erat pulpitum, et super id ascendebat poeta ut cantor, et sua carmina ut cantiones recitabat; extra vero erant mimi ioculatores, carminum pronuntiationem gestu corporis effigiantes per adaptationem ad quemlibet ex cuius persona ipse poeta loquebatur; unde cum loquebatur, pone de Iunone conquerente de Hercule privigno suo, mimi, sicut recitabat, ita effigiabant Iunonem invocare Furias infernales ad infestandum ipsum Herculem; et si tale pulpitum seu domunculum ascendebat poeta qui de more villico caneret, talis cantus dicebatur comedia." The explanation of *mimi* as *ioculatores* is in Papias, Huguccio, and Balbus. For Trevet, see Jenaro, *Trecento*, pp. 101–2.

14. 1 Pietro (Nannucci, pp. 9–10): "Nam dicitur a *comos*, quod est villa, et *oda*, cantus, quasi villicus cantus; et quod eius stylus erat in materia incipiente a tristi recitatione et finiente in letum, unde adhuc scribentes interdum loco salutationis dicunt 'Tragicum principium et comicum finem.' Et quod auctor iste ita scribere intendebat, incipiendo ab inferno et finiendo in paradisum, sic eius poema voluit nominari."

the vulgar tongue, just as rustics do, since as a *comicus* he had to be *humilis et remissus*. Pietro cites two authorities for this doctrine. The second is clear enough, namely, Isidore in Book 8: "Comedians are those who sang the acts of private men." But the first authority cited, *Ars poetica* 93–94, is a bit puzzling. If Pietro understands the lines properly, he may mean that, according to Horace, comedy usually speaks in humble tones because it only occasionally raises its voice. But then again he may think of raised voices and wrathful tumidity as characteristic not of high speech but of rustic "remissness"; or he may interpret *tollit* not as "raises" but as "lowers" (that is, "takes away") and *tumido ore* not as pompous bombast but as mealymouthed bickering—especially if he followed the reading of *timido*. Matthew of Vendôme understood Horace's following lines about tragedy in a corresponding way, as characterizing the high style of tragedy: he takes *proiecit ampullas* to refer to "hurling" vases rather than to "dropping" them.[15] However, in his next versions, as we will see, Pietro clearly interprets Horace to mean that comedy occasionally uses high style.

Pietro then speaks of tragedy, which he says is another poetic style and song: it is opposed to comedy, for it begins in joy and ends in sadness. It means "goat-song," because, according to Isidore, those who sang such things—that is, the old deeds and crimes of kings in a mournful song—were rewarded with a goat. Then he cites Horace's line about competing over a vile goat. He ends by saying that tragedy, or the tragic poet, speaks with loud and clamorous voice (*elate et clamose*), as is shown in Boethius's question about the *clamor tragediarum*; and for these reasons Seneca titled certain of his poems tragedies.[16]

Pietro concludes this section of his introduction by saying that there are other kinds of poetic songs that are named according to their meaning, namely elegiac (that is, desolatory), as in Boethius; bucolic (pastoral), as in Vergil's *Bucolics*; georgic (terrestrial), as in Vergil's *Georgics*; satiric (reprehensive), as in Horace, Juvenal, and Persius; and lyrical (delectable), as in Ovid.[17]

On the question of Pietro's unnamed sources, we can recognize, first of all,

---

15. Matthew of Vendôme, *Ars versificatoria* 2.5, ed. Edmond Faral, *Les arts poétiques du xiie et du xiiie siècles* (Paris 1924) pp. 109–93, esp. 153. Jenaro, *Trecento*, pp. 98–99, understands 1 Pietro in this way. Here is what Pietro says (1 Pietro, p. 10): "Item quod poeta in comedia debet loqui remisse et non alte, ut Terentius in suis comediis fecit; ad quod Horatius, 'Interdumque tamen vocem Comedia tollit, / iratusque Chremes tumido delitigat ore'; et Isidorus, *Ethimologiis*: 'Comedi sunt qui privatorum hominum acta cantabant'; per quod vide quare vulgariter Dantes ut comicus, humilis, et remissus scripsit, et loquendo vulgariter, ut faciunt rustici et quilibet idiota." I give variants for Pietro's Horace quotation below, p. 37 n. 4.

16. 1 Pietro (Nannucci, p. 10): "Tragedia vero est alius poeticus stylus et cantus, et oppositus comedie; nam incipit a letis et finit in tristibus. Et dicitur a *tragos*, quod est hirquus, et *oda*, cantus, quasi hirquinus cantus, quod talia canentibus, antiqua gesta videlicet et facinora regum luctuoso cantu, dabatur hirquus in premium, secundum Isidorum. Unde Horatius: 'Carmine qui tragico vilem certavit ob hirquum.' Et loquitur elate et clamose; unde Boetius in *Libro de consolatione*: 'Quid aliud tragediarum deflet clamor,' etc. Et ex his Seneca certa sua poemata tragedias titulavit."

17. 1 Pietro (Nannucci, p. 11).

that his definitions of comedy and tragedy clearly depend on Huguccio, whether in his own work or as repeated in Balbus; and since he cites Huguccio by name six times during the course of his work and Balbus not at all,[18] it is most likely that he was drawing on Huguccio directly. If so, we have an example of someone being able to find the accounts of tragedy and comedy under *oda*. Pietro's language is very close to that of the *Cangrande* Accessus. But while the Accessor could have derived his Huguccian material from Pietro without consulting Huguccio directly, the opposite is not true. For Pietro preserves Huguccio's terms (especially *tristia* and *leta*) where the Accessor does not; the Accessor seems rather to echo Guido da Pisa's phraseology.

It seems most likely, then, that the Accessor's phrases *remisse et humiliter* and *elate et sublime*[19] were inspired by Pietro (*sublime* echoes Guido's *sublimes persone*). The term *remissus* has been taken to be a nontraditional term in discussions of style;[20] however, the *Rhetorica ad Herennium* deals with *oratio remissa* in contrast to the usages of tragedy,[21] and this could well be the basis not only of Pietro's expression but also of Boccaccio's *istilo umilissimo e rimesso* in the prologue to the fourth day of the *Decameron*.[22] But the fact that Pietro cites Terence as an example may point to the intermediary of a commentary on Terence, perhaps one influenced by Donatus. Donatus says that Terence's plays are so tempered that they do not swell up into tragic height or fall into mimic vileness.[23]

When Pietro speaks not only of the style of comedy (which could come from

---

18. See Nannucci's index.

19. *Cangrande* 10.30; cf. 10.31: "remissus est modus et humilis."

20. Jenaro, *Trecento*, pp. 97–100.

21. *Rhetorica ad Herennium* 3.13.23: *sermo* is "oratio remissa et finitima cotidianae locutioni"; in 3.14.24 we are cautioned "ne ab oratoria consuetudine ad tragicam transeamus." This definition of *sermo* was cited by J. A. Scott in his review of Jenaro's book in *Modern Language Review* 71 (1976) 932–34, and Jenaro takes it up in his response, " 'Remissus est modus et humilis' (*Epistle to Cangrande*, §10)," *Lettere italiane* 31 (1979) 406–18, but neither he nor Scott notices its connection with tragedy in the *Rhetorica*. Jenaro objects that in the context of the *Rhetorica*'s third book *remissa* refers to tone rather than style, but admits that it could have been interpreted out of context to refer to style; he notes that it was in fact so taken in the *Accessus Horatii* of the *Accessus ad auctores* edited by R. C. B. Huygens, 2d ed. (Leiden 1970), pp. 49–53, esp. 51. As Scott points out, Jenaro himself notes that one of the meanings given by Balbus for *remissus* is *dimissus* (*Trecento*, pp. 99–100 n. 1). The same is true of Papias and Huguccio.

22. See Jenaro, *Trecento*, pp. 118–23.

23. Donatus-Evanthius 3.5: "eius fabulae eo sunt temperamento ut neque extumescant ad tragicam celsitudinem neque abiciantur ad mimicam vilitatem." As we will see in Chapter 6, Francesco da Buti does make use of the Donatus-influenced *Novem requiruntur* (see above, p. 1 n. 2, and below, p. 59). However, *Novem* not only lacks Donatus's statement on style, but it also says that Terence used the *levis* style (as opposed to *gravis* and *mediocris*): "Stilum servat levem. Stilus enim alius gravis, alius mediocris, alius levis. Gravis qui fit de maximis rebus sive personis, loquendo nimis alte et non vulgariter. Mediocris stilus est qui fit in mediocribus verbis et non tenet neque tantum vulgaria neque valde ponderosa. Levis stilus est qui de rebus levibus ac parvis loquitur planis et vulgaribus verbis, quod Terentius facit" (ed. G. V. Alessio, "Hec Franciscus de Buiti," *IMU* 24 [1981] 100–1, no. 67).

Huguccio) but also of tragedy as a style, he may be drawing on Jacopo Alighieri or on *2 Ottimo* or *3 Ottimo*, and the same may be true when he goes on to mention other categories of poetry. In his explanation of tragedy, Pietro's combination of material from Books 8 and 18 of the *Etymologies* is similar to the account in *3 Ottimo*, but it shows signs of a fresh reading of Isidore's texts, whether directly or by way of Trevet's commentary on Seneca.[24]

In Pietro's second commentary,[25] the text of his generic discussion is somewhat garbled, but his general meaning is clear. He says that Dante chose a suitable title for his work in calling it *Comedy*, in view of the "maternal and humble and sweet style" that he used, which he wished to hold good poetically for all persons, both those learned in Latin and those who knew only the vernacular.[26] Papias, he explains, defines comedy as a poetic song dealing with the deeds of private and humble persons in a middling and sweet style; and Horace points out that a high style is also sometimes used, when he says that Comedy raises her voice on occasion.[27]

Pietro then sums up the Huguccian material: comedy by its very nature should begin its songs and treatment with calamitous and adverse matters and

---

24. See Jenaro, *Trecento*, p. 101.

25. 2 Pietro is found in Florence Bibl. Laur. MS Ashb. 841; unfortunately, the text is often corrupt; a somewhat abridged version appears in Vatican MS Barb. lat. 4029, derived from the Ashburnam copy or its prototype (its variants therefore are either better readings or corrections—or fresh mistakes). I also indicate the corresponding pages in the faulty Della Vedova-Silvotti text (DVS).

26. 2 Pietro, Ashb. fol. 3 (cf. DVS p. 9). The text as abbreviated reads as follows (I italicize the words referring to the philosophy question): "qui sit libri titulus statī infra mōstrabo ī expositōe rubrice *cui pti·tā fy suppo.eandē ethice se morali*. Restat m̊ uidē de titulo lib᾿ p̂dći q̠ comedia dicitur. S_3 quare sic hūc suum librū auctor noīauit. & c᾿te merito ita ītitulauit eū· ɔsiderato stillo & mat᾿no & hūili & dulci quē tenē ītedebat poetice talia expectācia ad uniu᾿sas gētes *fy suppo·eadē ethice se morali*·lit᾿ratas quā uulgares canēdo." I expand and reconstruct the text as follows: "Qui sit libri titulus statim infra monstrabo in expositione rubrice. Cui parti tamen philosophie supponatur, [. . . dico quod supponitur] ethice seu morali. Restat modo videre de titulo libri predicti qui comedia dicitur. Sed quare sic hunc suum librum auctor nominavit, certe merito ita intitulavit eum, considerato stilo et materno et humili et dulci quem tenere intendebat poetice, talia expectancia ad universas gentes, [. . . tam] literatas quam vulgares, canendo." For the philosophy question, cf. 1 Pietro p. 11: "Nunc videndum cui parti philosophie supponatur. Unde dico quod supponitur ethice, idest morali philosophie." There is clearly something missing toward the end, for there is no referent to explain *talia expectancia*, the "such expectings" or "such expectant things" that Dante wished to sing to the world. The Barberini text stops short where the garbling is most obvious. It reads as follows, in expanded form: "Qui sit libri titulus statim infra monstrabo in exposicione Rubrice. Cui parti philosophie supponatur: Ethice, id est morali. Restat ergo uidere de titulo libri predicti qui comedia dicitur. Sed quare sic hunc suum librum auctor nominauit, et certe merito ita intitulauit, cum considerato stilio materno et humili et dulci quem tenere intendebat poetice talia spectantia ad vniuersas gentes" (fol. 1v).

27. 2 Pietro, Ashb. fol. 3: "Unde Papia dicit quod comedia est cantus poeticus qui priuatorum et humilium personarum gesta comprehendit mediocri stilo et dulci; ac etiam quandoque alto, unde in sua *Poetria* ait Oracius: 'Interdum tamen et uocem comedia tollit.' " (Barb. fol. 1v agrees.)

should finish in happy things, just as tragedy follows the opposite course—hence, the salutation of "tragic beginning and comic end." He goes on to say that perhaps it was this consideration of a happy end that led Dante to end each of the three books of the *Comedy* with the word "stars."[28] Another reason is that comedians, like tragedians and satirists, were allowed the liberty (according to Horace) of reprehending the wicked, and this was in keeping with Dante's intention.[29]

In his next try, Pietro tackles the question of why Dante called his work a comedy by citing Isidore, who defined comedy as the sort of poetic song that dealt with the deeds of private and humble persons in a modest style (Isidore in fact said nothing about style), exemplified by Plautus, Accius, and Terence, whereas tragedy was another kind of poetic work in high style, dealing for the most part with the sad deeds of kings.[30] He cites Horace as saying that the supreme style can also be used on occasion for comedy, and he notes that the gloss to the *Ars poetica* at this point gives an example from Terence.[31] Then he cites Huguccio by name for the plot criterion and the tragic-comic salutation.[32] Dante, in other words, wished to use a humble style, that is, the maternal language, and use it mainly to describe the deeds of private persons; but he also wanted to write at

28. Ibid.: "Preterea comedia de sui natura debet incipere sua carmina et tractatum a calamitosis et adversis rebus et debet finire in iocundis; unde consueuit scribi per antiquos in suis epistolis loco salutacionis, 'tragicum principium et comicum finem.' Nam tragedia alius cantus poeticus e contrario incipit et finit sua carmina. Nunc igitur cum auctor incoare ab inferno debeat et finire in paradiso, hoc suum poema recte comedia dici debuit, et forte hoc respectu auctor hoc suum poema in suis tribus libris semper finiuit ultimum verbum in 'stellis,' in rebus supernam felicitatem indagantibus [*lege* indicantibus] nobis." (The Barberini text agrees.)

29. Ibid. fol. 3r-v (DVS 10–11): "Item etiam quia comedis data est libertas reprehendi viciosos, ut tragedis et satiris, ut auctor facere intendebat; unde idem Oracius in *Poetria* ad hoc etiam ait: 'Successit uetus hijs comedia non sine multa / Ladem; sed inicium libertas excidit et uim / Dignam lege regi, etc." (The Barberini text, still on fol. 1v, omits the quotation from Horace, *Ars poetica* 281–83, which should read *Laude* for *Ladem* and *in uicium* for *inicium*.)

30. 3 Pietro, Vat. MS Ottob. lat. 2867, fols. 2v–3 (cf. DVS, pp. 10–11): "Circha quam primo queritur cur auctor hoc suum predictum poema nominatum [*lege* nominauerit] comediam; ad quod sciendum prenotandum est quod antiquitus, ut dicit Ysidorus, inter alios cantos poeticos erat quidam qui dicebatur comedia, scilicet quando aliquis poeta cantabat, idest sua carmina proferebat, circha gesta priuatorum personarum et humilium modesto stillo, ut Plautus, Accius, et Terrencius et alij comici poete fecerunt, sicut tragedia est alius cantus poeticus, quando aliquid sicilicet alto stillo describitur tangens tristia gesta regum, ut plurimum."

31. Ibid., fol. 3: "Quandoque tamen dicta comedia etiam suppremo stillo modullatur; vnde Oracius in sua poetria ait: 'Interdum tamen et vocem comedia tollit, / Iratusque Cremes tumido delitigat ore,' vbi glosa sic ait super dicto verbo *comedia tollit*, 'vt facit Terrencius in sua comedia dicens: "O celum, o terra, o maria Neptuni, proh summe Iupiter," etc.' Et ex hoc idem Oracius subdit in laudem talis stili comici sic: 'Successit verus [*lege* vetus] hijs comedia non sine multa/Laude,' etc."

32. Ibid., fol. 3: "Item prenotandum est quod prout scribit Ugucio, 'Comedia a tristibus incipit, sed in letis desinit. Tragedia vero e converso. Vnde in salutacione solemus mittere et optare tragicum principium et comicum finem, idest bonum et letum principium et bonum et letum finem.'"

times in the high and "elated" style about celestial things, and also to begin with sad things and end with celestial, and for this reason he ended each book with the word "stars."[33] We might note that Pietro's finding of three comic endings in Dante's poem might have led him to conclude that the work consists of three comedies, but he nowhere makes such a conclusion evident.

Many of Pietro's observations in all three versions of his commentary come from the books of his profession, the texts and glosses of canon and civil law; but none of his citations have any bearing on the genres of comedy and tragedy.[34] In contrast, another lawyer, Alberigo da Rosciate, does adduce a legal gloss in his explanation of Dante's title. In his Latin translation of Lana's commentary, which he completed sometime before the middle of the fourteenth century, Rosciate draws on Accursius's Ordinary Gloss to Justinian's *Digest*, where comedians are defined as those who recite comedies in alternate fashion, with one singing and the other "subsinging" or responding.[35] He also refers to Trevet's commentary on Seneca's tragedies.

Rosciate characterizes comedy as a poetic form originally used by rustics to the accompaniment of flutes. Later comedians, that is, companions, recited comedies—that is, the great events that were occurring—in the alternating style noted in the *Digest* gloss and in the commentator's introduction to the *Tragedies*. He adds that such comedians can still be seen, especially in Lombardy, singing the deeds of great lords in verses, with the one declaring and the other responding.[36]

33. Ibid., fol. 3 (DVS 12): "Ad propositum ergo, volens noster auctor et intendens scribere humili stillo, scilicet vulgarj seu materno, poetice facta priuatarum (ut plurimum) personarum, ac etiam in parte stillo alto et ellato, scribendo de rebus celestibus, ut facit in *Paradiso*, ultimo suo libro, et incipiendo a tristibus, idest ab infernalibus, et finiendo in letis, idest in celestibus, ut facit—quo respectu etiam credo ipsum finire quemlibet librum dicte eius *Comedie* in vltimo verbo in 'stellis,' ut facit, ut in letis et splendidis rebus—merito hoc eius poema *Comediam* nominauit."

34. For Pietro's juristic citations, see Luigi Caricato, "Il *Commentarium* all'*Inferno* di Pietro Alighieri: Indagine sulle fonti," part 1, *IMU* 26 (1983) 125–50, and see below, pp. 40–41.

35. *Corpus iuris civilis*: *Digestum*, lib. 21, tit. 1 (*De aedilicio edicto*), lex 34 (*Cum eiusdem*) ad v. *comoedi*: "Qui pariter recitant comedias: unus cantando, alter succinendo vel respondendo." I use the edition of Lyons 1550, vol. 1, col. 1620. As can be seen in the text given in the next note, Rosciate also refers to *Digestum* lib. 9, tit. 2 (*Ad legem Aquiliam*), lex 22 (*Proinde si servum*) par. 1: "Item . . . si quis ex comoedis," etc. But Accursius gives no gloss here (see cols. 853–54). Rosciate in his own commentary on *Cum eiusdam* simply refers to the Ordinary Gloss for an explanation of *comedi* and adds a reference to *Proinde*. See his *Commentarii in Digestum*, 2 vols. (Venice 1585, repr. Bologna 1974–77) 2:173v; cf. 1:369.

36. Antonio Fiammazzo, ed., *Il commento dantesco di Graziolo de' Bambaglioli dal "Colombino" di Siviglia con altri codici raffrontato* (Savona 1915), p. 110: "De isto inferno et eius penis pulcerime et venuste tractat auctor iste venerabilis in ista prima parte que *Infernus* appelatur, et mirabiliter et bene, conformans penas quibuslibet pecatis in forma poeticha que appelatur chomedia, quia ab antiquo tractata fuit a rusticis et ex solitu [*lege* sonitu] fistularum; unde postea apparuerunt chomedi, idest socij, gui pariter recitabant comedias, hoc est magnalia que occurebant, unus videlicet cantando, aliter [*lege* alter] succinendo et respondendo, ut notatur in glosa ff. *de Edil. edito*. l. *cum eisdem*, et *Ad l. Aquil* l. *proinde* §finali, et in prohemio Tragediarum

It is remarkable that Rosciate takes over nothing from his other sources on comedy, including Trevet's work, which he cites, and Lana's commentary, which he translates. He follows only Accursius and alleged contemporary practice that corresponds to Accursius's account (though Rosciate must have found some learned source for his statement that the early comedians used pipes or flutes). No other commentator remarks on the sort of Lombard comedians that Rosciate describes, who went about performing "serious comedy" of the sort admitted by Papias. If they truly existed, and if Dante knew about them, perhaps their art played a role in Dante's choice of title for his work.

---

succincte per commentatorem. Et isti chomedi adhuc sunt in usu nostro: apparent enim maxime in partibus Lombardie aliqui cantatores qui magnorum dominorum in rithimis cantant gesta, unus proponendo, alius respondendo." Taken from Oxford Bodleian MS Canonici ital. Miscell. 449. For Rosciate, see Bruno Sandkühler, *Die frühen Dantekommentare und ihr Verhältnis zur mittelalterlichen Kommentartradition* (Munich 1967), pp. 181 n. 83, 193, 277; see also "Alberigo da Rosate (o Rosciate)," *ED* 1:94. For Rosciate's self-characterization as "in utroque iure peritus," see Fiammazzo, p. 130.

5

The Doctrine and Sources of the Proto-Accessus

Since the next certain commentator we know of is Boccaccio, and since it has been established that Boccaccio drew upon some form of the Accessus section of the *Epistle to Cangrande*, let us examine the Accessor's doctrine on tragedy and comedy and try to identify its sources or connections with other commentaries.

We can easily conclude that the Accessor follows Guido da Pisa in calling comedy a poetic narration, and also in taking over the terms he uses for describing tragic and comic plots, while syncopating Guido's etymology. We note that Guido's *grata* is here changed to *quieta* (though we will see *grata* appear later), and *miserie* to *rei*.

> Et est comedia genus quoddam poetice narrationis ab omnibus aliis differens. Differt ergo a tragedia in materia per hoc quod tragedia in principio est admirabilis et quieta [Guido: grata], in fine seu [Guido: sive] exitu est fetida et horribilis; et dicitur propter hoc a *tragos*, quod est hircus, et *oda*, [Guido: quod est cantus; inde *tragedia*] quasi cantus hircinus, id est fetidus ad modum hirci, ut patet per Senecam in suis tragediis. [More material of Guido's is omitted.] Comedia vero inchoat asperitatem alicuius rei [Guido: miserie], sed eius materia prospere terminatur, ut patet per Terentium in suis comediis.[1]

The Accessor then goes beyond Guido's account and mentions the tragicomic epistolary salutation:

> Et hinc consueverunt dictatores quidam in suis salutationibus dicere, loco salutis, tragicum principium et comicum finem.

This statement has usually been taken to come from Huguccio, who says:

> Unde in salutatione solemus mittere et optare amicis tragicum principium et comicum finem, id est, principium bonum et letum et bonum et letum finem.

But the Accessor's formulation is much closer to that of 2 Pietro, where the practice is characterized as a past custom:

---

1. *Cangrande* 10.29; cf. Guido, *Expositiones*, ed. Vincenzo Cioffari (Albany, N.Y., 1974), p. 4. Brugnoli reads *sive exitu*, but all of the MSS have *seu exitu*.

> Unde consuevit scribi per antiquos in suis epistolis loco salutationis, tragicum principium et comicum finen.

In contrast, Huguccio speaks of it as still practiced, as does 1 Pietro:

> Unde adhuc scribentes interdum loco salutationis dicunt tragicum principium et comicum finem.

So does 3 Pietro, where Pietro specifically cites Huguccio:

> Unde in salutacione solemus mittere et optare tragicum principium et comicum finem, id est, bonum et letum principium et bonum et letum finem.[2]

It may be, however, that the Accessor was following 1 Pietro but put the custom in the past tense because he had never encountered the practice and concluded that it was no longer current.

The Accessor's next statement clearly parallels 1 Pietro rather than 2 Pietro. 1 Pietro reads, in Nannucci's edition:

> Item quod poeta in comedia debet loqui remisse et non alte, ut Terentius in suis comediis fecit; ad quod Horatius:
>
> Interdumque tamen vocem comedia tollit,
> iratusque Chremes tumido delitigat ore.

The Accessor says:

> Similiter differunt in modo loquendi: elate et sublime tragedia, comedia vero remisse et humiliter; sicut vult Horatius in sua *Poetria*, ubi licentiat comicos ut tragedos loqui, et sic e converso:
>
> Interdum tamen et vocem comedia tollit,
> iratusque Chremes tumido delitigat ore;
> et tragicus plerunque dolet sermone pedestri,
> Telephus et Peleus, etc.[3]

If the Accessor was drawing directly on 1 Pietro, he must have had his own text of the *Ars poetica*, since he quotes a different version of line 93 and adds lines 95 and 96—unless, of course, the Accessor used a version of 1 Pietro with a different reading, or unless Pseudo-Dante inserted the different reading into the Proto-Accessus. The noninfluence argument could also be made to work in reverse: the fact that Pietro's first line is different (though it scans properly) might be taken as an indication that he was not drawing on the Proto-Accessus. The matter becomes more complicated when we note that the version of line 93 in both 2 Pietro and 3 Pietro is the same as that in the Accessus (2 Pietro gives *only* line 93 and not line 94). One possible solution is that 1 Pietro's citation of Horace was originally identical to that of *Cangrande*, but that the text of 1 Pietro as we have it is the result of scribal alteration. It is instructive to see how many variants to lines

2. See above, p. 31 n. 32, for the full text of 3 Pietro and his citation of Huguccio.

3. *Cangrande* 10.30, quoting *Ars poetica* 93–96. For the term *remissa* or *remissus*, see above, p. 29 n. 21.

93 and 94 are to be found in the manuscripts of the commentary.[4] At all events, it is certain that the Accessor used the *Ars poetica* independently of Pietro, for it inspired him to come up with a new list of literary genres.[5]

1 Pietro leaves unspoken what he obviously takes to be the meaning of Horace's lines, and what the Accessor spells out, namely, that comic poets can sometimes use the language of tragedians, and vice versa. As we have seen, this interpretation of Horace is made explicit in 2 Pietro and 3 Pietro.[6]

When the Accessor applies his doctrine to Dante, he parallels 1 Pietro in interpreting the humble mode as the vernacular, but instead of Pietro's example of rustics or any unlearned person, he mentions "womenfolk." 1 Pietro reads:

> Per quod vide quare vulgariter Dantes ut comicus, humilis, et remissus scripsit, et loquendo vulgariter, ut faciunt rustici et quilibet idiota.

The Accessor says:

> Et per hoc patet quod *Comedia* dicitur presens opus. Nam si ad materiam respiciamus, a principio horribilis et fetida est, quia infernus, in fine prospera, desiderabilis,

---

4. I have examined only some of the manuscripts. To begin with, there is Vatican Library lat. 4782, a manuscript of the fifteenth century that Nannucci belatedly decided contained a text better than the three Florentine manuscripts and the one other Vatican text that he used; it is listed as no. 11 by John Paul Bowden, *An Analysis of Pietro Alighieri's Commentary on the Divine Comedy* (New York 1951), p. 23. The Horatian lines are given on fol. 14ra, and contain the variant *iratoque* (not given by Nannucci in his list at the end of his text, p. i). Vat. Capponi 176, likewise of the fifteenth century (Bowden, no. 10), which Nannucci also consulted, has *Interdum* in the first line but not the metrically necessary *et* before *vocem*, and *timido conlitigat* in the second line (fol. 9v); these variants are not given by Nannucci in his apparatus, and he does not note any variants from his Florentine texts. Vat. Barb. lat. 4098, of the fourteenth century (Bowden, no. 3), has *timido* (fol. lvb). Vat. Barb. lat. 4007, also of the fourteenth century (Bowden, no. 4), gives the lines exactly as they appear in Nannucci's text (fol. 2), as do four Florentine MSS, one of the fourteenth century: Laurentiana Plut. 90 sup. 118 fol. 55 (Bowden, no. 13), and three of the fifteenth: Laur. Plut. 40.38, fol. 3, Riccardiana 1075, fol. 1, and Bibl. Naz. Cent. Panciatichiano 4, fol. 5 (Bowden, nos. 5–6, 9), except that Plut. 40.38 reads *dellitigat hore*. Most modern editions of Horace give lines 93–94 as they appear in 3 Pietro and *Cangrande*. Of the above-noted variants, only *timido* is given in the apparatus of the edition by Otto Keller, *Opera* (Leipzig 1869), 2: 338, found in the eleventh-century scholiast manuscript, Paris B. N. lat. 7975, and even there it is corrected to *tumido*.

5. See below. In his review of Della Vedova-Silvotti in *Aevum* 54 (1980) 381–83, Giuseppe Frasso draws attention to another citation of the *Ars poetica*, that of line 339. It is given correctly as "Nec quodcumque velit poscat sibi fabula credi" by 1 Pietro (Nannucci, p. 6) and 3 Pietro (fol. 2), whereas the reading of 2 Pietro is: "Nec quodcumque uelit possit sua sibi fabula credi," according to the Barberini text (fol. l^{v}). But in the Ashburnam copy the line runs, "Nec quodcumque uelit possit sua sibi ba fabula credi" (fol. 2). The *possit* is underlined and the correct *poscat* is given in the margin by a later hand, and *sua* is crossed out—presumably by the same later corrector. But the meaningless *ba* remains untouched. The DVS reading (which Frasso has to rely on) is, "Nec quodcumque velit possit sibi fabula credi" (p. 6).

6. See Chapter 4, nn. 27, 31. I do not agree with those who, like Brugnoli, "Orazio," *ED* 4:175, think that such an interpretation misses Horace's meaning.

> et grata [here is Guido's word], quia Paradisus; ad modum loquendi, remissus est modus et humilis, quia locutio vulgaris in qua et muliercule comunicant.[7]

When the Accessor goes on to name other kinds of "poetic narration," he parallels 1 Pietro in listing bucolic verse, elegy, and satire. He omits 1 Pietro's georgic and lyric, but adds a genre that he thinks he has found in the *Ars poetica*, namely, the *sententia votiva.*[8]

What are we to make of the similarities between Pietro's commentaries and the *Cangrande* Accessus? Antonio Canal has suggested that Guido da Pisa was the author of *Cangrande*,[9] which of course would put the Accessus before Pietro's time of writing. It is conceivable, I suppose, that Guido could have drawn on his commentary to write an introduction to the *Paradiso* and addressed it to Cangrande in 1328 or 1329 (Cangrande died in the latter year). But it is unthinkable that Guido would have posed as Dante in so doing. It might be argued that the initial salutation of the Dedication is spurious (added later by the Compiler, I would say), like the single reference to Verona in the first paragraph of the Dedication, and meant originally for some other eminent patron. The author (whether Guido or someone else) would be dedicating not the *Paradiso* itself but only the enclosed copy of the "sublime canticle." However, even if one were to limit Guido's authorship to the Accessus (or rather Proto-Accessus) alone, there is so much in it that is new or alien to his known views that such an attribution must seem highly unlikely.

A pre-Pietro date would have to be given to the Proto-Accessus if it could be shown that any version of the *Ottimo commento* draws upon it. Francesco Mazzoni has demonstrated a clear connection between *3 Ottimo* and the *Cangrande* Exposition;[10] and Bruno Nardi suggests that the Accessus-Exposition portion of *Cangrande* was written by an Augustinian friar at Verona in accord with the doctrine of Giles of Rome, and that it was used by the unknown Thomist who produced *3 Ottimo.*[11] However, since the Exposition has an elaborate Thomistic analysis of *esse* and *essentia* and *3 Ottimo* does not, I think it much more likely that the analysis was added to *Cangrande* than that it was excised from *3 Ottimo.* I suggest, then, that the Compiler wrote the Exposition and made use of *3 Ot-*

---

7. *Cangrande* 10.31.

8. *Cangrande* 10.32: "Sunt et alia genera narrationum poeticarum, scilicet carmen bucolicum, elegia, satira, et sententia votiva, ut etiam per Oratium patere potest in sua *Poetria*; sed de istis ad presens nichil dicendum est." Cf. *Ars poetica* 76: "Post etiam inclusa est voti sententia compos." For Guido's four genres, see above, p. 13 n. 6.

9. Antonio Canal, *Il mondo morale di Guido da Pisa interprete di Dante* (Bologna 1981), pp. 68–69.

10. Francesco Mazzoni, "Per l'*Epistola a Cangrande*," in *Studi in onore di Angelo Monteverdi* (Modena 1959), pp. 498–516, esp. 511–13, singling out *Cangrande* 20.54–57, 21.61, 22.64–65, 28.77, and 30.85.

11. Bruno Nardi, *Il punto sull'Epistola a Cangrande* (Florence 1960), pp. 36–40; "Osservazioni sul medievale *accessus ad auctores* in rapporto all'*Epistola a Cangrande*" (1961), repr. in Nardi's *Saggi e note di critica dantesca* (Milan 1966), pp. 268–305, esp. 303–5.

timo at the same time that he subsumed the Proto-Accessus into his pseudepigraphous composition. Since there is no sign that Boccaccio saw the Exposition, the addition would have been made to his copy of the Proto-Accessus only after his death or, perhaps more likely, to another copy of the Proto-Accessus which he did not see.

If there is no reason to put the Proto-Accessus before the time of Pietro, we must ask if Pietro himself was the author. My response is the same that I gave for Guido's authorship, namely, that there is so much in the Accessus that is foreign to Pietro that the possibility seems unlikely. In his various versions, Pietro shows himself to be independent of other commentators and also to be scrupulous about citing his sources. It would be hard to imagine his taking over large sections from Guido without acknowledgment. Just so, it would be contrary to his modus operandi to draw on the Proto-Accessus without indicating that he was doing so. The probability is, then, that the Accessor drew on Pietro. We have noted points of similarity between the Accessus and both 1 Pietro and 2 Pietro, so that it is possible that he used both versions. The question could perhaps be cleared up by a full-scale comparison of the Accessus and Pietro's texts, including all the manuscript copies. My examination has been chiefly limited to the discussions of the kinds of poetry. But I agree with Jenaro that there is no indication of other connections between 1 Pietro and *Cangrande*, and I can see no further connections between 2 Pietro and *Cangrande*. The fact that both 2 Pietro and 3 Pietro adopt a fourfold sense for the *Comedy*, thereby paralleling Guido and *Cangrande*, as opposed to the sevenfold presentation of 1 Pietro, does not seem significant in view of the abundant earlier sources available for the fourfold analysis of Scripture. One is cited by name in 3 Pietro: the *Breviloquium* of St. Bonaventure.[12]

Even in 1 Pietro it is clear that one of Pietro's main sources is a fourfold analysis of Scripture, based on the example of Jerusalem, which he uses for his second, fifth, sixth, and seventh senses. Although there were several possible sources for this explanation, including Papias and Balbus,[13] he may have found

12. 3 Pietro, fol. 2v (DVS 9).

13. For Papias, see Violetta De Angelis's edition, *Elementarium*, vols. 1–3: *Littera A* (Milan 1977–80), s.v. "allegoria" (2:173, no. 64). After the example of Solomon's temple, he says: "Similiter 'Lauda Hierusalem Dominum,' etc. [Psalm 147.12], ipsam civitatem et homines, ecclesiam, animam, et patriam caelestem significat." Balbus, citing Papias, has: "Similiter Iherusalem ipsam civitatem et homines, ecclesiam, animam, et patriam celestem significat." Papias gets his examples from Bede, *De schematibus et tropis*, cap. 12; see the edition of C. B. Kendall in *Bedae opera*, Corpus Christianorum series latina 123A (Turnhout 1975), pp. 168–69. Bede in turn could have drawn on John Cassian, *Collatio* 14.8 (PL 49:963–64). A similar explanation occurs in the very popular *Summa de ecclesiasticis officiis* of John Beleth (ca. 1165), ed. Herbert Douteil, Corpus Christianorum continuatio medievalis 41–41A (Turnhout 1976), cap. 113 (pp. 212–13): "Similiter in hoc nomine Ierusalem ista quatuor inveniuntur: hystoria ut de civitate illa ad quam vadunt peregrini, allegoria ut militans ecclesia, tropologia ut quelibet fidelis anima, anagoge ut celestis Ierusalem." Beleth may have been drawing on the so-called *Miscellanea* attributed to Hugh of St. Victor, 3.54 (PL 177:670–71).

it in the commentaries on Gratian's *Decretum*, since he supports the first of his seven senses, the literal, with a statement supposedly found in Gratian.[14] The Decretists, beginning with Laurence of Spain, use the four meanings of Jerusalem to explain the canon *Ieiunium quarti*.[15] Laurence's predecessor, Huguccio, rested content with explaining *anagoge*,[16] pretty much in keeping with the definition in the *Magne derivationes* but with a different etymology.[17] Laurence, in contrast, explains how Jerusalem has four meanings: historically, it refers to the earthly city of that name; allegorically, it stands for the Church; morally or tropologically, it designates the faithful soul; and anagogically, it refers to the heavenly Jerusalem. Laurence's gloss was taken over by John Teuton in his *Glossa ordinaria* and was preserved in Bartholomew of Brescia's updated version.[18] Pietro

14. 1 Pietro (Nannucci, p. 5): "Et ut scribitur in *Decretis*: 'Licet in veteri lege multa sub figura ponantur, tamen quedam ad literam sunt sola intelligenda, ut in precepto illo, "Non occides, non mechaberis," etc.' " This passage has not yet been found in Gratian's *Decretum*. See Luigi Caricato, "Il *Commentarium* all'*Inferno* di Pietro Alighieri," *IMU* 26 (1983) 134: the first of his *loci non inventi*. Caricato uses the page numbering of the Della Vedova-Silvotti reprinting of Nannucci, which is even more defective than their transcription of 2–3 Pietro. Especially noteworthy for our present discussion is the following error: instead of giving 1 Pietro's sixth sense ("Sexto utitur alio sensu, qui dicitur *tropologicus*," etc., Nannucci, p. 7), the DVS text has: "Sexto utitur quodam alio sensu, qui dicitur *anagogicus*," etc. (p. 7). In other words, the tropological sense is skipped altogether and the anagogical is given as the sixth and last sense.

15. Gratian, *Decretum* 1.76.7, ed. Emil Friedberg, *Corpus iuris canonici*, 2 vols. (Leipzig 1879–81, repr. Graz 1959), 1:269–70, from Jerome's commentary on Zechariah 8.18–19, specifically at the point where he explains 8.14 ("cogitavi in diebus istis ut beneficiam Hierusalem et domui Iuda") supposedly by way of anagogy, "iuxta anagogem."

16. Huguccio, *Summa super Decreto*, Vat. MS lat. 2280, fol. 72, ad v. *iuxta anagogem*: "id est, iusta superiorem et spiritualem intellectum; sic intelligitur uerbum proprium he[braicum?]; hoc datur intelligi in eo, *quia tunc*, etc. [referring to the following words of the canon, Friedberg, col. 270]. *Anagoge* dicitur intellectus ductiuus ad superiorem uel habitus de supernis; *ana*, id est, sursum, *goge*, ducem, inde *a[na]gogem*, cuius sensus, id est, ducens superiora; scilicet, cum recedimus a significatione sententie et concipimus intellectum de Deo, de angelis. Et ponitur hic anagoge pro moralitate uel tropologia." Cf. the copy of Huguccio's *Summa* in Admont MS 7, fol. 162; it omits the first part of the gloss and begins at "hoc datur intelligi," and reads *ductus* for *ductiuus*.

17. Huguccio, *Magne derivationes*, fol. 8: "*Anagoge*, excelsus intellectus, vti de Deo et de angelis. Sic dictus ab *ana* et *Ge*, quod est terra. Vnde *anagogeticus*, *-a*, *-um*, qui tractat de celestibus."

18. Laurentius Hispanus, *Glossa palatina in Gratiani Decretum*, Vat. MS Regin. lat. 977, fol. 54; Iohannes Teutonicus, *Glossa in Decretum*, Vat. MS lat. 1367, fol. 52; Bartholomaeus Brixiensis, *Glossa ordinaria in Decretum*, in *Corpus iuris canonici*, 3 vols. (Rome 1582, repr. Lyons 1606), 1:367. I give only the latter text: "*Anagogen*, id est, superiorem et spiritualem, vel moralem, intellectum. Nam *ana*, supra, *goge*, ducere: inde *pedagogus*, quasi ductor. Hoc modo exponitur: his est enim quidam intellectus historicus, allegoricus, moralis sive tropologicus, et anagogicus, sicut diximus supra, Dist. 37, *Vino* [Gratian 1.37.4]. Sic hec vox, Hierusalem, historice signat civitatem illam terrestrem, allegorice Ecclesiam, moraliter animam fidelem, anagogice celestem Hierusalem. Moralis intellectus attendit que iuxta nos sunt, allegoricus que intra nos, anagogicus que supra nos. Hic ergo ponitur anagogicus pro allegorico." The Teutonicus and Brixiensis glosses shorten the Hispanus treatment at the canon *Vino*, which reads (*Glossa palatina*, fol. 25v) ad v. *secundum tropologiam*: "id est, secundum moralitatem; *tropos* enim conuersio, *logos*

could also have been drawing on the *Rosarium* of the Archdeacon, Guido of Baysio, which was finished in the year 1300. Guido adds from Isidore an etymology of *historia*[19] that corresponds to the one given by Pietro.[20] Pietro, of course, was perfectly capable of quoting from the *Etymologiae*, as he does in 2 Pietro and 3 Pietro in this context; but the fact that he does not cite Isidore by name here may indicate that he is using the intermediary source of the Archdeacon's commentary. In 2 Pietro and 3 Pietro, Pietro drops the third and fourth senses of 1 Pietro (namely, the apologetical and metaphorical) and incorporates the second (historical) into the first (literal): the literal level, he says, is used both for history and for fiction. He also drops the example of Jerusalem, and cites other texts and authorities.[21] The Accessor, of course, uses the Exodus rather than Jerusalem as an example.

To sum up, I suggest that the Accessor put together his commentary on Dante's *Comedy* by drawing on Guido of Pisa's commentary (and possibly on one or more commentaries dependent on it), on one or two versions of Pietro Alighieri's commentary, and on the *Ars poetica*, at least to arrive at his treatment of literary genres. If he used only 1 Pietro, and if his Accessus was used by Boccaccio only in his *Esposizioni*, the termini of the Accessus would be 1340 and 1373. If however we decide that the Accessor used 2 Pietro and that his work was used by Boccaccio in his *Trattatello*, we would have to date the Accessus to ca. 1350.

---

sermo, quasi conuersiuus sermo, quando scilicet illud quod loquimur ad mores conuertimus infirmandos [*lege* informandos]. Et est quadruplex modus exponendi sacras scripturas. Historicus est cum habetur respectus ad historiam, ut xxvi q. v. *Nec mirum* [*Decretum* 2.26.5.14]; tropologicus, quasi sermo conuersiuus, ut hic: *De penitentia*, dist. i, *Super tribus* [*Decretum* 2.33.3 *De pen.* 1.71]; allegoricus, quasi mixtus sermo ex terrenis et celestibus: *De consecratione*, dist. iiii, *Propter* [*Decretum* 3.4.69]; anagogicus, ab *ana*, quod est sursum, quando scilicet de terrenis transferimus nos ad celestia, ut *De cons*. dist. iiii, *Ecclesia* [*paradiso*] [*Decretum* 3.4.45]; *De pen.*, dist. ii, *Principium* [*Decretum* 2.33.3 *De pen.* 2.45].

19. *Rosarium domini Guidonis Archidiaconi Bononie super Decreto* (Strassburg ca. 1473) on *Decretum* 1.76.7 ad gl. *historicus*: "Adde, historia secundum Isidorum in primo libro *Ethymologiarum* dicitur ab *historin* grece, quod est latine cognoscere uel uidere. Apud veteres enim nullus scribebat historiam nisi qui interfuisset." Cf. Isidore 1.41.1.

20. 1 Pietro (Nannucci, p. 5): "Secundo utitur quodam sensu qui dicitur historicus, dictus ab historia, que historia dicitur ab *historin*, quod est videre, ex eo quod ea que in historia narrantur ac si essent subiecta visui declarantur: et continet res veras et verisimiles. Nam hec vox Hierusalem historice intelligitur ipsa civitas terrestris que est in Syria, in illa parte que dicitur Palestina, etc., idest [*var*: et eius] gesta."

21. The text of 2 Pietro is clearly corrupt in the beginning section on the literal level. The Ashburnham copy reads (I italicize some of the erroneous matter): "Namque *Nam*quandoque scribit in eo aliqua que superficialiter solummodo intelligi debent pro ut simpliciter litera sonat *ad co* ystorias recitando *ad hoc* et ut poeta suas fictiones faciendo" (fol. 2). The Barberini text reads: "Namque quandoque scribit in eo aliqua que superficialiter solummodo intelligi debent, prout simplex littera sonat ad historias recitandum et poeticas suas sermones faciendo" (fol. 1v). Pietro's meaning is made clear in 3 Pietro (fol. 2): "Nam interdum scribet aliqua que solum ut littera profert intelligenda erunt sine aliquo mistico intellectu, ut moris est scribentium uel fabulose uel ystorice."

6

Maramauro and Boccaccio, Benvenuto and Buti, and the Anonymous of Florence

After the flurry of activity around mid-century, the next datable commentary on Dante's *Comedy*, apart from Boccaccio's *Trattatello*, is that of a Neapolitan scholar, Guglielmo Maramauro (or Maramaldo). The existence of his commentary was not known until the *Inferno* portion was discovered recently by Pier Giacomo Pisoni. Maramauro was a correspondent of Petrarch's, and he says that his commentary was written with the assistance of Petrarch and others, including Boccaccio.[1] According to Maramauro, he began writing in the year of the Incarnation 1369 (no doubt dating the start of the year on 25 March) and spent a little more than four years on the project.[2] He would therefore have finished, or nearly finished, his commentary on the whole *Comedy* before Boccaccio began his formal lectures on the *Inferno* in October of 1373.

The first part of Maramauro's commentary is missing, and the surviving portion takes up in the middle of a discussion of the kinds of literature. He may have begun by speaking of tragedy, but we have only his concluding remarks on (presumably) satire. He divides this genre into two classes, reprehensory and derisory, and gives Horace and Juvenal as examples (perhaps he means that Horace is reprehensory and Juvenal derisory).[3]

---

1. Guglielmo Maramauro, Commentary on the *Inferno* contained in Isola Bella, Archivio e Biblioteca di Palazzo Borromeo MS Borromeo L.ii.54, cited by Pier Giacomo Pisoni, "Guglielmo Maramauro, commentatore di Dante e amico del Petrarca," *Studi petrarcheschi* n.s. 1 (1984) 253–55: "Con l'aiuto de miser Zoan Bochacio e de miser Francescho Petrarcha e del pivan Forese e de miser Bernardo Scanabechi io me mossi a volere prendere questa dura impresa" (p. 255). Two of Petrarch's *Seniles* (11.5 and 14.5) are addressed to Maramauro. See Rosario Coluccia, "Due nuove canzoni di Guglielmo Maramauro, rimatore napoletano del sec. xiv," *GSLI* 160 (1983) 161–202, esp. 162–63. Coluccia gives his birth as occurring between 1315 and 1320 and his death ca. 1380. In his commentary, as Pisoni reports, he describes himself as "negli anni de *sua* età de cinquantadoi" when he started it in 1369 (p. 255); I take this to mean that he reached the age of fifty-two sometime after he began his work, therefore in the mid or latter part of 1369 or in 1370 before 25 March; he would have been born, then, in 1317 or 1318.

2. Maramauro quotes two lines of Petrarch's *Africa*, namely, 6.901–2, but he mistakenly attributes them to Book 9 (Pisoni, "Guglielmo Maramauro," p. 255 and n. 7). They come from the passage of thirty-four lines at the end of Book 6 which was circulated without Petrarch's permission in 1343. See Nicola Festa, *Saggio sull'Africa del Petrarca* (Palermo 1926), pp. 10–11. The text of the whole work was not available until 1377 (ibid., pp. 36–37).

3. I cite from Sig. Pisoni's transcription of fol. 1r of Maramauro's commentary, which he

Next, and last, he comes to authors who "composed their works through comedies." Comedy means "rustic song," of the sort that begins with vile, base, and dolorous things and ends with things honorable, worthy, and gracious. Dante had good reason for calling his work a comedy, because its lyric verses are singable, and because the whole work resembles the writings of Plautus, Ennius, "Enievius," and Eron (that is, Aesop). Dante, like them, begins with the basest and most dolorous possible place, namely, hell; then, lifting his matter, he comes to purgatory; and finally, he arrives at the ultimate beatitude of heaven, where the divine essence is seen face to face. Maramauro adds that what Dante claims to have seen he saw by his own genius, through the eyes of reason and faith.[4]

We note that Maramauro seems to base his generic distinctions solely on content, not on style. Although he accepts the one reason that Boccaccio will put forth for calling Dante's work a comedy, there does not seem to be any resemblance between his formulation and Boccaccio's, and no telling resemblances between his accessus and the remarks of any other commentator that we have examined. He shares with Guido da Pisa, the Accessor, and Boccaccio the division of form into *forma tractatus* and *forma tractandi*, but this feature cannot be made to provide a clear indication of dependency or indebtedness. Maramauro does not elaborate on the point, or on any of the other common "Accessory" topics, except for a comment on the part of philosophy to which the poem belongs.[5]

Let us now see what use Boccaccio made of whatever commentaries he did

---

very kindly sent to me. The opening words, on satire, labeled section 1, read as follows: "de alchuno vicioso. Et questa ha doi modi: l'uno a dir contra altrui reprehendendo'lo a nome, e l'altro modo è de menar befa de lui per alchuna cossa la quale esso creda sapere e non sa, e voglia contrastare con colloro chi la sapeno bene. Epero se dicono doi modi da reprehendere: l'uno reprehensorio e l'altro derisorio. E cosi scripse Oratio nostro venusino et Iuvenale nostro regnicolla."

4. Ibid., sec. 2: "Altri composero lor opere per comedie. Et è a dire comedia canto villano, el quale se comenza da cosse vile, basse, e dolorose, e finisse in cosse honorate, digne, e gratiose; e canta'sse ne li lochi ove se congregano li vilani le feste. Epero non senza cagione Dante intitola questa soa opera *Comedia*, e per versi lirici li quali se solean cantare ne la * * * de' poeti. E cosi scripse Plauto poeta comico, Ennio, Enievio [= e Nievio? e Mevio?] et Eron cioe Ysopo. E Dante, seguendo costoro, comenza ad exorire la sua materia de l'inferno como dal piu basso e doloroso locho che sia; e poi, alzando la materia, pervene al purgatorio; et ultimo pervenne a l'ultima nostra beatitudine, nel paradiso, la ove se vede a facia a faza la essentia divina. E questo intenda ciaschuno che vole intrare a legere questa opera: che cio che dante dice che esso vidde, esso el vidde per alteza de inzegno. Et primo quanto ala ragione humana, dopo quanto per fede."

5. Ibid., sec. 3: "Io faria la divisione de questo libro: de la materia e de la forma e del titolo del libro e a que parte de phylosophia se sotomete, et anchora de la forma del tractato, et anchora de la forma del tractare. Ma, per non fare prolixita de parole, yo lo pretermeto e solo ala parte de phylosophia naturale io reduco questa opera, pero che segondo el mal operare homo merita pena, et segondo el bene operare homo merita premio de salute." This is the end of the first page of the transcript sent to me by Sig. Pisoni, and I have not yet seen the immediate continuation. He did send as well some excerpts from farther on in the commentary, concerning Vergil's *Aeneid* and Guido Cavalcanti, but they do not enlarge on the generic questions discussed at the beginning. For other similarities between Maramauro and Guido da Pisa, and between Maramauro and Villani, see below, p. 71 n. 38.

have at hand, which included the Proto-Accessus, when he set about lecturing on Dante's *Comedy*. We note, first of all, that Boccaccio lists tragedy along with satire, comedy, bucolic, elegy, and lyric as examples of different kinds of poetic narrative; he therefore substitutes lyric for the Accessor's "votive sentence."[6] But like Rosciate he limits his discussion to comedy and does not define or describe tragedy or the other genres. However, one can deduce some of his ideas of tragedy from what he says about comedy. One such deduction would be that ancient tragedy, like ancient comedy, was a theatrical enterprise of the sort explained by Pietro Alighieri: the poet recited the lines while actors pantomimed the actions.[7] A false deduction that has been made about Boccaccio is that he considered the episodes of his *De casibus* to be tragedies. This misconception has been fostered especially by students of English literature, but it is shared by the editor of the new edition of the *De casibus*.[8]

Boccaccio addresses the question of why Dante called his work a comedy by noting several meanings of comedy that are inappropriate to the great poem. The first of these is the etymological definition of comedy as a rustic song that deals with base matters, like the tending of livestock, or boorish love stories.[9] When he turns to the question of comic style, he seems to be following the Proto-Accessus, for he characterizes the style of comedy as humble and "remiss" and the language of *feminette* (translating the Accessor's *muliercule*). But, in contrast to his position in the *Trattatello*, he decisively rejects the Accessor's conclusion that the style of Dante's *Comedy* is comic. Rather, he says, it is polished,

6. Boccaccio, *Esposizioni*, Accessus 17 (p. 4): "Appresso, si dimostra nel titolo questo libro essere appellato *Comedia*. A notizia della qual cosa è da sapere che le poetiche narrazioni sono di più e varie maniere, sì come è tragedia, satira, e comedia, buccolica, elegia, lirica, ed altre. Ma volendo di quella sola che al presente titolo apartiene vedere, vogliono alcuni mal convenirsi a questo libro questo titolo, argomentando primieramente dal significato del vocabolo e, appresso, dal modo del trattare de' comici, il quale pare molto essere differente da quello che l'autore serva in questo libro."

7. For his description of the theatrics of comedy, see *Esposizioni* Accessus 23 (n. 12 below) and 1.1.84–86 (pp. 37–38). Unlike 1 Pietro, Boccaccio considers the scene not to be a pulpit but a little house that also served the actors as a changing room. This is a concept of some of the commentators on Terence. See Claudia Villa, *La lectura Terentii* (Padua 1984), 1: 249. Villa does not document any examples earlier than the fifteenth century, but she says that they are very common.

8. Vittorio Zaccaria, *De casibus virorum illustrium*, ed. Pier Giorgio Ricci and V. Zaccaria, *Tutte le opere* 9 (Milan 1983), p. xlviii: the structure of the *De casibus* is "attuata secondo il canone retorico medievale della *tragedia*." Chaucer is the real inventor of *de casibus* tragedies; see H. A. Kelly, "Chaucer and Shakespeare on Tragedy," *Leeds Studies in English* 20 (1989).

9. Boccaccio, *Esposizioni*, Accessus 18: "Dicono adunque primieramente mal convenirsi le cose cantate in questo libro col significato del vocabolo, per ciò che 'comedia' vuole tanto dire quanto 'canto di villa,' composto da *comos*, che in latino viene a dire *villa*, e *odos*, che viene a dire *canto*: e i canti villeschi, come noi sappiamo, sono di basse materie, sì come di loro quistioni intorno al cultivare della terra, o conservazione di loro bestiame, o di loro bassi e rozi inamoramenti e costumi rugali; a' quali in alcuno atto non sono conformi le cose narrate in alcuna parte della presente opera, ma sono di persone eccellenti, di singulari e notabili operazioni degli uomini viziosi e virtuosi, degli effetti della penitenzia, de' costumi degli angeli e della divina essenzia."

graceful, and sublime. He does admit, however, that the style could have been even more sublime if Dante had written it in Latin.[10] Boccaccio's characterization of Dante's style resembles what the Accessor says about *tragic* style, namely, the *modus elate et sublime loquendi.*[11]

Boccaccio then takes up the dialogic form of comedy, in which only the characters or the persons of the comedy speak. Dante's poem does not fit this criterion, for Dante often narrates the story or speaks of himself. Similarly, comedy uses no similes or examples, whereas Dante's poem does. Moreover, comedy deals with fiction, while Dante concerns himself with the truth. Finally, parts of comedies are called scenes, whereas the parts of Dante's work are cantos.[12] He concludes this part of his discourse by saying that it seems from what has been said that the term comedy is inappropriate to the work. He adds that we cannot solve the problem by alleging that the title was wrongly applied to the work, because Dante himself calls it a comedy in canto 21 of the *Inferno.*[13]

Boccaccio goes on to admit in effect that Dante, who is acknowledged to have been a very sagacious person, must have had a good reason for so naming his work. The only acceptable reason that Boccaccio himself can think of is a

---

10. Ibid., 19: "Oltre a questo, lo stilo comico è umile e rimesso, acciò che alla materia sia conforme, quello che della presente opera dire non si può, per ciò che, quantunque in volgare scritta sia, nel quale pare che comunichino le feminette, egli è nondimeno ornato e leggiadro e sublime, delle quali cose nulla senti il volgare delle femine. Non dico però che, se in versi latini fosse, non mutato il peso delle parole volgari, ch'egli non fosse più artificioso e più sublime molto, per ciò che molto più d'arte e di gravità ha nel parlare latino che nel materno." For the *Trattatello*, see above, pp. 17–18.

11. *Cangrande* 10.30.

12. Boccaccio, *Esposizioni*, Accessus 20–23: "E, appresso, dell'arte spettante al comedo: mai nella comedia non introducere se medesimo in alcuno atto a parlare; ma sempre a varie persone, che in diversi luoghi e tempi e per diverse cagioni deduce a parlare insieme, fa ragionare quello che crede che apartenga al tema impreso della comedia; dove in questo libro, lasciato l'artificio del comedo, l'autore ispessissime volte e quasi sempre or di sé or d'altrui ragionando favella. (21) E similemente nelle comedie non s'usano comparazioni ne recitazioni d'altre storie che di quelle che al tema assunto apartengono: dove in questo libro si pongono comparazioni infinite e assai storie si racontano che dirittamente non fanno al principale intento. (22) Sono ancora le cose che nelle comedie si racontano cose che per avventura mai non furono, quantunque non sieno sì strane da' costumi degli uomini che essere state non possano: la sustanziale istoria del presente libro, dell'essere dannati i peccatori, che ne' loro peccati muoiono, a perpetua pena, e quegli che nella grazia di Dio trapassano essere allevati alla eterna gloria, è, secondo la catolica fede, vera e stata sempre. (23) Chiamano, oltre a tutto questo, i comedi le parti intra sé distinte delle loro comedie 'scene'; per ciò che, recitando li comedi quelle nel luogo detto 'scena,' nel mezzo del teatro, quante volte introduceano varie persone a ragionare tante della scena uscivano i mimi trasformati da quegli che prima avevano parlato e fatto alcuno atto, e, in forma di quegli che parlar doveano, venivano davanti dal popolo riguardante e ascoltante il comedo che racontava; dove il nostro autore chiama 'canti' le parti della sua *Comedia.*"

13. Ibid., 24: "E così, acciò che fine pognamo agli argomenti, pare, come di sopra è detto, non convenirsi a questo libro nome di comedia. Né si può dire non essere stato della mente dell'autore che questo libro non si chiamasse comedia, come talvolta ad alcuno d'alcuna sua opera è avvenuto, con ciò sia cosa che esso medesimo nel xxi canto di questo prima cantica il chiami *Comedia*, dicendo: 'Cosi di ponte in ponte altro parlando, / che la mia *Comedia* cantar non cura.'"

figurative use of the term. Dante's poem has an overall structure that is similar to the comedies of Plautus and Terence, in that they begin turbulently, full of uproar and discord, but end in peace and tranquility. Dante begins in the sorrows and tribulation of hell and ends in the repose, peace, and glory enjoyed by the blessed in eternal life.[14]

Boccaccio's statements both here and in the *Trattatello* are conclusive proof that the *De vulgari eloquentia* was not available to him, at least when he was writing or lecturing on the *Comedy*. He does not know that Dante permitted the middle style to comedy, and he does not know or remember that Dante considered the vernacular capable of the highest style, that of tragedy. We may also take his treatments as proof that he did not know the *Epistle to Cangrande* in its form of a letter by Dante himself, since he shows himself willing to accept any reason that Dante might have had in calling his poem a comedy. It is also clear that Boccaccio had read Dante's *Eclogues* in the proper spirit and attributed the reference to *comica verba* (where *comica* according to Boccaccio's gloss means *vulgaria*) not to Dante himself but to Dante's characterization of Giovanni del Virgilio's opinion of comedy.[15]

Though Boccaccio's language in his conclusion does not especially resemble that of *Cangrande*, he may have been somewhat influenced by the Proto-Accessus in his formulation. He doubtless accepted the Accessor's assertion that the opposite kind of structure is a prime feature of tragedy, and he presumably has this characteristic in mind when he says in his commentary on canto 4 that Seneca's *Apocolocyntosis* is in the form of tragedy.[16] But if he had reached canto 20 in his commentary, where Dante has Vergil call the *Aeneid* a tragedy, he would have had to choose some other criterion than plot structure to justify the appellation. The most obvious one would have been that of style; but since he believed that Dante's poem was in a sublime style, he would have to say that on the basis of style both works should be classified as tragedy—figuratively speaking, of course. But since Vergil wrote in Latin, no doubt Boccaccio would have acknowledged that the *Aeneid* had a "higher" tragic style than the style of Dante's vernacular poem. If he had proceeded to comment on canto 21, where Dante

14. Ibid, 25–26: "Che adunque diremo alle obiezioni fatte? Credo, con ciò sia cosa che occulatissimo uomo fosse l'autore, lui non avere riguardo alle parti che nelle comedie si contengono, ma al tutto, e da quello avere il suo libro dinominato, figurativamente parlando. Il tutto della comedia è, per quello che per Plauto e per Terrenzio, che furono poeti comici, si può comprendere, che la comedia abbia turbulento principio e pieno di romori e di discordie e poi l'ultima parte di quella finisca in pace e in tranquillità. (26) Al qual tutto è ottimamente conforme il libro presente: per ciò che egli incomincia da' dolori e dalle tribulazioni infernali, e finisce nel riposo e nella pace e nella gloria, la quale hanno i beati in vita eterna."

15. See above, p. 5 n. 21.

16. Boccaccio, *Esposizioni* 4.1.338 (pp. 253–54): "Compuose . . . un altro . . . il quale è molto più poetico che morale ed è in prosa ed in versi, in forma di tragedia: e in quello discrive come Claudio Cesare fosse cacciato di paradiso e menatone da Mercurio in inferno. . . . E quello libretto per tutto non è altro che far beffe di Claudio e della sua poco laudevol vita." Boccaccio may be saying, however, that the mixture of prose and verse is a characteristic of tragedy.

refers to his poem as a comedy in contrast to Vergil's high tragedy, he might have reconsidered his ideas on why the *Comedy* was so called.

Benvenuto da Imola was one of the auditors of Boccaccio's lectures on Dante in 1373–74, but Benvenuto is pretty much independent of Boccaccio in his own treatments of the *Comedy*. Benvenuto's commentary exists in three forms: the *recollectae* or student notes of Stefano Talice da Ricaldone, taken during Benvenuto's lectures at Bologna in early 1375 (1 Benvenuto); Benvenuto's "first redaction," identified by Carlo Paolazzi as having been made while Benvenuto was lecturing at Ferrara in the winter of 1375–76 (2 Benvenuto); and his final version, which seems to have been published shortly after his death in 1386 or 1387 (3 Benvenuto).[17]

The Ferrara course, or Benvenuto's redaction of it, may have been abbreviated, since 2 Benvenuto omits material found in both 1 Benvenuto and 3 Benvenuto, notably references to the tragedies of Seneca.[18] Since the sense and accuracy or completeness of both early versions are questionable, I will concentrate my analysis on his final version. As a preface, I should note that though Benvenuto drew extensively on the first and last parts of Herman Alemannus's translation of Averroes's commentary on the *Poetics*, he did not penetrate far enough into the treatise to see that it dealt with tragedy under the guise of "the art of praise."[19]

In his Ferrarese redaction, Benvenuto objects to the notion of some interpreters that the *materia* of Dante's poem is comedy. Comedy, he insists, is not the matter but the style of the poem,[20] while its matter or "subjective part" is the various states of the soul. "Style" for Benvenuto refers to the three kinds of poetry indicated by the terms tragedy, satire, and comedy, signifying respectively high, middle, and low forms of writing. Of the first, he says in his final version:

> Tragedy is a high and proud style; for it deals with memorable and horrifying deeds, like changes of kingdoms, the uprooting of cities, conflicts in war, deaths of kings, the destruction and slaughter of men, and other great disasters; and those who describe such things are called *tragedi* or *tragici*, like Homer, Vergil, Euripides, Statius, Simonides, Ennius, and many others.[21]

---

17. The three versions are to be found as follows:

1 Benvenuto: ed. Vincenzo Promis and Carlo Negroni, *La Commedia di Dante Alighieri col commento inedito di Stefano Talice da Ricaldone*, 2d ed. 3 vols. (Milan 1888).

2 Benvenuto: Florence, Bibl. Laur. MS Ashb. 839. See Carlo Paolazzi, "Le letture dantesche di Benvenuto da Imola a Bologna e a Ferrara e le redazioni del suo *Comentum*," *IMU* 22 (1979) 319–66, esp. 322–47.

3 Benvenuto: *Comentum super Dantis Aldigherij Comoediam*, 5 vols., ed. James Philip Lacaita (Florence 1887). See Paolazzi, p. 361.

18. H. A. Kelly, "Aristotle-Averroes-Alemannus on Tragedy," *Viator* 10 (1979) 203 n. 201.

19. Ibid. 200–4. See above, p. 9 n. 38.

20. 2 Benvenuto fol. 2v: "Aliqui dicunt quod materia huius libri est comedia, sed non est uerum; imo est stilus, non materia."

21. 3 Benvenuto 1:18: "Deinde tangitur in titulo stylus poeticus. Ad quod notandum est quod

Benvenuto's failure to mention Seneca in this list is strange. It may be that he was thinking primarily of narrative rather than dialogic or dramatic tragedy here; or it may have been a matter of pure forgetfulness, since as I have noted he refers to Seneca's tragedies elsewhere in his commentary and cites them a dozen times. He may even have annotated the plays,[22] in which case he would certainly have known about their dramatic structure. But if Benvenuto did forget to mention Seneca here, his oversight was of long standing, since he also omitted him from his list of tragic authors in his Ferrarese redaction[23] (as well as omitting all references to his plays later in the commentary).

Benvenuto goes on to characterize satire as a middle and temperate style, like that used by Horace, Juvenal, and Persius. Comedy, in contrast, is a low and humble style dealing with the common and vile deeds of rustics, and so on, as practiced by Plautus, Terence, and Ovid.[24]

He then says that just as every form of philosophy is contained in Dante's poem, so too it can be regarded as appertaining to each of the three literary genres: it is a tragedy, satire, and comedy. It is a tragedy, first of all, in that it deals with popes, princes, barons, and other magnates and nobles. It is a satire because it reprehends all vices and spares no dignity or power; therefore (from this point of view) it could more properly be titled *Satire* rather than *Tragedy* or *Comedy*. Nevertheless, it is a comedy as well, Benvenuto insists; but rather than drawing on his previous discussion of comedy, he provides a new characterization: Dante's poem can be called a comedy because it fulfills Isidore's definition by beginning with sad *materia* and ending with joyful.[25]

Isidore, however, nowhere defines comedy in this way. Rather it is the sort

---

est triplex stylus, scilicet, tragedia, satyra, et comedia. Tragedia est stylus altus et superbus; tractat enim de memorabilibus et horrendis gestis, qualia sunt mutationes regnorum, eversiones urbium, conflictus bellorum, interitus regum, strages et cedes virorum, et alie maxime clades; et talia describentes vocati sunt tragedi, sive tragici, sicut Homerus, Virgilius, Euripides, Statius, Simonides, Ennius, et alii plures."

22. Kelly, "Aristotle," p. 204.

23. 2 Benvenuto fol. 3: "Nam comedia stilus est. Vbi nota quod poetarum triplex est stilus. Est tragedia que tractat de rebus altis cum superbo et alto stilo, sicut subuersiones regnorum, dil[u]uia, cedes, strages magnorum ducum; sicut fuit Homerus, Vergilius, Lucanus, Statius, etc." See also 3 Benvenuto 1:154: "Licet Homerus, Vergilius, et Lucanus scripserint in alto stilo, scilicet tragedia, tamen Horatius scripsit in mediocri stilo, puta satira, et Ovidius in basso, scilicet comedia. Dicendum breviter quod unusquisque istorum in genere suo alios superavit; ita quod Horatius superat alios satiros, Ovidius alios comicos, etc."

24. 3 Benvenuto 1:18–19: "Satyra est stylus medius et temperatus; tractat enim de virtutibus et viciis; et talia describentes vocantur satyri sive satyrici. Sunt enim satyri vitia reprehendentes, sicut Horatius, Iuvenalis, et Persius. Comedia est stylus bassus et humilis; tractat enim vulgaria et vilia facta ruralium, plebeiorum, et humilium personarum; et talia describentes vocantur comedi sive comici, sicut Plautus, Terentius, Ovidius." Cf. 2 Benvenuto fol. 3: "Secundus stilus dicitur satira, stilus mediocris; et est reprehensorius uitiorum, ut Oratius, Iuuenalis, Persius. Est et comedia, que tractat de rebus infimis et plebeis."

25. 3 Benvenuto 1:19: "Modo est hic attente notandum quod, sicut in isto libro est omnis pars philosophie, ut dictum est, ita est omnis pars poetrie. Unde si quis velit subtiliter investigare, hic est tragedia, satyra, et comedia. Tragedia quidem, quia describit gesta pontificum, principum,

of characterization given to comedy by Huguccio or by Osbern of Gloucester,[26] one of Huguccio's sources, or by Andrea Lancia in *2 Ottimo*. Benvenuto did in fact use *2 Ottimo* in his philosophical classification of the *Comedy*,[27] and perhaps he was also influenced by it in saying that Ovid was a writer of comedy. One might suppose that Benvenuto was thinking of what we tend to think of as Ovid's comic works, such as the *Ars amatoria* and *Remedia amoris*, even though they do not deal predominantly with rustics. But since *2 Ottimo* names the *Metamorphoses*, perhaps Benvenuto was thinking of this work. However, though *2 Ottimo* says that comedy moves from misery to felicity, neither it nor Huguccio nor Osbern mentions Isidore, whereas Benvenuto's major source on the point must have connected Isidore with the sad-to-joyful plot, or at least named Isidore in such a way that Benvenuto assumed the connection.

After Benvenuto suggests the "Isidorian" reason for our calling Dante's work a comedy, he admits that Dante's own reason for calling it a comedy was different. Dante named his work *Comedy* because he wrote it in the lowest style—lowest, that is, from the viewpoint of language—namely, the vernacular. (Benvenuto hastens to add that, as a vernacular poem, it is sublime.)[28] In other words, Dante did not consider his poem a comedy from the viewpoint of characters or events or even "style" but only from the "literal" aspect of its language: it was in Italian rather than in Latin.

---

regum, baronum, et aliorum magnatum et nobilium, sicut patet in toto libro. Satyra, idest reprehensoria; reprehendit enim mirabiliter et audacter omnia genera viciorum, nec parcit dignitati, potestati, vel nobilitati alicuius. Ideo convenientius posset intitulari *Satyra* quam *Tragedia* vel *Comedia*. Potest etiam dici quod sit comedia, nam secundum Isidorum comedia incipit a tristibus et terminatur ad leta. Et ita liber iste incipit a tristi materia, scilicet ab inferno, et terminatur ad letam, scilicet ad paradisum, sive ad divinam essentiam." Cf. 2 Benvenuto fol. 3: "Sed sicut dixi de philosophia, ita dico quod in isto opere est omnis pars poesis siue poesie. Est tragedia quia tractat de papis, imperatoribus, regibus, cardinalibus, marchionibus, ut patebit, et ista est primarie(?) tanquam tragedia. Potest dici satira; nullus enim fuit qui nulli parcens ita audacter increparet uitia, nec indulserit et deluerit(?) alicui dignitati uel potestati. Comedia etiam potest dici propter stilum bassum et vulgarem, et quia incipit, ut dicit Ysidorus *Ethimologiis*, a rebus tristibus et finit in letis. Vnde concludo quod potius potest dici tragedia quam comedia et potius satira quam uel comedia uel tragedia."

26. Osbern of Gloucester, *Derivationes* (ca. A.D. 1150), ed. Angelo Mai as *Thesaurus novus latinitatis*, Classici auctores e vaticanis codicibus editi 8 (Rome 1836); see pp. 111, 143, 593. In the last-named place is the entry: "Tragedia, carmen luctuosum, quia incipit a letitia et finit in tristitia, cui contrarium est comedia, quia incipit a tristitia et finit in letitia."

27. See Luis Jenaro-MacLennan, *The Trecento Commentaries on the Divina commedia and the Epistle to Cangrande* (Oxford 1974), p. 92n: he calls Benvenuto a plagiarist in using *2 Ottimo*'s idea of classifying Dante's poem under various sciences, but says that Benvenuto blunders in considering theology a part of philosophy (3 Benvenuto 1:17), while *2 Ottimo* considers it to be a different and "supernatural" science. He does not say how he knows that Benvenuto is wrong and *2 Ottimo* right on this point.

28. 3 Benvenuto 1:19: "Sed dices forsan, lector, 'Cur vis mihi baptizare librum de novo, cum autor nominaverit ipsum *Comediam*?' Dico quod autor potius voluit vocare librum *Comediam* a stylo infimo et vulgari, quia de rei veritate est humilis respectu literalis, quamvis in genere suo sit sublimis et excellens."

The same point is made, but more clearly, in the Ferrarese account: even though Dante knew that his vernacular style excelled all other vernacular writings, nevertheless, since it was in the lowest class from the viewpoint of "literal" style, he humbly called it a comedy.[29]

In his early Bolognese series, Benvenuto introduced his whole generic discussion by provocatively suggesting that *Tragedy* would have been a more suitable title for Dante's work, if it had to be named after its style. Tragedy deals with high poetic subjects and with great evils like the death of kings and downfall of kingdoms; just so, Dante's work tells of the deeds of all magnates. Similarly, it could be called *Satire*, because satire is the style of reprehension, used for reprehending vices and commending virtues; just so, Dante's poem reprehends vices and praises virtues, and it also varies the subject matter and the style, which is another feature of satire.[30] To judge from his final version, Benvenuto seems to mean that satire ranges over every level of society—hence, including both the high and low subjects of tragedy and comedy—in order to deal with its own proper subject of vice.

Benvenuto concludes that Dante's work contains, or consists of, every style. But so far in this first version he has not defined comedy or told us how Dante's poem can be a comedy except in the sense that a satire includes the subject matter of comedy. He now gives the explanation that he will put at the end of his finished commentary: "But Dante himself called it a comedy, because from the viewpoint of literal style a comedy is so called from its being in the vernacular."[31]

So ends Benvenuto's generic discussion in this lecture series, but he goes on to discuss reasons why such a great man should have decided to write in the vernacular. Ricaldone reports Benvenuto as saying:

> Sed est dubium que est causa qua homo tantus deduxit se ad describendum vulgariter. Ratio prima est ista que habetur in sua epistola, ut faceret fructum et delectationem pluribus gentibus, tam literatis quam illiteratis; unde, si descripsisset literaliter, tunc ipsum vulgares non intellexissent; unde novum stilum voluit capere et etiam ut faceret fructum Italicis. Secunda ratio est, quoniam ipse consideravit quod reges et principes, qui olim delectabantur et quibus opera poetarum intitulabantur, nunc ipsam poesim neglexerunt, et viciis dediti sunt; ideo se reduxit ad istum stilum. Primo enim noster incepit literaliter sic: "Ultima regna canam

29. 2 Benvenuto fol. 3: "Sed auctor, sapiens et cognoscens quod quantumcumque stilus suus omnes alios maternos excesserit, tamen infimus est ratione literalis stili, ideo *Comediam* humiliter appellavit." Given by Paolazzi, "Letture," p. 323.

30. 1 Benvenuto 1:7: "Et cum dicitur *Comedie*, tangitur stilus libri. Sed videtur quod debeat intitulari *Tragedia* et non *Comedia* prius. Nam tragedia est materia poetica que est alta et describit magna mala, sicut mortes regum, regnorum subversiones; ideo debet vocari *Tragedia* quia ipse describit facta omnium magnatum. Etiam potest intitulari *Satira*, unde satira est stilus reprehensionis, et habet reprehendere vicia, commendare virtutes. Unde liber iste reprehendit vicia et laudat virtutes, et etiam mutat materiam et stilum sicut satira facit."

31. Ibid.: "Et sciendum est hoc, quod hic est quilibet stilus. Sed ipse Dantes vocavit *Comediam*; quoniam, respectu stili literalis, dicitur comedia unde vulgaris est."

> fluido contermina mundo." Alia ratio est, quia vidit stilum suum non esse sufficientem materie de qua inceperat; sed sic faciendo omnes vicit. Et sic fuit unde dicens Petralca: "Magna opinio huius hominis; ad omnia scivisset se optime applicare."[32]

Paolazzi has argued that the letter referred to in this passage, as the source of the first reason that Benvenuto considers, was the *Epistle to Cangrande*.[33] However, *Cangrande* does not discuss Dante's motives for writing in the vernacular, but simply explains why Dante called the work a comedy (one reason being that it was written in the vernacular); and Benvenuto does not take up the sort of explanation found in *Cangrande* in his own accounts of Dante's motives for choosing his title. Moreover, Ricaldone's report is quite clearly garbled. We are fortunate to have what must have been the original sense of the passage, or close to it, in Benvenuto's final version, but postponed to his discussion of canto 2 of the *Inferno*. It reads:

> Hic autem oritur questio que solet sepe fieri, et merito: quare, scilicet, vir tante literature et scientie scripsit vulgariter et materne? Dicendum breviter, multis de causis. Primo, ut pluribus proficeret, et maxime Italicis, qui pre ceteris in poeticis delectantur, imo quasi soli. Si enim scripsisset literaliter, non profecisset nisi literatis, nec omnibus literatis, sed paucis. Fecit ergo opus nunquam factum, in quo literatissimi et sapientissimi viri possunt speculari. Secundo, quia autor, videns liberalia studia, potissime poetica, esse deserta a principibus et nobilibus, qui principaliter solebant in poeticis delectari, et quibus opera poetica solebant olim intitulari, et ob hoc opera Virgilii et aliorum excellentium poetarum iacere neglecta et despecta, cautius et prudentius se reduxit ad stilum vulgarem, cum iam literaliter incepisset sic:
>
> Ultima regna canam, fluido contermina mundo,
> Spiritibus que lata patent, que premia solvunt
> Pro meritis cuicumque suis,
>
> et cetera. Alii tamen et multi comuniter dicunt, quod autor cognovit stilum suum literalem non attingere ad tam arduum thema; quod et ego crederem, nisi me moveret autoritas novissimi poete Petrarce, qui loquens de Dante scribit ad venerabilem preceptorem meum Boccatium de Certaldo: "Magna mihi de ingenio eius oppinio est: potuisse eum omnia quibus intendisset."[34]

The only letter mentioned in this authentic passage is the one Petrarch wrote to Boccaccio in the spring of 1359, beginning *Multa sunt in literis tuis*. Petrarch says that their fellow countryman ("conterraneus noster") is a noble poet by reason of his subject, but a popular one by reason of his style ("popularis quidem quod ad stilum attinet, quod ad rem hauddubie nobilis").[35] Benvenuto quotes

---

32. Ibid.

33. Paolazzi, "Letture," pp. 323–24.

34. 3 Benvenuto 1:78–79.

35. Petrarch, *Familiares res* 21.15.1. I follow the edition of Umberto Bosco, *Le familiari*, 4 (Florence 1942), 94–100.

the letter to counter the third reason he has brought up (which he says is frequently alleged by others) to explain why Dante wrote in Italian—namely, that Dante's Latin style was not adequate for the purpose. Petrarch was of the opposite opinion, and clearly wished that Dante had written in Latin.[36]

In a recent study, Paolazzi suggests that it was Benvenuto's master Boccaccio himself who had provided him with a copy of this and other letters of Petrarch that he cites.[37] He also argues persuasively that Petrarch in his 1359 letter was responding not only to a letter of Boccaccio's (now lost), but also to the first version of Boccaccio's *Trattatello*.[38] It is in fact in the *Trattatello* that we find the first two reasons that Benvenuto discusses for Dante's writing in Italian: first, that he wanted his work to be profitable to many people, especially Italians, even those who did not know Latin; and second, since the Latin poets were neglected by princes and nobles (who presumably were capable of understanding Latin), he decided to try the vernacular. Boccaccio's text reads:

> Muovono molti, e intra essi alcuni savi uomini, generalmente una quistione così fatta: che con ciò fosse cosa che Dante fosse in iscienzia solennissimo uomo, perché a comporre così grande, di sì alta materia, e sì notabile libro, come è questa sua *Comedia*, nel fiorentino idioma si disponesse; perché non più tosto in versi latini, come gli altri poeti precedenti hanno fatto? A così fatta domanda rispondere, tra molte ragioni, due a l'altre principali me ne occorrono. Delle quali la prima è per fare utilità più comune a' suoi cittadini e agli altri Italiani: conoscendo che, se metricamente in latino, come gli altri poeti passati, avesse scritto, solamente a' letterati avrebbe fatto utile; scrivendo in volgare fece opera mai più non fatta, e non tolse il non potere essere inteso da' letterati, e mostrando la bellezza del nostro idioma e la sua eccellente arte in quello, e diletto e intendimento di sé diede agl'idioti, abandonati per addietro da ciascheduno. La seconda ragione, che a questo il mosse, fu questa. Vedendo egli li liberali studii del tutto abandonati, e massimamente da' prencipi e dagli altri grandi uomini, a' quali si soleano le poetiche fatiche intitolare, e per questo e le divine opere di Virgilio e degli altri solenni poeti non solamente essere in poco pregio divenute, ma quasi da' più disprezzate; avendo egli incominciato, secondo che l'altezza della materia richiedea, in questa guisa:
>
> Ultima regna canam, fluvido contermina mundo,
> Spiritibus que lata patent, que premia solvunt
> Pro meritis cuicunque suis,
>
> etc., i lasciò istare; e, immaginando invano le croste del pane porsi alla bocca di coloro che ancora il latte suggano, in istile atto a' moderni sensi ricominciò la sua opera e perseguilla in volgare.[39]

36. The whole passage that Benvenuto draws on reads as follows: "Nam quod inter laudes dixisti, potuisse illum si voluisset alio stilo uti, credo edepol—magna enim michi de ingenio eius opinio est—potuisse eum omnia quibus intendisset" (*Fam.* 21.15.22).

37. Carlo Paolazzi, "Petrarca, Boccaccio, e il *Trattatello in laude di Dante*," *SD* 55 (1983) 165–249, esp. 242–43.

38. Ibid., pp. 184–98.

39. Boccaccio, *1 Trattatello* 190–92 (ed. Ricci, pp. 486–87).

In the revised version, and in response to Petrarch's letter (as Paolazzi shows), Boccaccio begins with the second reason and only touches very lightly on the first at the end;[40] And in the *Esposizioni* he eliminates the first reason altogether.[41]

Perhaps, then, Ricaldone misunderstood Benvenuto's reference to Petrarch's letter to be a reference to a letter by Dante himself. But there is in fact another letter involved, which purports to give Dante's own reasons, speaking in the first person, for his writing in Italian. I refer to the transparently inauthentic *Epistle of Brother Ilaro*, which is the source of the second reason originally given by Boccaccio, and the source also of the Latin beginning that Dante allegedly wrote for his work. The letter is preserved in Boccaccio's notebook, and Giuseppe Billanovich has argued that it was composed as a rhetorical exercise by Boccaccio himself.[42] Supporting this thesis is the fact that Boccaccio in his writings on Dante does not cite it as a letter giving Dante's views, but rather uses it as the source of various opinions on Dante. This at least is true in both versions of the *Trattatello*, when he attributes the notion of Dante's triple dedication of the *Comedy* to the reasoning of "some person" or "some persons."[43] But, as we have seen, Boccaccio throughout treats the *Ultima regna* verses as authentically Dante's.

Brother Ilaro's letter is addressed to Huguccio de Fagiola; he sends him a copy of the *Inferno*, glossed by Ilaro himself, at Dante's request. He informs him that the poet dedicated the cantica to Huguccio, and says that he intends to dedicate the *Purgatorio* to Moroello Malaspina and the *Paradiso* to King Frederick. In recounting the conversation he had with Dante, Ilaro says that he marveled at Dante's writing his poem in the vernacular, since it seemed to him that it would have been almost impossible, as well as unfitting, to express his meaning properly in that medium.[44] Dante responded that he had indeed begun his work in Latin, in the verses that we have seen.[45] He accounted for his change of mind thus:

> Sed cum presentis evi conditionem rependerem, vidi cantus illustrium poetarum quasi pro nicilo esse abiectos; et hoc ideo (quod) generosi homines, quibus talia

40. Boccaccio, *2 Trattatello* 128–30 (pp. 528–29); see Paolazzi, "Petrarca, Boccaccio," pp. 221–22.

41. Boccaccio, *Esposizioni* Accessus 74–77.

42. Giuseppe Billanovich, "La leggenda dantesca del Boccaccio: Dalla lettera di Ilaro al *Trattatello in laude di Dante*," *SD* 28 (1949) 45–144; his reasons are summed up on p. 138 n. 1. He gives an edition of the letter on pp. 141–44. I am grateful to Professor Billanovich for his personal assistance in enabling me to identify Benvenuto's source, and for his advice and help on other aspects of this study.

43. Boccaccio, *1 Trattatello* 193–94; *2 Trattatello* 131. For the texts, see below, p. 69 n. 34.

44. *Epistle of Brother Ilaro* (Billanovich, "Leggenda," p. 143): "Cui me super qualitate sermonis admirari respondi, tum quia difficile, ymo inoppinabile videbatur intentionem tam arduam vulgariter exprimi potuisse, tum quia inconveniens videbatur coniunctio tante sententie amiculo populari."

45. Billanovich gives the first word as *ultime* rather than *ultima*; but *ultimē* does not scan, and *ultima* is the reading of all of the texts of Boccaccio and Benvenuto, and also of Villani (see below, p. 71).

> meliori tempore scribebantur, liberales artes—pro dolor!—dimisere plebeis. Propter quod lirulam qua fretus eram deposui, aliam preparans convenientem sensibus modernorum. Frustra enim mandibilis cibus ad ora lactentium admovetur.[46]

Boccaccio's second reason, that Latin poetry is now disregarded because the sort of people who used to patronize it no longer study the liberal arts, is clearly taken from this passage of Ilaro's letter. His first reason, that it would benefit both those with and those without Latin, which resembles 2 Pietro's observation that Dante sang for both literate and vulgar *gentes*, is also easily derivable from the explanation that "Dante" gives to Ilaro: for doubtless many members of the patron class would have been so negligent in their studies that they knew no Latin at all, or at least not enough to understand Latin verse.

It is possible, then, that Ricaldone was accurate in reporting that Benvenuto attributed the first reason (or first two reasons) for Dante's writing in Italian to "Dante's letter"—or at least to Ilaro's letter in which Dante is quoted. But the question remains of how and when Benvenuto would have heard about the letter, since Boccaccio does not identify it either in the first version of the *Trattatello*, to which Benvenuto's account is closest, or in the written version of his lectures. He may have spoken of the letter in the oral version, which Benvenuto attended, or he may have mentioned it in correspondence, say, at the time of providing Benvenuto with a copy of Petrarch's letter (and perhaps a copy of his early *Trattatello*).

In the later versions of his commentary, Benvenuto removed the discussion about Dante's reasons for writing in Italian from his prologue, and rested content with saying that Dante surpassed all vernacular styles and poets. We will see that Villani takes this point further and considers that Dante's Italian style is superior to any Latin style—at least any Latin style that Dante himself could have written. Benvenuto was tempted to agree to a corollary of this conclusion, as we have seen, and only hesitated because of Petrarch's conviction that Dante could have accomplished his goals by writing in Latin.

To repeat, Benvenuto's failure to draw on the reasons given in *Cangrande* for Dante's choice of title is an indication that he did not know the Proto-Accessus and certainly did not know the *Cangrande* Compilation in its final form as a letter written by Dante himself. It is true that in his second and third versions Benvenuto does put forth an explanation of comedy similar to the Accessor's (that is, a work with a sad beginning and happy ending), but he attributes it to Isidore. Moreover, far from saying that it was Dante's reason for calling the poem a comedy, he gives it as his own reason for considering it to be in the comic style, and he contrasts it with Dante's reason (Dante's reason being that the poem was in Italian).

Now that we have seen what Benvenuto has to say in the three versions of his introduction, it should be clear that he not only uses *stilus* in the traditional

46. *Epistle of Ilaro* (pp. 143–44).

sense of "diction," which was Huguccio's meaning, but also takes the word to mean "literary genre." Thus, according to 2 Benvenuto, tragedy is a style written in a high style about high things. He uses the word in a third way when he speaks of "literal style," to designate the language in which a work is written (Latin being high style, any vernacular being low style). A fourth usage appears later in his commentary, at the point in canto 20 of the *Inferno* where Vergil calls the *Aeneid* his high tragedy: here Benvenuto identifies the poem itself as a style. He says that the *Aeneid* is so called because "it is a high style and it deals with high things."[47] (I should add that when Dante calls his own work a comedy in the next canto, Benvenuto explains *mia comedia* as meaning "my vernacular book.")[48]

Although Benvenuto posits a Huguccian chain of events for comedy (which he attributes to Isidore), he does not do so for tragedy. He does not mention the movement from happiness to sadness, except implicitly, in that tragedy is said to deal with disasters. But stories of disaster can begin in disaster and stay there, like Seneca's tragedies, or can end in prosperity, like the *Aeneid*. Moreover, the "high things" of tragedy, which Benvenuto attributes to the *Aeneid*, are not limited to disasters. Furthermore, it is clear that the disasters of tragedy are not necessarily iniquitous; sometimes they are simply calamitous. There is no emphasis in Benvenuto on criminal elements in the kings or others whose downfall or slaughter is related in tragedy. It is noteworthy that while the *Aeneid* is said to deserve the name of tragedy because it contains high things (presumably both characters and events), Dante's work is judged to be a tragedy by Benvenuto only because it deals with high-ranking men. Benvenuto's use of the term *magnates* may reflect at least an indirect influence from Huguccio.

We turn now to a commentator who is specifically indebted to Boccaccio and his *Esposizioni*, in its written form—namely, Francesco di Bartolo da Buti. According to some reckonings, Buti began his lectures on Dante's poem in 1385 or a little earlier. But when commenting on *Paradiso* 6.1–9, he himself gives the year of writing as 1393; and the chief manuscript says that the commentary was concluded on 11 June 1395.[49]

In the prologue of his commentary, Buti notes that Dante called his work a comedy in cantos 16 and 21 of the *Inferno*, and says that he probably did so because comedy has a troubled beginning and a joyful end. But rather than enlarging on this point, he says that for the moment he will not bring up the objections that could be raised against the title, or the answers to such objections. He puts the question aside, not only for the sake of brevity, but also because Boccaccio has sufficiently touched on the matter.[50] As we have seen, Boccaccio argues

47. 3 Benvenuto 2:88: "Quia est stylus altus, et de rebus altis tractans."

48. 3 Benvenuto 2:95.

49. See Francesco Mazzoni, "Francesco di Bartolo da Buti," *ED* 3:23–27; Aldo Vallone, "Buti nella critica dantesca del Trecento," *Accademie e biblioteche d'Italia* 45 (1977) 422–37.

50. Francesco da Buti, *Commento sopra la Divina comedia*, ed. Crescentino Giannini, 3 vols.

against various suggested reasons for calling the poem a comedy and accepts only the reason that Buti mentions. Buti does not discuss the matter further in his prologue, except to say that the various parts are called *canti* not only to correspond to the *cantiche* but also from the analogy with comedy, which means *canto villesco*.[51]

He does not deal with comedy when he comes to canto 16 of the *Inferno*, but he does treat of tragedy when he comments on canto 20. He seems to say that Dante calls Vergil's poem high because it is in high style, and a tragedy because it deals with the deeds of princes and begins with joyful things and ends in sadness and adversity. Tragedy, Buti explains, is the noblest of all poems, because it is in high style and treats of the highest possible matter—gods, kings, and princes—and begins in felicity and ends in misery.[52] This interpretation of the *Aeneid* demonstrates either that Buti was not familiar with it or was not thinking clearly.[53] It is interesting to note that he adds gods to kings and princes as the subjects of tragedy. I have seen no one else do this except Placidus.[54] Since it is unlikely that Buti had access to Placidus, the idea is probably his own.

He goes on to give the most ingenious explanation of the etymology of tragedy thus far encountered: it means "goat song" because a goat has the look of a prince in front by reason of its horns and beard, while at the rear it is filthy and shows its bare buttocks. Thus too tragedy begins in felicity and ends in misery; and therefere a goat was among the gifts that were given to the reciters of tragedy.[55]

(Pisa 1858–62), 1:7: "E la cagione che il mosse credo che fosse questa, che la comedia à torbido principio e lieto fine, e così à questo poema, che prima tratta dell'inferno e de' vizi, che sono turbulenta, e all' ultimo tratta delle virtù e della felicità de' beati, che è cosa lieta. Le ragioni che si pottrebbono far contra, a mostrare che questo nome no si convenia a questa opera, e le soluzioni a ciò, al presente lascio per osservare la brevità, e perchè messer Giovanni Boccacci nella sua lettura che cominciò assai sofficientemente le tocca."

51. Ibid., 7–8.

52. Ibid., 531–32: "Dice Vergilio che la sua *Eneide* è alta tragedia; questo finge Dante per dimostrare che in alto stile è fatta, e che si dee chiamare tragedia con ciò sia cosa che tratti de' fatti de' principi, e comincia dalle cose liete e finisce nelle triste et avverse. Tragedia è poema più nobile che tutti li altri, pero che in alto stile, e tratta della più alta materia che si possa trattare: cioè delli idii e de' re e delli principi, et incomincia da felicità e termina in miseria."

53. The explanation of Hollander (see above, p. 5 n. 22) that Buti was thinking of the *Aeneid* and considered it a tragedy "since it ends with the death of Turnus or, as he says, 'with sad and adverse things' " (TDC 252; cf. TC 130 n. 21, TDI 216 n. 197), is not convincing.

54. Placidus, *Glossae*, S 21 *scaena*, ed. J.W. Pirie and W.M. Lindsay, *Glossaria latina* 4 (Paris 1930, repr. 1965), p. 34: "Tragoedia est enim genus carminis quo poetae regum casus durissimos et scelera inaudita vel deorum res alto sonitu describunt."

55. Buti, 1:532: "Et interpretarsi tragedia canto di becco, chè come il becco à dinanzi aspetto di principe per le corna e per la barba, e dietro è sozzo, mostrando le natiche nude, e non avendo con che coprirle. Così la tragedia incomincia dal principio con felicità e poi termina in miseria: e però tra li altri doni che si davano a' recitatori della tragedia si dava il becco." Presumably no animal was readily producible to dramatize or symbolize the effect of comedy; for it would have to have had a mournful face, if not a disgusting one, and splendid hindquarters.

This explanation is also given by the Anonymous of Florence in his commentary.[56] Although scholars sometimes speak of the Anonymous as writing after Buti,[57] I have not seen Buti noted as a source for him, and I suppose it is possible that he is the source for Buti. The Latin etymology in the Anonymous's explanation[58] shows that he is drawing on some source other than the commentaries that have been named as his sources—the Italian commentaries of Jacopo Alighieri, Lana, Lancia, and Boccaccio, and the Latin commentaries of Pietro Alighieri and Benvenuto.

The Anonymous explains comedy in the more conventional terms of plot, as the opposite of tragedy; but he complicates matters by suggesting that comedy can deal with the same content as tragedy (except in reverse order). He says that tragedy begins with the prosperity of lords or with great deeds and ends in adversity or misery, whereas comedy begins in misery and ends in prosperity.[59]

When Dante refers to his own poem as a comedy in canto 21, shortly after having Vergil call the *Aeneid* a high tragedy, Buti pauses to discuss the matter. Comedy, he says, means "song of villagers." It deals with middling persons and should be written in a middling style; it begins in adversity and ends in felicity. Such are the fables of Terence and Plautus. There might be some doubt whether this poem should be called a comedy, but since the author so wished it, the name should be allowed. Buti adds that Petrarch, in a letter that begins *Nec te laudasse peniteat*, takes up this point and says that he does not see why Dante called it a comedy.[60]

Where did Buti acquire his notion of comedy as middling in style and persons? Papias and Balbus, we have seen, pass on Placidus's idea of middling style for comedy. Only Donatus has anything of the sort to say about the characters of comedy: it deals, he says, with *homines mediocris fortunae*. The Donatus-Evanthius account of comedy was not yet available in its entirety, but excerpts

---

56. *Commento alla Divina commedia d'Anonimo Fiorentino del secolo xiv*, ed. Pietro Fanfani, 3 vols. (Bologna 1866–74) 1:451–52: "Tregedia e quello stilo poetico che tratta di signori o di gran fatti di fortuna. Et dicitur ab *tragos* grece quod latine dicitur hircus, però che nella faccia dinnanzi i fatti de' signori, di che i poeti trattono, sono cose grandi, belle, et dilettevoli, poi nel fine sono rustiche et villane le loro eversioni, et molt[o] simili al becco, ch' è bello dinnanzi et fetido dirietro."

57. See Francesco Mazzoni, "Anonimo Fiorentino," in *ED* 1:291–92.

58. The passage "Et dicitur ab *tragos* grece quod latine dicitur hircus" in note 56.

59. *Anonimo*, 461: "Quello che vuol dire commedia altre volte è detto: una differenzia hae fra l'altre dalla tragedia: quella comincia da prosperità di signori o di gran fatti, et finisce in avversità et in miserie; questa in contrario, chè viene, da miserie, in prosperità seguendo."

60. Buti, 1:543: "*La mia comedia*: cioè questa opera la quale l'autore chiama comedia. Comedia s'interpetra canto di villani, e tratta delle persone mezzane, et in mezzano stilo si dee comporre, et incomincia da avversità e finisce in felicità, come fanno le favole di Terenzio e di Plauto. Sarebbe dubbio se questo poema dell'autore si dee chiamare comedia o no; ma poi che le piacque chiamarla comedia debbalisi concedere. Messer Francesco Petrarca in una sua epistola che comincia, *Nec te laudasse peniteat*, ec., muove questa questione e dice: 'Nec cur comediam vocet video.' " On Petrarch, see above, pp. 52–53, and see Vallone. "Buti," p. 429.

or remnants of its doctrine did appear in commentaries on Terence.[61] One such commentary, with the incipit of *Novem requiruntur*, was used by Buti for his own accessus to Terence, and it does follow Donatus on the point of characters: "In comedia mediocres persone habentur."[62] But it deviates from Donatus in ascribing a "light" style to Terence.[63] In the longer version of Buti's accessus, which may be his original text, Buti matches style with content. He follows a threefold stylistic paradigm of tragedy, comedy, and satire, with tragedy requiring a sublime style and comedy a middling one.[64] The sublime style deals with the greatest things and persons, with high rather than common speech; the middling style deals with middling persons or things, and it does not imitate things that are either too vulgar or too weighty; the low style deals with small and low things or persons in plain and common words, as is shown in satires.[65] Terence's comedies, of course, are in the middling style.

In sum, the source of Buti's doctrine of comic style is not clear. But it is clear that he is consistent in applying it to both Terence and Dante.

---

61. See M. D. Reeve and R. H. Rouse, "New Light on the Transmission of Donatus's *Commentum Terentii*," *Viator* 9 (1978) 235–49, esp. 246 n. 29.

62. Ed. G. V. Alessio, "Hec Franciscus de Buiti," *IMU* 24 (1981) 99 (no. 54).

63. See above, p. 29 n. 23.

64. Buti, *Accessus to Terence*, ed. Alessio, "Hec Franciscus de Buiti," pp. 109–16, esp. 114 (no. 22): "Ideo tragedia requirit sublimem stilum, comedia vero mediocrem."

65. Ibid., p. 116 (no. 31), long version: "Stilus vero est mediocris, quia stili sunt tres: sublimis, mediocris, et infimus. Sublimis est qui fit de maximis rebus et personis, loquendo alte et non vulgariter; mediocris vero qui fit de mediocribus rebus sive personis nec imitatur tantum vulgaria ned tantum ponderosa; infirmus est qui tractat de rebus parvis et infimis sive personis, planis et vulgaribus verbis, ut patet in Satiris. Et hec sufficiant ad prefationem dicti autoris. Et cetera." In the short version, which appears in Sozomeno da Pistoia's manuscript, we find the following: "Stilus autem est mediocris. Stili autem tres sunt: sublimis, mediocris, et infimus. Sublimis, ut heroicus; mediocris, ut comicus; infimus, ut satirus, ut buccolicus, georgicus. Hec Franciscus de Buiti."

7

Pseudo-Dante, Villani, and Dante

According to the hypothesis I have developed in this study, an unknown student of Dante's *Comedy* set to work sometime in the last quarter of the fourteenth century to create an introduction to the *Paradiso* that he attributed to Dante himself. He made use of a preexisting Accessus to the whole *Comedy*, prefaced it with a Dedication to Cangrande, and followed it with an Exposition of the beginning of *Paradiso*. The resulting Compilation we now know as the *Epistle to Cangrande*.

Within the general framework of this hypothesis, a number of variations can be formulated. For instance, the Dedication, or the first part of it, may be based on an authentic letter of Dante's; or it may be a forgery by someone other than the Compiler and only used by him, whether he believed it to be authentic or not. If there was an early forgery of this sort, we would have to distinguish between two Pseudo-Dantes—namely, Pseudo-Dante the Dedicator and Pseudo-Dante the Compiler. Such a view would fit the theory of Ettore Paratore, who suggests that the Dedication was apocryphal and that a later forger added the Accessus-Exposition.[1] It is also possible that the Compiler was not the same person as the Expositor, but someone who found ready-made not only the Proto-Accessus but also a Proto-Exposition. This scenario is set forth by Colin Hardie,[2] except that he believes that there was also a Proto-Dedication (to use my terminology) by someone other than Dante. He suggests a date of ca. 1324–27 for the whole Proto-Compilation, and a date of ca. 1390 for the final Compiler's transformation of it into a letter by Dante to Cangrande in Verona. However, in light of the conclusions we have established, we must put the Proto-Accessus after 1 Pietro and before Boccaccio's *Esposizioni*, if not before his *Trattatello*, and date the Exposition (or Proto-Exposition) after *3 Ottimo*. Furthermore, we must say that when Boccaccio used the Proto-Accessus it was not attached to a Proto-Exposition, since there is no sign that he knows the contents of the Exposition.

1. Ettore Paratore, "L'eredità classica in Dante" (1965), revised version in *Tradizione e struttura in Dante* (Florence 1968), pp. 55–121, esp. 110–11 n. 50.

2. C. G. Hardie, "The *Epistle to Cangrande* Again," *Deutsches Dante-Jahrbuch* 38 (1960) 51–74, esp. 74.

We would therefore have to assign different dates for each, say ca. 1350 for the Accessus and ca. 1380 for the Exposition. The Expositor himself may have prefaced his Exposition with the Accessus before the Dedicator-Compiler added his Dedication, or before the Compiler took a preexisting Dedication and joined it to the Accessus-Exposition.

If we posit that the Dedicator, Expositor, and Compiler were one and the same person, namely, Pseudo-Dante, we must conclude that he worked in isolation from Boccaccio, Benvenuto da Imola, and Francesco da Buti, the great Dantists of his day, for he shows no awareness of their work nor they of his. He did, however, come across an introduction to the *Comedy* that Boccaccio had drawn on for his commentary. This work, which I have called the Proto-Accessus, was taken over now in great part by the Compiler to serve as an introduction to his Exposition of the *Paradiso.* He adjusted it in order to fit his context of a commentary on the third canticle of Dante's poem—for instance, by inserting the phrase "whole and part" now and then. We have seen that one of these phrases was already in the Proto-Accessus, taken over from Guido, in the clause, "quia non ad speculandum sed ad opus inventum et fictum est totum et pars."[3] Let me note here that neither the Accessor nor the Compiler made an adjustment in the ending of this sentence to convert it to a preferred *cursus.* But in another case, where the Accessor simply copied a nonrhythmical cadence of Guido's, "iustitie premiandi et puniendi *obnoxius est,*"[4] the Compiler in applying it to *Paradiso* twice converts it into a standard cursus: "est iustitie premiandi et *puniéndi obnóxius*" (*tardus*) and "obnoxius est *iustítie premiándi*" (*velox*).[5] In another instance, the Accessor or the Compiler changes Guido's *admirábilis et gráta,* which Dante at least would have considered nonrhythmical, to the velox *admirábilis et quiéta;* but a form identical to the original, *desiderábilis et gráta,* is given later.[6] In the case of Guido's tardus *alicúius misérie,* the Accessus has the nonrhythmical *alicúius réi,*[7] whereas in place of Guido's *ópere est dúplex* (the same form as his *admirábilis et gráta*), the Accessus has *véro est dúplex,* an acceptable *planus* form.[8]

We encounter a difficulty in cursus analysis when we come to *suis tragediis* and *suis comediis.*[9] If Guido da Pisa followed Dante in regarding *tragedia* and *comedia* as paroxytone,[10] the cadences, though Ciceronian, would be unacceptable to Dante; but if Guido, or the Accessor or the Compiler, considered them

---

3. See above, p. 15.

4. Guido, *Expositiones,* p. 3; *Cangrande* 8.25.

5. *Cangrande* 11.34.

6. Guido, *Expositiones,* p. 5; *Cangrande* 10.29, 10.31. See below at n. 27 for the suggestion that *admirábilis et gráta* (and, of course, *desiderábilis et gráta*) was an acceptable form for later writers.

7. Guido, *Expositiones,* p. 6; *Cangrande* 10.29.

8. Guido, *Expositiones,* p. 3; *Cangrande* 9.26.

9. See Guido, *Expositiones,* pp 5–6; *Cangrande* 10.29.

10. See above, pp. 9–10.

to be proparoxytone, in keeping with classical quantities and the practice of some medieval Latinists (which prevailed in modern times), then each phrase would be transformed into a tardus. The same difficulty comes with the twice-occurring cadence *sua poetria* in the Accessus,[11] referring to Horace's *Ars poetica*; a paroxytone reading of the medieval word *poetria* would produce a Ciceronian cadence, a proparoxytone a tardus. A further difficulty comes from the fact that four of the six manuscripts read *poetica* ($VM^1M^2M^3$), one has *poetia* (*R*: for *poesia*?), and only one reads *poetria* (*Me*). Boffito assumes that the sixteenth-century scribe of the last-mentioned manuscript changed the authentic reading of *poetica* to *poetria* because Dante consistently uses *poetria* in his authentic writings,[12] and presumably other modern editors, including even Brugnoli, have themselves chosen *poetria* for the same reason. The same impulse must account for editors' use of the Dantean form *rithimus*, even though all of the manuscripts have *rhythmus* or some similar disyllabic spelling. There is a difference in rhythm between the nonrhythmical *divíditur in ríthimos* and the form *divíditur in rhýthmos* (the *admirábilis et gráta* cadence that may have become acceptable later in the century).[13] The manuscript reading *cántuum et rhythmórum* is velox, whereas the editorially emended *cantuum et rithimorum* is nothing.[14]

These examples show that there are many pitfalls in analyzing cadences, and sometimes the conclusions to which such analyses lead are far from convincing. Nevertheless, I believe that a brief consideration of the prose rhythms to be found in *Cangrande* will be helpful in discussing questions of divided authorship.

I follow in general the method recently set forth by Peter Dronke,[15] except that I do not restrict myself to the ends of sentences, but analyze as well the cadences of major pauses within sentences (details are given in Appendix 2). The rhythmical cursus were especially cultivated by writers of formal epistles, and modern scholars have assumed that no such usage can be found in technical treatises, except at the beginnings and perhaps again at the ends. This was the early conclusion of Paget Toynbee for Dante's *De vulgari eloquentia* and *De*

---

11. *Cangrande* 10.30, 32.

12. Giuseppe Boffito, *L'Epistola di Dante Alighieri a Cangrande della Scala* (Turin 1907), p. 27. The only time I have seen *poetria* used in medieval quantitative verse is in the following couplet on Geoffrey of Vinsauf's *Liber versuum* (which later came to be called *Poetria nova*) in Munich Bayer. Staatsbibl. CLM 4603 fol. 136ra:

Esse poema metrum, fictorem dico poetam;
Arsque poetria; sed sit fictio dicta poesis,

where it is scanned *pŏētrĭă*. See the edition by Marjorie Curry Woods, *An Early Commentary on the Poetria nova of Geoffrey of Vinsauf* (New York 1985), p. 487, where however *poetrie* is mistakenly put for *poetria*. See my review in *Manuscripta* 32 (1988) 54–58, where I make this point, and where I argue that Geoffrey himself did not title his work *Poetria nova*.

13. *Cangrande* 9.26. See below at n. 27. Boccaccio, apparently translating this passage in the *Trattatello*, uses *rittimi*, according to the Ricci edition (see p. 17 above); but Ricci does not note variants. *Divíditur in rhýthmis* is classified as a *spondaicus* (S^5); see Appendixes 2 and 3.

14. *Cangrande* 12.35.

15. Peter Dronke, *Dante and Medieval Latin Traditions* (Cambridge 1986), pp. 13, 103–11.

monarchia as well as for all but the beginning epistolary portion of *Cangrande*.[16] But he later came to realize that "in the *De vulgari eloquentia* the *cursus* is observed, not in occasional passages only, but systematically throughout the treatise, in almost every passage where the nature of the subject allows."[17] Toynbee did not draw the conclusion about the authenticity or inauthenticity of other works in the Dantean corpus, specifically *Cangrande*, that such a finding should have suggested. Dronke, however, has since found a similarly high percentage of rhythmical cadences in the *De monarchia* as well as in the *De vulgari eloquentia*, but only about half the proportion in the body of *Cangrande*.[18] In the *De vulgari eloquentia*, he says, "a distinctive pattern of cadences can be seen, which is so startlingly different from that of the fitful cadences in the exposition to Cangrande that it is very difficult indeed to imagine that both could stem from the same author."[19]

My analysis of all "clauses" (meaning phrases as well), including periods, yields results that confirm Dronke's findings. His study of the 96 periods (in Mengaldo's punctuation) after the opening sections of the *De vulgari eloquentia* shows that 71 (74 percent) follow the rhythmical cursus (counting only the three regular cadences, velox, planus, and tardus, and their proclitic substitutes). In my own analysis, I find only 28 velox endings as opposed to Dronke's 30, giving a total of 69 rhythmical endings (71.9 percent). The same passage yields 387 clauses, of which 232 (59.9 percent) end rhythmically. This is a somewhat larger differential than is to be found in other writings. For instance, in Guido da Pisa's Prologue of 87 periods, 50 or 53 (57.5 or 60.9 percent) end rhythmically (depending on the pronunciation of words like *tragedia*), while of the 259 clauses in the Prologue, between 131 and 135 (50.6 and 52.1 percent) fit the cadences. In the first version of Pietro Alighieri's commentary, after his elaborate first two sentences, there are 29 periods (in Nannucci's edition), 13 or 14 (44.8 or 48.3 percent) of which end rhythmically, and 162 clauses, of which 61 or 63 (37.7 or 38.9 percent) are rhythmical. Both of Pietro's initial periods are rhythmical, while of the 21 clauses in them, 17 (81 percent) are rhythmical. Similarly, all six of the periods in the first section of the *De vulgari eloquentia* are cadenced, whereas only 29 (87.9 percent) of the 33 clauses follow suit.

In the Dedication of *Cangrande*, 17 out of the 18 periods (94.4 percent) are cadenced; these periods yield 71 clauses, of which 57 (80.2 percent) follow the cadences. This compares well with the first half of Dante's sixth epistle, which

16. Paget Toynbee, "Dante and the *Cursus*: A New Argument in Favor of the Authenticity of the *Quaestio de aqua et terra*," *Modern Language Review* 13 (1918) 420–30, expanded as Appendix C: "Dante and the *Cursus*" in his edition of the *Epistolae* (1920), pp. 224–47; see esp. p. 231 and n. 2.

17. Paget Toynbee, "The Bearing of the *Cursus* on the Text of Dante's *De vulgari eloquentia*" (14 March 1923), *Proceedings of the British Academy* 10 (1921–23) 359–77, esp. 359.

18. Dronke, *Dante*, pp. 105–6.

19. Ibid., p. 13. In saying that the *DVE* "has not hitherto been analyzed for its use of rhythmic prose," Dronke shows that he is unaware of Toynbee's 1923 study.

Dronke takes as equivalent in length to the Dedication: of the 18 periods, 17 are cadenced; of the 97 clauses, 77 (79.4 percent) are cadenced. The whole letter has 36 periods, of which 33 (91.7 percent) have standard forms, while 139 (82.2 percent) of the 169 clauses follow suit.

According to Dronke's findings, the 96 sentences of the Accessus-Exposition have 36 (37.5 percent) that are rhythmical. My own method of calculation counts 102 sentences, of which 37 to 41 (36.3 to 40.2 percent) are rhythmical. The same text yields 394 clauses, of which 149 to 155 (37.8 to 39.3 percent) are rhythmical. In other words, there is no falloff at all between sentences and clauses in these sections of *Cangrande* taken as a whole.

These figures support the conclusion that, whereas the Dedication shows a global consistency with Dante's epistolary and introductory style, the Accessus and Exposition fall far short of his expository style. But let us look more closely at the various parts of *Cangrande*.[20] First of all, we note in the Dedication that the cadences are observed with great regularity until the final paragraph (4.12–13), where there is a series of five nonrhythmical clauses in a row. Toynbee was led to suspect the integrity of the text; he accepted several emendations that "restored" the cursus (these emendations show how easily one can write rhythmically if one has the mind to do so).[21] But the state of the text might just as easily lead one to suspect the intervention of another writer who altered or added to an existing letter without maintaining the strict cursus forms—or who was writing at a later time and using forms not acceptable to Dante's period.

The Dedication proper does end in a regular tardus (*urgébat ultérius*), and there are two more such cadences in the following transition sentence of the Compiler (*consumáta epístole* and *compendióse aggrédiar*). The Compiler then begins to introduce the Accessus by quoting Aristotle's *Metaphysics* in the translation of James of Venice,[22] followed by a quasi-philosophical discussion in which there are nine nonrhythmical clauses and only two rhythmical (both tardus). In the paragraphs that follow, however, a somewhat higher percentage of rhythmical cadences is found in passages assignable to the Compiler than in those assignable to the Accessor. The Expositor too has a quite low incidence of rhythmical cadences, explained in part perhaps by his technical philosophical discussions. When the Compiler concludes by addressing Cangrande again, in the final two paragraphs, when he should resume the epistolary style with its strict observance of the cursus, cadenced endings are suprisingly scarce; he does manage

20. See the marked text of *Cangrande* in Appendix 3.

21. Toynbee, *Epistolae*, p. 171: he changes *conferri videri potest* to *potest conférri vidéri* (planus); changes *videbar* to *videar* to create a velox (*vídear expressísse*); and changes *vitam* to *invidiam* to make another velox (*invídiam parvipéndens*). In the first part of the first sentence of the paragraph, which the earlier Oxford edition gave as "Illud quoque praeterire silentio simpliciter, inardescens non sinit affectus," Toynbee eliminates the comma, taking *simpliciter* with *inardescens*, thereby avoiding the nonrhythmical cadence *silentio simpliciter*. He could have noted that this interpretation creates a tardus, *preteríre siléntio*.

22. *Cangrande* 5.14. See above, pp. 15–16, and Appendix 1.

to conclude strongly by going from two planus endings to a velox, but Dante himself preferred to go from a velox or a tardus to a planus.[23]

If we look only at periods, 11 can be assigned to the Accessor (apart from direct quotations from Guido), of which only four (36.4 percent) are rhythmical; of the 65 periods belonging to the Expositor, 24 or 25 (36.9 or 38.5 percent) are rhythmical; and of the 22 assignable to the Compiler, 10 or 11 (45.4 or 50 percent) are rhythmical. The spread is closer when we look at the clauses: for the Accessor, 17 to 20 of 49 (36.1 to 43.9 percent); for the Expositor, 87 of 240 (36.3 percent); and for the Compiler, 37 or 38 of 84 (44.0 or 45.2 percent).

As I noted previously, in these calculations I have been recognizing only the three regular forms of cadence plus any "proclitic" substitutes that find a mention in two or more of the Italian theorists; these substitutes turn out to be three forms of velox and one each of planus and tardus. But it is clear that by Dante's time the third velox substitute (which I label V^4) was not in favor with Dante or any other writer whose works I have analyzed or seen analyzed, except for Cola di Rienzo.[24] Moreover, there was at least one other cadence not mentioned by the theorists that Dante expressly singled out for disfavor, namely the "enclitic" planus (which I label P^3); Dante gives the example of *dóminam Bértam*. He calls it *insipidus*, which I take to mean "amateurish," "not in the best taste."[25] This must mean that some stylists were allowing it. And when we look at Petrarch, Boccaccio, and later writers, we see that it has outstripped the proclitic form (P^2) in popularity, whether by deliberate choice or as the result of "natural selection."[26]

Dante did not avoid the P^3 form as consistently as he did the V^4 form. There is one P^3 among the 33 clauses of the introductory section of the *De vulgari eloquentia*, and 17 among the following 387 clauses; but there is only one out of all 169 clauses in Epistle 6—in the first clause after the salutation ("Eterni pia *providéntia Régis*"). Out of the 214 periods in all of Dante's authentic letters, there are only three P^3 endings. But there are two such among the 71 clauses of the Dedication of *Cangrande*, one in the middle (par. 2.8: *supérius díxi*), and the other at the end (4.13: *grátie véstre*). The number of P^3 cadences among the 394 clauses of the Accessus-Exposition is 17 or 18, which is comparable with the incidence in the *De vulgari*. But only three of these are in the Accessus portion,

23. See his discussion in *DVE* 2.6, treated in Appendix 2, pp. 80–82.

24. See the tables in Appendix 2. Dante has no instances of the V^4 cadence in the clauses of Epistle 6 and the first ten sections of *DVE* or in the periods of his other authentic epistles, and neither does Pietro in the clauses of his commentary that I have analyzed. Guido has three instances, and *Cangrande* also has three (two of which I assign to the Expositor and one to the Compiler). Out of 1,000 sentences, Petrarch has only four V^4 endings and Salutati only two, while out of 620 sentences Boccaccio has none. Cola di Rienzo has 39 V^4 cadences out of 1,377 sentences; they amount to 3.4 percent of his total of 1,305 velox cadences.

25. *DVE* 2.6.4–5.

26. Out of the sample of 1,000 Petrarch sentences, 47 are P^1, 18 are P^2, and 24 are P^3; out of Boccaccio's 620 sentences, the figures are 79, 19, and 44; and most later writers are more extreme: see Table 5 in Appendix 2 (p. 89).

and one of them is taken over from Guido, while the other two are attributable to the Compiler. The Exposition, then, has 14 P^3 endings (or 15, counting *hierarchia* in par. 21.60 as proparoxytone), of which one is a translation of Dante's Italian (par. 20.53: *áliqua mínus*) and three are to be assigned to the Compiler at the end, when he returns to addressing Cangrande (32.88: *magnificéntia véstra*; 33.89: *quólibet órbe*; 33.90: *vidélicet Déo*).

If we proceed farther in this direction and take Petrarch's example as an indication of mid-fourteenth-century practice, we can postulate two acceptable enclitic forms of the tardus cadence, and also find a completely new kind of cadence, which modern scholars call *trispondaicus*, but which I will call simply *spondaicus*, or spondaic. The regular form is that of Cicero's favored ending, *ésse videátur*, and I have isolated two proclitic forms and two enclitic forms. An example of the second enclitic, which I label S^5, is Guido's *admirábilis et gráta*.[27]

As one would expect, works or passages with a fairly low percentage of regular and proclitic forms register the highest increase in acceptable cadences when enclitic and spondaic forms are admitted into the fold. For instance, there is a 23.7 percent increase in rhythmical cadences in the clauses of sections 2–10 of the *De vulgari*, but only a 10.3 percent increase in the first section of the same work. Presumably in both cases the increase is a "natural" or unintended one. That is, Dante surely did not give preference to the enclitic and spondaic forms over other kinds of endings that he considered equally nonrhythmical.

I will not venture to say if the increase in any of the cases I give in my tables in Appendix 2 is statistically significant. I will, however, point out where the "new-fangled" cadences occur most frequently in some representative works. In the first half of Dante's *Epistle 6*, which, as we have seen, is equivalent in length to the Dedication of *Cangrande*, there are 97 clauses, of which 77 (79.4 percent) are regular and proclitic, and an additional six are enclitic or spondaic, an increase of 7.8 percent; in the whole letter, there are 169 clauses, of which 139 are regular-proclitic (82.2 percent) and another 13 are enclitic-spondaic, an increase of 9.4 percent. The enclitic and spondaic cadences are scattered throughout the letter, beginning, as noted previously, in the first sentence, and ending in the closing cadence of the final sentence: "Est enim quoniam peccator percutitur, ut sine retractatione moriatur." But the final spondaic *retractatióne moriátur* is the result of editorial emendation. Since the manuscripts end in a trisyllabic, *rivantur*, I suggest a trisyllabic emendation, such as *ruatur*, which would produce a regular planus; this, combined with the tardus earlier in the sentence (*peccátor percútitur*), results in the effect that Dante praises the most, calling it "et sapidus, et venustus, etiam et excelsus" and classifying it as the "gradus constructionis excellentissimus."

In the *Cangrande* Dedication, of the 71 clauses, 57 (80.2 percent) are regular or proclitic, and another eight are enclitic or spondaic, an increase of 14 percent. Three enclitic tardus forms come early (1.3: *Jerúsalem pétiit*; 2.4: *inspícere*

---

27. See above, p. 62.

líbeat; and 2.7: *nóscere dátum est*); I have mentioned the enclitic planus at 2.8 (*supérius díxi*); another tardus comes in the third section (3.11: *cóngruum cómperi*); and in the fourth section, there are two spondaics (4.12: *vidébar expressísse*; and 4.13: *vítam parvipéndens*) in addition to the enclitic planus (4.13: *grátię véstre*).

Of the 84 clauses I have attributed to the Compiler, 37 or 38 are regular or proclitic, while an additional 17 are enclitic or spondaic, an increase of 45.9 or 44.7 percent. I have noted the three enclitic planus forms he uses at the end of the Exposition when he reverts to addressing Cangrande. He also uses a number of spondaics at this point (33.89: *íllis animábus*; 33.90: *princípio seu prímo*, *ultérius querátur*, *Á[lfa] et O[méga]*, *princípium et fínis*). The usual editorial reading *Alfa et O* is based on Dante's usage in *Paradiso* 26.17, which is not relevant if Dante did not write *Cangrande*. Neither letter is spelled out in any of the manuscripts. *V*, for instance, has "AΩ" (contrary to the Boffito-Toynbee reading). The whole passage is based on Apocalypse 1.8: "Ego sum A et ω, principium et finis," found in various forms in medieval copies of the Vulgate. We note that *principio seu primo* could easily be tranformed to a velox by using *sive* for *seu*, but all six manuscripts have *seu*.

I must conclude that these results are too problematic to add much cogency to any particular distribution of authorial responsibility in *Cangrande*. Perhaps the most plausible case is that these figures support the idea of an early form of the Dedication in strict cursus form (whether by Dante himself or an imitator) that was altered at the end and joined to the Accessus-Exposition by a later Compiler who had a more Petrarchan standard for epistolary cadences. By assigning paragraph 4.12–13a to the Compiler, we do not change his stylistic statistics by much; but by removing the paragraph entirely from the Dedicator, we bring the resulting epistle closer to Dantean perfection. Of the 16 periods it contains (in Brugnoli's punctuation), 14 are regular and the other two are proclitic. The 64 clauses have an 85.9 percent regular-proclitic proportion (as opposed to 80.2 percent when paragraph 4.12–13a is counted).

I do not see any stylistic objection to the idea that the Compiler is the author of the entire Exposition. If he was, we must conclude that he made use of *3 Ottimo* and fleshed it out with some Thomistic distinctions on existence. Alternatively, there could have been a preexistent Exposition by someone else, which was used independently by the author of *3 Ottimo* and the Compiler.[28] The Exposition has a reference to Chapter 2 of Book 2 of the *Metaphysics* of Aristotle;[29] since this chapter comes immediately after the passage quoted by the Accessor (drawing on Guido) and quoted again by the Compiler (using a different translation), we may wish to take it as a sign that the Compiler was also responsible for the citation in the Exposition, whether or not he was responsible for the whole of the Exposition.

---

28. See above, pp. 38–39.

29. *Cangrande* 20.56: "Et cum esset sic procedere in infinitum in causis agentibus, ut probatur in secundo *Metaphysice*, erit devenire ad primum, qui Deus est." This is the reading of *V*; the other five MSS mistakenly cite the third book and abbreviate the title: "in 3° methaph.," etc.

If the Compiler used *3 Ottimo* for the Exposition, he did not take the opportunity to incorporate its doctrine on comedy and tragedy into the Accessus. The Exposition does not touch on the generic aspects of literature at all, except in drawing upon Cicero's *De inventione*. It refers to Cicero's work as *Nova rhetorica*, which is contrary to Dante's own usage of calling it *Rhetorica prima*.[30] It designates the subject matter of the *Paradiso* as admirable ("cum ergo materia circa quam versatur presens tractatus sit admirabilis"),[31] which according to Brugnoli contradicts the definition of comedy in the Accessus and is more in keeping with the Accessor's definition of tragedy. However, though it is true that the Accessor, when dealing with the criterion of *materia*, says that tragedy is admirable in the beginning, he adds (in effect) that comedy is the opposite.[32] In the case of Dante's poem, therefore, the matter of *Paradiso* would be admirable. At least on this point, then, the Expositor would seem to be consistent with the Accessor; and he also agrees with the Dedicator in characterizing *Paradiso* as the sublime canticle, or a sublime canticle, of the *Comedy*.[33] In one aspect the Expositor differs from the other commentators who wrote in Latin, namely, Guido, Pietro, and Benvenuto: when he quotes Dante's poem, he translates the Italian into Latin rather than giving the original. This practice differs from Dante's own method of dealing with vernacular poetry in his Latin treatise, *De vulgari eloquentia*. At the end, the Compiler has Dante uncharacteristically characterize himself as beset with *familiaris angustia* (though he does in this case produce a regular tardus). Many readers have found this statement to be at odds with the Dantean persona of the Dedication as well as with Dante's real nature and the circumstances of his life when he was writing the *Paradiso*.

If the Compiler himself was the author of the Dedication, he must have been inspired by the report that Boccaccio records, after naming the three dedicatees specified in Brother Ilaro's letter, that the whole *Comedy* was dedicated to Cangrande.[34]

Pseudo-Dante the Compiler had finished and published his pseudepigraphon in time for it to be read and cited by Filippo Villani in his commentary on the

30. *Cangrande* 19.49 and Brugnoli's note (in *Opere minori*, vol. 2, ed. P. V. Mengaldo et al. [Florence 1979], pp. 626–27), referring to Dante's citation of the *Rhetorica prima* in *De monarchia* 2.5.2.

31. *Cangrande* 19.50.

32. *Cangrande* 10.29.

33. *Cangrande* 3.11.

34. Boccaccio, *1 Trattatello* 193–94 (p. 487): "Questo libro della *Comedia*, secondo il ragionare d'alcuno, intitolò egli a tre solennissimi uomini italiani, secondo la sua triplice divisione, a ciascuno la sua, in questa guisa: la prima parte, cioè lo *'Nferno*, intitolò a Uguiccione della Faggiuola, il quale allora in Toscana signore di Pisa era, mirabilmente glorioso; la seconda parte, cioè il *Purgatorio*, intitolò al marchese Moruello Malaspina; la terza parte, cioè il *Paradiso*, a Federigo III re di Cicilia. (194) Alcuni vogliano dire lui averlo intitolato tutto a messer Cane della Scala; ma, quale si sia di queste due la verità, niuna cosa altra n'abbiamo che solamente il volontario ragionare di diversi; né egli è sì gran fatto che solenne investigazione ne bisogni." In *2 Trattatello* 131 (p. 529), he attributes the idea of the triple dedication to more than one person: "secondo che ragionano alcuni." See above, p. 54. In *2 Trattatello* 132, instead of dismissing both

Comedy. Since Villani was the first person to come across the letter of "Dante" to Cangrande with its elaborate explanation of the poem, we might expect that he would have regarded it as a sensational discovery and drawn extensively upon it in his own lectures. Surprisingly, however, he refers to it only matter-of-factly[35] and makes very limited use of it.

Scholars have been unable to date Villani's lecturing on Dante with any precision; they can only tell us that sometime between 1391 and 1402 he was mandated by the Studio Fiorentino to give a course on the *Comedy*.[36] But since he uses Buti's idea of the front and rear ends of a goat as corresponding to the structure of tragedy, if we accept 1395 for the completion of Buti's commentary, a date of "ca. 1400" should be acceptably safe for Villani's written commentary.

Villani begins his discussion of the title of Dante's work by drawing on *Cangrande* for the etymology of comedy and for the plot structure of tragedy. He then introduces the goat-form idea, adding that all of the plays of Seneca bear out this configuration. He finds it confirmed as well in Fortune's rhetorical question in Boethius's *Consolation of Philosophy*.[37] Therefore, he says (rather illogically), Dante's poem is rightly titled *Comedy*. He proceeds to give the plot movement of comedy, only adding to the *Cangrande* account by specifying a middle as well as a beginning and end: there is fear and trembling at the beginning, good promise and hope in the middle, and happy and complete sweetness and joy at

---

ideas as speculation, he expresses preference for the second: "Alcuni voglion dire lui averlo intitolato tutto a messer Can della Scala; e io il credo più tosto, per la maniera che tenne di mandar prima a lui quello che composto avea che ad alcuno altro." See Giuseppe Billanovich, "La leggenda dantesca del Boccaccio," *SD* 28 (1949) 108–14, who takes Boccaccio's treatment as an indication that he was drawing on *Cangrande*. But Boccaccio speaks of the whole *Comedy* as dedicated to Cangrande, whereas *Cangrande* gives no sign that Dante had dedicated the first two parts to him before his dedication of the *Paradiso*. I admit, however, that a similar objection could be brought to bear in the opposite direction: just as *Cangrande* would not inspire Boccaccio to think that the whole *Comedy* was dedicated to Cangrande, so too Boccaccio's account would not inspire the Compiler to think that only the *Paradiso* was dedicated to Cangrande. But I do not postulate that the Compiler drew on Boccaccio; I suggest only that he and Boccaccio drew on the same report.

35. Filippo Villani, *Il commento al primo canto dell'Inferno*, ed. Giuseppe Cugnoni (Città di Castella 1896), p. 28: "Noster vero poeta in quodam introductorio suo super cantu primo *Paradisi*, ad dominum Canem de la Scala destinata, de sex agere videtur, que fa[c]tum, agentem, formam, finem, libri titulum, et genus philosopye comprehendunt."

36. See Bruno Basile, "Villani, Filippo," *ED* 5:1011–13.

37. Villani, *Commento*, pp. 34–35: "Ad quorum intelligentiam scire debemus quod ab hoc greco nomine *comos* quod latine villa sonat, et *oda*, cantus, dicitur *comedia*, hoc est, villanus cantus. Et est comedia narrationis poetice genus, a reliquis differens. Nam tragedia, in materia sua, in principio est admirabilis et quieta, in fine vero turbulenta, orribilis, et fetida, et ostendit similitudo animalis a quo deducitur tale nomen: nam *tragos* grece, latine yrcus dicitur, et, ut supra dictum est, *oda*, cantus; unde *tragedia* grece, latine yrcinus cantus. Et sane yrcus prima fronte et pulcer et imperiosus ostenditur; at, cum posteriora converterit, turpis et fetidus invenitur. Hanc bestie figuram, et figurata per bestiam, omnes Senece tragedie sane intelligentibus ostendunt; et id Boetii verba confirmant, dicentis: 'Quid enim aliud tragediarum clamor deflet, nisi incerto ictu Fortunam felicia regna vertentem?' "

the end.[38] He then makes a comment, still drawing on *Cangrande*, on the differences between the styles of comedy and tragedy, but without applying the differences to Dante's poem, and concludes with the *Cangrande* list of other poetic narratives (omitting however, the *sententia votiva*).[39]

Later in his commentary, Villani takes up the question of why Dante wrote his poem in Italian. He cites the two and a half Latin hexameters and the reasons that Brother Ilaro ascribed to Dante, but only as anonymously reported in Boccaccio's accounts.[40] He goes on to say that his uncle, Giovanni Villani, who had been a friend of Dante's, was told by him that he wrote in Italian for the following reasons. First, when he compared his Latin verses with those of Vergil, Statius, Horace, Ovid, and Lucan, it seemed to him that it was like comparing sackcloth with "the purple." Therefore, when he found himself to be very skilled at vernacular verses, he applied his genius to this form of writing. Second, he wished to ennoble his native tongue and extend its capabilities. Finally, he wished to show that even the most difficult aspects of the sciences could be properly treated in the vernacular.[41] This series of considerations has the ring of authenticity about it, since it encompasses Dante's interest in *elocutio vulgaris*. The same is true of Villani's shorter explanation in his *Life of Dante*, where he uses the phrase *vulgaris eloquentia*.[42] The Barberini version of the *Life* refers to the Latin

38. Ibid., p. 35: "Bene, igitur, si diligenter opus totum nostri comici spectetur, rite *Comedia* titulabitur, cum in sui principio, hoc est in inferno, orribilis sit, tremenda sit et fetida; in medio vero, hoc est in purgatorio, bone spei et aliquid gratie promittens; in fine, hoc est in paradiso, prospera, desiderabilis, et amena. Et, ut sic, comedie materia in principio pavida et tremebunda est; in medio bone promissionis et spei; in ultimis felix et plena dulcedinis et letitie." Guido da Pisa also speaks of purgatory as the middle site of the narrative, in which there is hope of ascending to glory. See the passage quoted above, p. 13. Maramauro deals with purgatory also when he says that Dante elevates his matter in the second part of the *Comedy*, and he also characterizes the end point (and the beginning point as well) with a series of three adjectives. See above, p. 44 n. 4.

39. Ibid.: "Modus vero loquendi poete, quantum ad comicum attinet, humilis, remissus, et vulgaris est, mulierculis quodammodo pervius; ubi apud tragedos elatum et sublime. Sunt et alia poeticarum narrationum genera: buccolicum, scilicet, et elegiacum ac satiricum, quos qui velit cognoscere, et in *Poetria* Oratii poterit invenire."

40. Ibid., pp. 78–79; see Billanovich, "Leggenda," p. 133 n. 2.

41. Villani, *Commento*, p. 79: "Audivi, patruo meo Iohanne Villani hystorico referente, qui Danti fuit amicus et sotius, poetam aliquando dixisse quod, collatis versibus suis cum metris Maronis, Statii, Oratii, Ovidii, et Lucani, visum ei fore iuxta purpuram cilicium collocare. Cumque se potentissimum in rithmis vulgaribus intellexisset, ipsis suis accomodavit ingenium. Amplius aiebat vir prudens, id egisse ut suum idioma nobilitaret et longius veheret; addebatque, sic se facere ut ostenderet etiam elocutione vulgari ardua queque scientiarum posse tractari."

42. Villani, *De vita et moribus Dantis poete comici insignis*, ed. Angelo Solerti, *Le vite di Dante, Petrarca, e Boccaccio* (Milan [1904–5]), pp. 82–90, esp. 88: "Conatus est poeta dum poeticis studia cumularet heroico metro divinum opus suum in latinum componere, sicque opus suum ceptitavit: 'Ultima regna canam fluido contermina mundo.' Cumque iam capitula septem vel circiter eleganti satis metro edidisset, intellexit non satis ad votum opus respondere. Cumque se potentiorem ea vulgari eloquentia sentiret, que rithmos modulatur pedibus mensuratis, se ad componendum vulgarem famosissimam *Comediam* convertit."

form of his work as a tragedy, or even gives it the title of *Tragedia*.[43] Thus it follows the non-Dantean and pseudo-Dantean notion that a tragic poem in Latin would have to be called a comedy in the vernacular or that the vernacular is not able to rise to tragic style.

I have finished my review of the various reasons given by Dante's commentators for the title of his poem and the characteristics they consider to belong to comedy and tragedy. Let me try to summarize their teachings in terms of Huguccio's three *differentiae* between tragedy and comedy—namely, plot, characters or subject, and style—and his fourth requirement for tragedy, that it deal with crimes (whether the "protagonist" is the perpetrator or the victim of the criminal actions).

Dante himself discriminated between tragedy and comedy primarily on the basis of style and subject matter, tragedy having high style and noble subjects, comedy having middle or low style and an undisclosed subject matter. He does not speak in terms of characters or persons, sequence of events, crimes or sins, or joy and sorrow.

Guido da Pisa singles out plot movement as the distinguishing characteristic of tragedy and comedy; the one goes from good to bad events and the other from bad to good. Tragedy, however, does not deal so much with the criminal as with the horrible. Or more precisely, it does not deal with horrible crimes (like Huguccio's "very cruel deeds" of killing one's father or mother or eating one's child), but rather with the horrible punishment of sins. Moreover, when Guido thinks of Dante as tragic, he thinks only of the great deeds of sublime characters in the *Comedy*. Jacopo della Lana also distinguishes tragedy and comedy by plot, but avoids speaking of sin and punishment and is silent about crime as well. He speaks only of splendor and the lack of it, and of high and low esteem. Vergil's account of the fall of Troy in the *Aeneid* is a tragedy that is written in high style, but style does not seem to be a defining component of tragedy or comedy. Jacopo Alighieri concentrates on subject matter: tragedy deals with the magnificent, comedy with all subjects. Andrea Lancia in *2 Ottimo* combines the two approaches of Jacopo and Guido: he takes over the subject-matter specifications of Jacopo (which he expresses as low, middle, and high things) and the plot-movement criterion of Guido. In *3 Ottimo*, however, the plot criterion is dropped, and Papias's descriptions are adopted: Isidore's criminous subject matter and lamentation motif for tragedy, and the mix of low persons, middle style, historical events, and great persons for comedy. Thereby *3 Ottimo* comes to much the same topic-assessment of comedy as Jacopo and *2 Ottimo*, namely, "all things" or "all men," but does so by a different route.

Pietro Alighieri's encounter with medieval notions of the ancient theater did

43. Ibid. p. 88 n. 6: "Conatusque est heroico metro inire *Tragediam*, sed cum animadvertisset se potentiorem ea vulgari eloquentio, que rythmos mensuratis pedibus modulatur, ad componendum *Comediam* famosissimam se convertit."

not affect his understanding of the genres of tragedy and comedy, and he dropped all theatrical references in the second and third versions of his commentary. Pietro draws directly on Huguccio and takes over all of his generic specifications; he also cites Isidore, Boethius, and Horace. Tragedy has the Isidorian subject matter of the crimes of wicked kings (which combines Huguccio's requirements of great crimes and great characters); it uses high style, and it moves from joy to sadness. Comedy moves from sadness to joy, uses a humble and remiss style, and deals with private men. We are left to make the inference that Terence could write his comedies in Latin, since Latin was his vernacular; but if Dante wanted to write a comedy, he had to use Italian, the language of the rustics of his own time.

Pietro was clearly not satisfied with his first-version account of tragedy and comedy as an explanation of why his father called his poem a comedy. In his second version, therefore, he sought an explanation of Dante's "maternal, humble, and sweet style" in Papias, as Lancia had done in *2 Ottimo*. But in addition to using Papias's combination of humble and private persons with middling and sweet style, he clarified his earlier allusion to Horace's *Poetics* and explained that high style could also be used in comedy when appropriate. To these stylistic considerations, Pietro joined Huguccio's plot movements for comedy and tragedy, but no longer spoke of Isidore's criminous subjects for tragedy.

In his third version, Pietro incorrectly cites Isidore as saying that comedy uses a modest style for its subject matter of the deeds of humble and private persons, as contrasted with the high style that tragedy uses for the sad deeds of kings. He adds Horace's high-style license for comedy and Huguccio's plot sequences. By writing in the vernacular, Dante automatically used a humble style; for this reason, and also because he was dealing mainly with private persons and because he brought the events to a happy conclusion, he called his poem a comedy. This designation also allowed him to write in high style about celestial matters (Pietro does not notice the contradiction here: Dante writes in high style while using the low vernacular).

Alberigo da Rosciate, a contemporary of Pietro's, translated Jacopo della Lana's Italian commentary into Latin and presumably passed on Lana's notions. But Rosciate gives his own interpretation of comedy based on a legal gloss and on contemporary practice: comedies are poetic accounts of great events recited in alternating fashion by pairs of minstrels.

The Accessor who composed the Proto-Accessus later used by Boccaccio and Pseudo-Dante had several of the earlier commentaries at his disposal, notably that of Guido of Pisa and the first and perhaps the second version of Pietro's work. The Accessor accepts the plot criterion as primary in the differentiation between tragedy and comedy, and chooses to follow Guido for his terminology—for instance, he specifies horror rather than sadness (Pietro's term), and associates Seneca with the goatish fetidness of tragedy. But he follows 1 Pietro in discussing the stylistic requirements of tragedy ("elated") and comedy (remiss). He also refers to the tragicomic salutation, not, however, as a current custom (as in

Huguccio, 1 Pietro, and 3 Pietro), but as a former practice (as in 2 Pietro).

Boccaccio made use of the Proto-Accessus in compiling his own commentary and paid attention particularly to the characteristics of comedy derived from Pietro (remiss style) and Guido (turbulent beginning and peaceful end). He rejects the first as inapplicable to Dante, but accepts the second. A similar criterion had been applied to Dante shortly before Boccaccio's time of writing by an acquaintance of his, Guglielmo Maramauro. Most of Boccaccio's other ideas about comedy, none of which he finds to be pertinent to Dante's poem, seem to come from his knowledge of Terence or the commentaries on Terence: this is especially true of the characteristics of dialogue, the lack of examples and similes, fictional subjects, and division into scenes. Perhaps because Boccaccio thinks of Terence's plays as comedies properly so called, he considers Dante's use of the term to be figurative.

Benvenuto da Imola distinguishes tragedy by high style and great and horrifying events—or, when speaking of the tragic aspect of Dante's poem, great persons. Comedy, in contrast, uses low style and deals with lowly persons. Neither of these comic features is verified in Dante's poem, unless style is taken in the linguistic sense—Latin being high style and the vernacular low. This was in fact the reason that Dante called his poem a comedy, Benvenuto says, but it was the best low-style work ever written. The only "respectable" criterion by which Benvenuto can classify the poem as a comedy or comic is the one chosen by Boccaccio, of movement from sad to joyful matter; but Benvenuto mistakenly attributes the idea to Isidore.

Francesco da Buti uses three of Huguccio's criteria for tragedy: a tragedy is in high style and treats of the highest possible matter, and begins in felicity and ends in misery. He does not include the content of great crimes. Comedy has the opposite plot movement, but in respect of style and subject it is not the opposite of tragedy. Rather, it is simply one step down from tragedy in a three-tiered system, as it was for Dante. But whereas Dante's series was tragedy, comedy, and elegy, Buti follows the series of tragedy, comedy, and satire, which he got from the Terence commentaries. The Anonymous of Florence parallels Buti's plot analysis of tragedy and comedy and also uses his goat analogy: the goat's noble head and foul hindquarters correspond respectively to the beginning and end of tragedy.

Finally, Filippo Villani was the only commentator of the century who was misled by Pseudo-Dante's fraud of attributing the Proto-Accessus to Dante. But he seems also to have had privileged information about Dante's interest in *vulgaris eloquentia*. He accepts the Huguccian (and non-Dantean) criteria of plot and style, including the characterization of comic style as *humilis, remissus, et vulgaris*, at the same time that he reports Dante's intention of ennobling the *lingua vulgaris* by means of his poem.

Dante's name was attached to the doctrines of the Accessor too late in the fourteenth century for it to have had any important effect. It has done far more damage in subsequent times. The Accessor in fact was simply repeating the authoritative but misguided opinions invented by earlier commentators on Dante's poem, who did not have access to the odd notions of tragedy and comedy that Dante explains in the *De vulgari eloquentia*.

Of all the commentators who tried to explain Dante's understanding of comedy, probably the closest to the mark was his son Jacopo, with his simple statement that comedy deals with all subjects. This idea was taken over by Andrea Lancia in *2 Ottimo*; then Lancia (or his reviser) in *3 Ottimo* hit upon what I take to have been the basis of Dante's notion—that is, Papias's combination of both low and high persons, historical events, and middle style. Pietro Alighieri arrived at the same solution in the second version of his commentary, though his explanation was still contaminated with the non-Dantean explanations of plot movement and low style—specifically, understanding the vernacular as automatically entailing low style.

I believe that very few of the commentators went along with Dante's notion that tragedy and comedy were living genres, even though many of them occasionally spoke of them in the present tense. Boccaccio at an early stage called one of his own works a comedy (*Comedy of the Florentine Nymphs*), apparently because it is partially in the *terza rima* of Dante's *Comedy*. But by the time he came to prepare his commentary, he seems to have accepted the ancient dramatic works of Terence and Plautus as the only true kind of comedy. Rosciate alone refers to contemporary poetic works (or at least recitations) as comedies.

Petrarch deserves credit for confessing puzzlement over Dante's reason for choosing *Comedy* as the title of his poem. For this is as much as to say that Petrarch rejected all the explanations that had been given by the commentators. But he doubtless would have been dumbfounded by the real explanation—Dante's own idiosyncratic understanding of comedy. Dante's remarks in the *De vulgari eloquentia* betray a concept almost totally foreign to the usual notions of comedy. But his presentation is so incomplete and inadequate in the face of his later achievement in the genre of comedy that it proves to be very unsatisfactory, especially his limitation of comedy to middle and low style and his implied limitation of it to less-than-tragic subjects. Pietro Alighieri may well be right in thinking that Dante, with or without Horace's permission, admitted high style as well as the middle and low styles to the genre of comedy—especially when, with Papias's authorization, comedy deals with high subjects. Dante undoubtedly considered some or all of his canzoni to be tragedies—that is, written in the *lingua vulgaris illustris* about the worthiest topics. He mentions that some poets' tragedies shade into elegy because of their metrical pecularities, if not because of miserable subject matter. There is no doubt that his *Comedy* deals with both the most sublime things and the most miserable things, to some extent. Since he called his work a comedy, we can assume that of the two comic styles he designates in the *De vulgari eloquentia*, the *mediocris* and the *humilis*, he considered it to be mainly in the *mediocris* and only occasionally, if at all, in the *humilis* style.

The question is whether he would consider his work to shade into tragedy at times, and employ the *illustris* style, especially when treating of subjects so exalted as to be beyond the powers of any comic or tragedic poet (as he expresses it in *Paradiso*).

It is this sort of speculation that we must limit ourselves to when discussing Dante's stylistic and generic intentions in the *Comedy*. We must put behind us the gropings in the dark encapsulated in the spurious *Epistle to Cangrande*, where they were given an authority and authenticity belied by their content. Pseudo-Dante has had a successful run, but now it is time to set him aside and return to Dante himself.

Appendix 1

The Five Translations of Aristotle's *Metaphysics*

As I showed on page 16, there are two quotations in the Accessus portion of the *Epistle to Cangrande* from the same paragraph of Aristotle's *Metaphysics*, Book 2, at the conclusion of chapter 1. One quotation, "ad aliquid et nunc speculantur practici" (*Cangrande* 16.41), is also to be found in the similar discussion of Guido da Pisa's commentary, and it clearly comes from the *Translatio Anonyma* or Moerbeke's revision. The other, "sicut res se habet ad esse, sic se habet ad veritatem" (*Cangrande* 5.14), is based on the translation of James of Venice.

I give below the passage in question, corresponding to lines 993b20–31 of the original Greek, as it was rendered in each of the five translations available in the fourteenth century. The *Translatio Iacobi*, *Translatio Anonyma*, and *Translatio Composita* are from the editions by Gudrun Vuillemin-Diem in Aristoteles latinus vol. 25.1–1a, 1970 (*Iacobi*, *Composita*) and vol. 25.2, 1976 (*Anonyma*); see notes 20 and 21 on page 16 above. The fourth translation is that attributed to Michael Scot, rendering the text as it appears in Arabic in Averroes's commentary; I use the edition of Gion Darms: Averroes, *In Aristotelis librum II (α) Metaphysicorum Commentarius* (Fribourg 1966), pp. 57–58. For Moerbeke's translation, I rely on the text that accompanies Thomas Aquinas's commentary (specifically, the Marietti edition of 1950, p. 84).

1. *Translatio Iacobi Venetici Greci (Vetustissima)*

   Speculative quidem enim finis veritas est, practice vero opus; et namque si quodam modo se habere intendant, non causam per se sed ad aliquid et nunc considerant practici. Nescimus autem verum sine causa; unumquodque autem maxime ipsum est aliorum secundum quod et aliis est quod univocum est (ut ignis calidissimus; et aliis enim causa hoc est caloris); quare verissima posterioribus causa est quod est veris esse. Unde eorum que semper sunt principia necesse est semper esse verissima (non enim aliquando vera, neque illis causa est aliqua ipsius esse, sed illa aliis), quare unumquodque sicut se habet ad esse, sic et[1] ad veritatem.

[1]sic et] ita se habet, *MS Wolfenbüttel, Bibl. Duc. 577 Helmst. (13th c.)*

2. *Translatio Anonyma (Media)*

Nam theorice finis est veritas et practice opus; et enim si quomodo se habet intendunt, non causam secundum se sed ad aliquid et nunc speculantur practici. Nescimus autem verum sine causa; unumquodque vero et id aliorum maxime secundum quod in aliis inest univocatio (ut ignis calidissimus; et enim aliis est causa hic caloris); est ergo verissimum quod posterioribus est causa inesse veris. Quapropter semper existentium principia semper esse verissima est necesse (non enim quandoque vera, nec illis causa aliqua est esse, sed illa aliis), quare unumquodque sicut habet esse, ita et veritatem.

3. *Translatio Composita (Vetus)*

Theorice namque finis veritas est, practice vero opus; et namque si quodam modo intendant practici habere causam, non causam secundum se ipsam considerant sed ad aliquid et nunc. Sed non sine causa verum scimus; unumquodque autem ipsum aliorum maxime est secundum quod aliis inest univocum (ut ignis calidissimus est; ipse namque et aliis causa caloris est); quare et verissimum quod posterioribus esse veris causa est. Unde rerum principia que semper sunt semper verissima esse necesse est (non enim aliquando vera sunt, nec illis inest causa in esse, sed illa aliis), quare unumquodque sicut ad esse sic ad veritatem se habet.

4. *Translatio Scotti ex Arabico (Nova)*

Finis enim scientie speculative est veritas et finis scientie operative operatio. Operantes enim, licet considerent in eo quod agant, tamen non perscrutantur de causa propter seipsam, sed respectu eius quod agunt. Et nos non scimus veritatem absque eo quod sciamus causam eius. Et unumquodque principiorum proprie est causa eorum secundum que sunt alie res que conveniunt in nomine et intentione, verbi gratia ignis in fine caliditatis. Ex quo oportet, quod illud quod est maxime verum, sit illud quod est causa veritatis rerum que sunt post. Et ideo necesse est, ut principia rerum que sunt semper, sint semper in fine veritatis, quia non sunt vera in aliquo tempore et in aliquo non, neque habent causam in esse vera in eo quod sunt vera, sed illa sunt causa in hoc aliarum rerum. Quapropter necesse est, ut dispositio cuiuslibet rei in esse sit dispositio sua in rei veritate.

5. *Translatio Guillelmi de Moerbeka (Nove Translationis)*

Nam theorice finis est veritas, et practice opus. Etenim si quo modo se habet, intendunt, non tamen secundum se, sed ut ad aliquid et nunc speculantur practici. Nescimus autem verum sine causa. Unumquodque vero maxime id ipsum aliorum dicitur, secundum quod et in aliis inest univocatio. Puta ignis calidissimus, etenim est causa aliis hic caloris. Quare et verissimum quod posterioribus est causa ut sint vera. Quapropter semper existentium principia esse verissima necesse est. Non enim quandoque vera, quandoque non vera; nec illis causa aliqua est ut sint, sed illa aliis. Quare unumquodque sicut se habet ut sit, ita et ad veritatem.

Appendix 2

The Analysis of Prose Cadences

I wish to supplement the observations made in Chapter 7 on the incidence of rhythmical cursus in some of the Latin writings that I have discussed, especially Dante's authentic works and the *Epistle to Cangrande*. As noted there, I have followed the lead of Peter Dronke's excursus, "The *Epistle* to *Cangrande* and Latin Prose Rhythm,"[1] in his method of analysis, especially in setting forth the various kinds of acceptable cursus forms. Dronke in turn draws on Tore Janson's study of earlier prose works.[2] In the following scheme, *p* means paroxytone (accented on the penult) and *pp* means proparoxytone (accented on the antepenult); a preceding number notes the number of syllables in a word that follows the initial word in a cadence.

Velox	V^1	*pp 4p*	*dénique recomméndo*	Regular form
	V^2	*pp 1 3p*	*doctíssimum et amícum*	Proclitic form
	V^3	*pp 2 2*	*magnália vèstra vídi*	Proclitic form
	V^4	*pp 1 1 2*	*variátio est a tóto*	Proclitic form
Planus	P^1	*p 3p*	*fuísse constábit*	Regular form
	P^2	*p 1 2*	*sectári non décet*	Proclitic form
Tardus	T^1	*p 4pp*	*segregáta percénsui*	Regular form
	T^2	*p 1 3pp*	*símul et tétigi*	Proclitic form

1. Peter Dronke, *Dante and Medieval Latin Traditions* (Cambridge 1986), pp. 103–11.

2. Tore Janson, *Prose Rhythm in Medieval Latin from the Ninth to the Thirteenth Century*, Studia latina stockholmiensia 20 (Stockholm 1975), esp. pp. 28–29. See the long review by Giovanni Orlandi, *Studi medievali* 3.19 (1978) 701–18; Dronke draws on Orlandi to supplement Janson's application of the Pearson (chi-squared) statistical test. But in my opinion the test cannot be meaningfully applied to a document as brief as *Cangrande*—even if it were not the product of more than one author.

As noted, V^1, P^1, and T^1 are the primary types. V^2, P^2, and T^2 are types generally allowed as substitutes. They are called proclitic because they are formed by substituting a monosyllabic word for the first syllable of the final word. V^3 and V^4 are additional proclitic types listed by some of the Italian medieval authorities,[3] but by the fourteenth century at least they were very rarely used, and V^4 was boycotted altogether by Dante (as far as I have been able to see). I include them in my study nonetheless; since they are of such infrequent occurrence, they will make little statistical difference; and since I include the data on their incidence, they can be siphoned off at will.

It is arguable from Gudrun Lindholm's statistics that by the time of Boccaccio and Petrarch additional cadences of an "enclitic" type were admitted, formed by adding a syllable to the first word in the cadence, as follows:

Planus	P^3	*pp 2*	*trístia bélla*	Enclitic form
Tardus	T^3	*pp 3pp*	*necessárium dúxerim*	Enclitic form
	T^4	*pp 2 1*	*hauddúbie Róma est*	Enclitic form

P^3 is the form that Dante labeled *insipidus* (in the example *dóminam Bértam*). Of the T^3 and T^4 forms, the latter is usually very rare, but Petrarch has twice as many T^4 instances as T^3. In addition, there is the type called by modern scholars *trispondaicus*; in order to use a distinctive letter for it (S), I call it simply *spondaicus*. I distinguish five forms, based on Petrarch's most frequent examples:

Spondaicus	S^1	*p 4p*	*quídem arbitrárer*	Regular form
	S^2	*p 1 3p*	*vidétur res exémplo*	Proclitic form
	S^3	*p 2 2*	*habére mecum pótest*	Proclitic form
	S^4	*pp 3p*	*ítaque premíssis*	Enclitic form
	S^5	*pp 1 2*	*partícipes non cúlpe*	Enclitic form

S^1, S^2, and S^3 correspond to V^1, V^2, and V^3, and S^4 and S^5 more or less to the enclitic tardus forms, T^3 and T^4. One might think that Petrarch would be attracted to the cadence because of Cicero's *ésse videátur* formula, an S^1 type; but in fact Petrarch's examples of S^4 outnumber the four other types put together.

---

3. Gudrun Lindholm, *Studien zum mittellateinischen Prosarhythmus: Seine Entwicklung und sein Abklingen in der Briefliteratur Italiens*, Studia latina stockholmiensia 10 (Stockholm 1963), pp. 13–19.

In the tables that follow, I will show the incidence of the traditional regular and proclitic forms first, and then the enclitic and spondaic forms, in the hope that the various frequencies can tell us something about the time as well as the style of writing.

Dronke does not discuss the possibility of obsolete or new forms in the fourteenth century, and he does not advert to the differences between classical and medieval stress. He follows, for instance, the classical norm of saying *monárchia*, whereas many speakers in the Middle Ages, including Dante, said *monarchía*.[4] Furthermore, he does not note the problems involved in relying on different editors for determining the rhythms of period endings. Apart from their varying choices of readings and emendations, editors disagree on when to end sentences—and modern notions of complete sentences are unlikely to correspond fully to medieval ideas. In the Dedication section of *Cangrande*, Brugnoli marks off eighteen sentences, whereas Toynbee has twenty-one and Boffito has twenty-two, and some of Brugnoli's are different from theirs. Even where they coincide, a different variant or spelling can affect the rhythm, as I have noted in my discussion in Chapter 7. There is also the consideration that some authors write longer sentences than others. To take an extreme example, the first two sentences of 1 Pietro, excluding quotations, contain 196 words, whereas the first 159 words of Guido da Pisa's commentary (or 157, counting *idest* as one word) are divided into seven sentences by his editor. I have avoided some of these problems by not limiting myself to periods but including all clauses and notable phrases (I make the term "clauses" do service for both). There is, of course, the difficulty that my choices do not correspond to medieval ideas of division. Nevertheless, I can be assured of a certain amount of uniformity because I use the same criteria of division for different works, no matter how variously their editors have punctuated them.

We can be certain that Dante and other authors did extend their practice of cursus to clauses. Here are the examples that Dante gives in the *De vulgari eloquentia*[5] (I label the clauses as outlined above):

1. *insipidus*: Petrus amat multum dominam Bertam.^{P3}
2. *sapidus*: Piget me cunctis pietate maiorem,^{P1} quicumque in exilio tabescentes,^{V1} tantam sompniando revisunt.^{P1}

4. See above, pp. 9–10, 62. As with *comedía* and *tragedía*, I assume Dante's pronunciation of specific words from the stress he gives to the Italian cognates, like the following in the *Comedy*: *barrattería* (1.22.53), *Elía* (2.32.80), *empiréo* (1.2.21), *filosofía* (1.11.97), *gerarcía* or *gerarchía* (3.28.121), *melodía* (2.29.22; 3.14.32; 3.23.97, 109), *parlasía* (1.20.16), *salmodía* (2.33.2), and *teodía* (3.25.73). I infer that he said *monarchía* from his saying *hierarchía* (which I infer from *gerarcía*)

5. Dante, *DVE* 2.6.4–5.

3. *sapidus et venustus*: Laudabilis discretio marchionis Estensis,$^{P^1}$ et sua magnificentia preparata,$^{V^1}$ cunctis illum facit esse dilectum.$^{P^1}$

4. *sapidus et venustus et excelsus (gradus constructionis excellentissimus)*: Eiecta maxima parte florum (V^3) de sinu tuo Florentia,$^{T^1}$ nequicquam Trinacriam (T^1) Totila secundus adivit.$^{P^1}$

Note that in the final sentence it would be possible to find four regular cursus; but I assume that Dante intended to count only the T^1 *túo Floréntia* and the P^1 *secúndus adívit.*

In order to show the correspondences between the rhythmic structure of periods (as punctuated by modern editors) and that of all clauses, I give both sets of data in the following tables. Like Dronke, I omit from consideration quotations, titles, and foreign words and single-word translations of foreign words. I also exclude cues introducing quotations. But I include multiple-word translations into Latin (for example, in etymologies), specifically the Expositor's translations of Dante's Italian; but in this latter case I also give figures with these endings subtracted. As I have not considered "Seneca in suis tragediis" to designate a title, so I treat "Oratius in sua poetria" in the same way. For such words as *tragedia* and *poetria* where the accent could go on the penult or the antepenult, I give both, with the penult or paroxytone form (*p*) listed first. In the case of *rith(i)mus* in its two oblique appearances in *Cangrande*, I treat the longer form first, then the shorter. I have set aside all questions of dubious or shifting accent (for example, in composite words and words with enclitics or variously placed prepositions), which Balbus treats in great detail, except for Greek-based words ending in *ia* (and also *empireum*). In all other such cases, I have followed the simplified classical rules of accent; but I go on record as noting the differences or uncertainties of medieval practice.

Tables

Note. In all of the tables, the first column of the top tier gives the total of all periods (or clauses); the second column gives the total of all velox, planus, and tardus cadences (V + P + T), followed by the percentage. The next three columns give the breakdown of each into regular and proclitic cadences. The final column gives the number and percentage of nonrhythmical or uncadenced periods (or clauses). In the bottom tier, the first column, labeled V + P + T + S, gives the number of all cadenced periods (or clauses), now counting spondaic and enclitic planus and tardus cadences. The Planus column gives the total of all planus cadences, with the number of enclitic or P^3 cadences in parentheses. The Tardus column is similar, the Spondaic column gives all forms, and the final column gives the number and percentage of leftover uncadenced periods (or clauses). Where a second line of figures is given, introduced by a slash, it indicates the range of words with two possible accents. Thus, in Table 3, in the Velox column, "32" over "/27" means that there are 32 velox cadences when such words are accented on the penult (*tragedía*) and only 27 when they are accented on the antepenult (*tragédia*).

Tables 1 and 2 give the figures for periods (Table 1) and all clauses (Table 2) in some of Dante's authentic works. His epistolary style of course appears in his letters; the data for the periods in his nine genuine letters are derived from Lindholm (pp. 76–87), using Toynbee's edition. The figures for *Epistle 6* are based on my own analysis of the edition of Arsenio Frugoni (Dante, *Opere minori*, vol. 2, 1979, pp. 550–60). I analyze it in whole and in part (viz., the first half alone, to 4.15, the sentence ending "igne cremari"), since Dronke uses the first half as an example of Dante's style corresponding in length to the Dedication of *Cangrande*. Dante's introductory style is illustrated in the first section of the *De vulgari eloquentia*, and his expository style in the following sections, from 2 to midway through 10 (the sentence ending "dextrum et sinistrum" on p. 86 of P. V. Mengaldo's edition, *Opere minori* 2). Dronke has selected this passage as being equivalent in length to the Accessus-Exposition portion of *Cangrande*.

TABLE 1 Dante: Periods

PERIODS: REGULAR AND PROCLITIC

	Total	*V+P+T*	*%*	*Velox (V^1 V^2 V^3 V^4)*		*%*	*Planus (P^1P^2)*		*%*	*Tardus (T^1T^2)*		*%*	*Nonrhythmical*	*%*
Ep. 1–9	214	195	*91.1*	93	(80 9 4 0)	*43.5*	63	(56 7)	*29.4*	39	(29 10)	*18.2*	19	*8.9*
Ep. 6 (half)	18	17	*94.4*	8	(6 1 1 0)	*44.4*	4	(3 1)	*22.2*	5	(4 1)	*27.8*	1	*5.6*
Ep. 6 (all)	36	33	*91.7*	15	(13 1 1 0)	*41.7*	8	(7 1)	*22.2*	10	(9 1)	*27.8*	3	*8.3*
DVE 1	6	6	*100.0*	3	(3 0 0 0)	*50.0*	2	(1 1)	*33.3*	1	(1 0)	*16.7*	0	*0.0*
DVE 2–10	96	69	*71.9*	28	(20 4 4 0)	*29.2*	27	(25 2)	*28.1*	14	(9 5)	*14.6*	27	*28.1*

PERIODS: WITH ENCLITIC AND SPONDAIC

	V+P+T+S	*%*	*% of Increase*	*Planus (P^3)*		*%*	*Tardus (T^3 T^4)*		*%*	*Spondaic (S^1 S^2 S^3 S^4 S^5)*		*%*	*Nonrhythmical*	*%*
Ep. 1–9	203	*94.9*	*4.1*	66	(3)	*30.8*	42	(2 1)	*19.6*	2	(1 0 1 0 0)	*0.9*	11	*5.1*
Ep. 6 (half)	17	*94.4*	*0.0*	4	(0)	*22.2*	5	(0 0)	*27.8*	0	(0 0 0 0 0)	*0.0*	1	*5.6*
Ep. 6 (all)	34	*94.4*	*3.0*	8	(0)	*22.2*	10	(0 0)	*27.8*	1	(1 0 0 0 0)	*2.8*	2	*5.6*
DVE 1	6	*100.0*	*0.0*	2	(0)	*33.3*	1	(0 0)	*16.7*	0	(0 0 0 0 0)	*0.0*	0	*0.0*
DVE 2–10	79	*82.3*	*14.5*	28	(1)	*29.2*	17	(3 0)	*17.7*	6	(1 4 0 1 0)	*6.2*	17	*17.7*

TABLE 2 Dante: Clauses

CLAUSES: REGULAR AND PROCLITIC

	Total	*V+P+T*	*%*	*Velox (V^1 V^2 V^3 V^4)*	*%*	*Planus (P^1P^2)*	*%*	*Tardus (T^1T^2)*	*%*	*Nonrhythmical*	*%*
Ep. 6 (half)	97	77	*79.4*	17 (15 1 1 0)	*17.5*	34 (28 6)	*35.1*	26 (22 4)	*26.8*	20	*20.6*
Ep. 6 (all)	169	139	*82.2*	35 (29 4 2 0)	*20.7*	59 (51 8)	*34.9*	45 (37 8)	*26.6*	30	*17.7*
DVE 1	33	29	*87.9*	11 (7 4 0 0)	*33.3*	10 (8 2)	*30.3*	8 (6 2)	*24.2*	4	*12.1*
DVE 2–10	387	232	*59.9*	73 (55 11 8 0)	*18.9*	105 (84 21)	*27.1*	54 (37 17)	*13.9*	155	*40.1*

CLAUSES: WITH ENCLITIC AND SPONDAIC

	V+P+T+S	*%*	*% of Increase*	*Planus (P^3)*	*%*	*Tardus (T^3 T^4)*	*%*	*Spondaic (S^1 S^2 S^3 S^4 S^5)*	*%*	*Nonrhythmical*	*%*
Ep. 6 (half)	83	*85.6*	*7.8*	35 (1)	*36.1*	29 (3 0)	*30.0*	2 (1 0 0 1 0)	*2.1*	14	*14.4*
Ep. 6 (all)	152	*89.9*	*9.4*	60 (1)	*35.5*	52 (7 0)	*30.8*	5 (3 0 1 1 0)	*3.0*	17	*10.1*
DVE 1	32	*97.0*	*10.3*	11 (1)	*33.3*	8 (0 0)	*24.2*	2 (0 1 0 1 0)	*6.1*	1	*3.0*
DVE 2–10	287	*74.2*	*23.7*	122 (17)	*31.5*	64 (9 1)	*16.5*	28 (13 5 6 3 1)	*7.2*	100	*25.8*

Tables 3 and 4 show the data for the introductory sections of the commentaries of Guido da Pisa (ed. Cioffari, pp. 1–7) and Pietro Alighieri, the first version, up to the beginning of his discussion of the rubric of *Inferno* (ed. Nannucci, pp. 1–11). For 1 Pietro, I analyze the opening two sentences separately, since it seems obvious that he took special pains with the cadences in them.

TABLE 3 Guido and 1 Pietro: Periods

PERIODS: REGULAR AND PROCLITIC

	Total	*V+P+T*	*%*	*Velox (V^1 V^2 V^3 V^4)*	*%*	*Planus (P^1P^2)*	*%*	*Tardus (T^1T^2)*	*%*	*Nonrhythmical*	*%*
Guido, Prol.	87	53 /50	*60.9* *57.5*	32 (26 2 4 0) /27 (21 2 4 0)	*36.8* *31.0*	16 (14 2)	*18.4*	5 (4 1) /7 (6 1)	*5.7* *8.0*	34 /37	*39.1* *42.5*
1 Pietro, Proem	2	2	*100.0*	1 (0 0 1 0)	*50.0*	1 (1 0)	*50.0*	0 (0 0)	*0.0*	0	*0.0*
Intro.	29	14 /13	*48.3* *44.8*	5 (0 1 4 0)	*17.2*	1 (0 1) /2 (1 1)	*3.4* *6.9*	8 (5 3) /6 (4 2)	*27.6* *20.7*	15 /16	*51.7* *55.2*

PERIODS: WITH ENCLITIC AND SPONDAIC

	V+P+T+S	*%*	*% of Increase*	*Planus (P^3)*	*%*	*Tardus (T^3 T^4)*	*%*	*Spondaic (S^1 S^2 S^3 S^4 S^5)*	*%*	*Nonrhythmical*	*%*
Guido, Prol.	65 /62	*74.7* *71.3*	*22.6* */24.0*	20 (4)	*23.0*	5 (0 0) /7 (0 0)	*5.7* *8.0*	8 (5 1 0 0 2) /8 (3 1 0 1 3)	*9.2* *9.2*	22 /25	*25.3* *28.7*
1 Pietro, Proem	2	*100.0*	*0.0*	1 (0)	*50.0*	0 (0 0)	*0.0*	0 (0 0 0 0 0)	*0.0*	0	*0.0*
Intro.	21 /20	*72.4* *69.0*	*50.0* *53.8*	1 (0) /2 (0)	*3.4* *6.9*	8 (0 0) /6 (0 0)	*27.6* *20.7*	7 (3 2 1 1 0)	*24.1*	8 /9	*27.6* *31.0*

TABLE 4 Guido and 1 Pietro: Clauses

CLAUSES: REGULAR AND PROCLITIC

	Total	V+P+T	%	Velox (V^1 V^2 V^3 V^4)		%	Planus (P^1P^2)		%	Tardus (T^1T^2)		%	Nonrhythmical	%
Guido, Prol.	259	135	*52.1*	68	(46 13 6 3)	*26.2*	50	(39 11)	*19.3*	17	(10 7)	*6.6*	124	*47.9*
		/131	*50.6*	/62	(40 13 6 3)	*23.9*	/49	(38 11)	*18.9*	/20	(13 7)	*7.7*	/128	*49.4*
1 Pietro, Proem	21	17	*81.0*	9	(5 4 2 0)	*42.9*	8	(5 3)	*38.1*	0	(0 0)	*0.0*	4	*19.0*
Intro.	162	61	*37.7*	22	(14 2 6 0)	*13.6*	16	(13 3)	*9.9*	23	(16 7)	*14.2*	101	*62.3*
		/63	*38.9*	/23	(15 2 6 0)	*14.2*	/17	(13 4)	*10.5*	/23	(17 6)	*14.2*	/99	*61.1*

CLAUSES: WITH ENCLITIC AND SPONDAIC

	V+P+T+S	%	% of Increase	Planus (P^3)		%	Tardus (T^3 T^4)		%	Spondaic (S^1 S^2 S^3 S^4 S^5)		%	Nonrhythmical	%
Guido, Prol.	169	*65.7*	*25.2*	59	(9)	*22.8*	22	(5 0)	*8.5*	20	(9 2 1 1 7)	*7.7*	90	*34.7*
	/165	*63.7*	*/25.6*	58	(9)	*22.4*	25	(5 0)	*9.7*	/20	(6 2 1 3 8)	*7.7*	/94	*36.3*
1 Pietro, Proem	21	*100.0*	*23.5*	8	(0)	*38.1*	0	(0 0)	*0.0*	4	(0 0 1 3 0)	*19.0*	0	*0.0*
Intro.	101	*62.3*	*65.6*	24	(8)	*14.8*	30	(5 2)	*18.5*	25	(13 4 3 4 1)	*15.4*	61	*37.7*
			/62.3	/26	(9)	*16.0*	/31	(6 2)	*19.1*	/21	(9 4 3 4 1)	*13.0*		

Table 5 draws on the data provided by Lindholm (pp. 88–165) for the periods of Petrarch (letters from the year 1350), Boccaccio (d. 1375), Salutati (d. 1406), Leonardo Bruni (d. 1444), Gasparino Barzizza (d. 1431), and Poggio Bracciolini (d. 1459) to give a view of the epistolary style of these humanists.

Table 5 Petrarch and the Humanists: Epistolary Periods

PERIODS: REGULAR AND PROCLITIC

	Total	*V+P+T*	*%*	*Velox (V^1 V^2 V^3 V^4)*	*%*	*Planus (P^1P^2)*	*%*	*Tardus (T^1T^2)*	*%*	*Nonrhythmical*	*%*
Petrarch	1,000	658	*65.8*	359 (211 66 78 4)	*35.9*	65 (47 18)	*6.5*	234 (189 45)	*23.4*	342	*34.2*
Boccaccio	620	296	*47.4*	75 (49 10 16 0)	*12.1*	98 (79 19)	*15.8*	123 (96 27)	*19.8*	324	*52.3*
Salutati	1,000	748	*74.8*	401 (306 69 24 2)	*40.1*	182 (157 25)	*18.2*	165 (136 29)	*16.5*	252	*25.2*
Bruni	1,000	387	*38.7*	131 (112 7 10 2)	*13.1*	174 (157 17)	*17.4*	82 (67 15)	*8.2*	613	*61.3*
Barzizza	1,000	286	*28.6*	50 (22 7 16 5)	*5.0*	138 (125 13)	*13.8*	98 (83 15)	*9.8*	714	*71.4*
Bracciolini	1,000	336	*33.6*	125 (78 28 16 5)	*12.5*	138 (102 36)	*13.8*	73 (46 27)	*7.3*	664	*66.4*

PERIODS: WITH ENCLITIC AND SPONDAIC

	V+P+T+S	*%*	*% of Increase*	*Planus (P^3)*	*%*	*Tardus (T^3 T^4)*	*%*	*Spondaic (S^1 S^2 S^3 S^4 S^5)*	*%*	*Nonrhythmical*	*%*
Petrarch	804	*80.4*	*22.2*	89 (24)	*8.9*	270 (12 24)	*27.0*	86 (12 8 10 45 11)	*8.6*	196	*19.6*
Boccaccio	417	*67.3*	*41.0*	142 (44)	*22.9*	166 (37 6)	*26.8*	34 (11 2 3 13 5)	*5.5*	203	*32.7*
Salutati	851	*85.1*	*13.8*	209 (27)	*20.9*	192 (24 3)	*19.2*	49 (28 8 5 7 1)	*4.9*	149	*14.9*
Bruni	677	*67.7*	*74.9*	230 (66)	*23.0*	109 (26 1)	*10.9*	207 (102 5 26 64 10)	*20.7*	323	*32.3*
Barzizza	617	*61.7*	*115.7*	183 (45)	*18.3*	142 (42 2)	*14.2*	242 (105 29 27 76 5)	*24.2*	383	*38.3*
Bracciolini	638	*63.8*	*89.9*	216 (78)	*21.6*	101 (18 0)	*10.1*	196 (87 19 27 52 11)	*19.6*	362	*36.2*

Table 6 gives examples of curial epistolary style, beginning with the prime minister of Frederick II, Pietro della Vigna (d. 1249), Cola di Rienzo (d. 1354), the Avignon pope Clement VI (letters of 1344–52), the Roman pope Boniface IX (letters of 1389–94), and the postschism popes Martin V (d. 1431), Nicholas V (d. 1455), Pius II (d. 1464), Julius II (d. 1513), Leo X (d. 1521), and Clement VII (d. 1534). The data come from Lindholm (pp. 56–76 and pp. 165–96). We note that Pius II, the humanist Aeneas Silvius, first breaks away from the overwhelming preference for the velox and approximates the style of his fellow humanists. In the cases where there is not a break-down of spondaic cadences, the total number will be slightly too high, since Lindholm computes more than my five forms under the category of trispondaicus.

TABLE 6 Curial Epistolary Style: Periods

PERIODS: REGULAR AND PROCLITIC														
	Total	*V+P+T*	*%*	*Velox*	*(V^1 V^2 V^3 V^4)*	*%*	*Planus*	*(P^1P^2)*	*%*	*Tardus*	*(T^1T^2)*	*%*	*Nonrhythmical*	*%*
Pietro d. Vigna	322	301	*93.5*	222	(147 49 22 4)	*68.9*	74	(59 15)	*23.0*	5	(5 0)	*1.6*	21	*6.5*
Cola di Rienzo	1,377	1,305	*94.8*	1,153	(665 252 197 39)	*83.7*	136	(110 26)	*9.9*	16	(13 3)	*1.2*	72	*5.2*
Clement VI	363	350	*96.4*	299	(237 40 21 1)	*82.4*	46	(41 5)	*12.7*	3	(3 0)	*0.8*	13	*3.6*
Boniface IX	300	273	*91.0*	257	(227 23 7 0)	*85.7*	16	(15 1)	*5.3*	0	(0 0)	*0.0*	27	*9.0*
Martin V	134	104	*77.6*	83	(70 11 2 0)	*61.9*	14	(13 1)	*10.4*	7	(5 2)	*5.2*	30	*22.4*
Nicholas V	105	68	*64.5*	57	(51 2 2 2)	*54.3*	7	(6 1)	*6.7*	4	(4 0)	*3.8*	37	*35.2*
Pius II	379	183	*48.3*	34	(32 2 0 0)	*9.0*	85	(70 15)	*22.4*	64	(57 7)	*16.9*	196	*51.7*
Julius II	80	46	*57.5*	24	(15 6 1 2)	*30.0*	16	(12 4)	*20.0*	6	(4 2)	*7.5*	34	*42.5*
Leo X	500	158	*31.6*	60	(39 7 12 2)	*12.0*	59	(52 7)	*11.8*	39	(30 9)	*7.8*	342	*68.4*
Clement VII	214	69	*32.2*	35	(32 1 1 1)	*16.4*	20	(19 1)	*9.3*	14	(11 3)	*6.5*	145	*67.8*

PERIODS: WITH ENCLITIC AND SPONDAIC

	$V+P+T+S$	%	% of Increase	Planus (P^3)		%	Tardus (T^3 T^4)		%	Spondaic (S^1 S^2 S^3 S^4 S^5)		%	Nonrhythmical	%
Pietro d. Vigna	315	*97.8*	*4.7*	77	(3)	*23.9*	8	(2 1)	*2.5*	8	( )	*2.5*	7	*2.2*
Cola di Rienzo	1,336	*97.0*	*2.4*	139	(3)	*10.1*	20	(4 0)	*1.4*	24	(18 2 3 1 0)	*1.7*	41	*2.8*
Clement VI	354	*97.5*	*1.1*	46	(0)	*12.7*	4	(1 0)	*1.1*	5	(4 0 0 1 0)	*1.5*	9	*2.5*
Boniface IX	292	*97.3*	*7.0*	17	(1)	*5.7*	0	(0 0)	*0.0*	18	( )	*6.0*	8	*2.7*
Martin V	122	*91.0*	*17.3*	16	(2)	*11.9*	10	(3 0)	*7.5*	13	( )	*9.7*	12	*9.0*
Nicholas V	87	*82.9*	*27.9*	8	(1)	*7.6*	4	(0 0)	*3.8*	18	( )	*17.1*	18	*17.1*
Pius II	275	*72.6*	*50.3*	110	(25)	*29.0*	80	(16 0)	*21.1*	51	(29 8 1 12 1)	*13.5*	104	*27.4*
Julius II	57	*71.3*	*23.9*	19	(3)	*23.8*	9	(3 0)	*11.3*	5	(4 0 1 0 0)	*6.2*	23	*28.8*
Leo X	324	*64.8*	*51.2*	75	(16)	*15.0*	60	(21 0)	*12.0*	129	(71 6 20 26 6)	*25.8*	176	*35.2*
Clement VII	131	*61.2*	*47.3*	28	(8)	*13.1*	18	(4 0)	*8.4*	50	(37 4 1 8 0)	*23.4*	73	*34.1*

Tables 7 and 8 provide the data on the clauses of the Dedication portion of the *Epistle to Cangrande*, first of all to the end, up to the Compiler's transition to the Accessus in paragraph 4.13, and then without paragraph 4 altogether. The style of the letter up to the end of paragraph 3 corresponds to Dante's own preferences for the traditional cadences, whereas paragraph 4 either shows a lack of concern or reflects the style of a later period, when enclitic and spondaic cadences were acceptable. See above, pp. 65, 67–68. The precise distribution of cadences in the whole *Epistle to Cangrande* can be seen in Appendix 3.

TABLE 7 — *Epistle to Cangrande*, Dedication: Periods

PERIODS: REGULAR AND PROCLITIC

	Total	*V+P+T*	*%*	*Velox (V^1 V^2 V^3 V^4)*		*%*	*Planus (P^1P^2)*		*%*	*Tardus (T^1T^2)*		*%*	*Nonrhythmical*	*%*
Dedication	18	17	*94.4*	6	(4 2 0 0)	*33.3*	7	(7 0)	*38.9*	4	(4 0)	*22.2*	1	*5.6*
Without par. 4	16	16	*100.0*	6	(4 2 0 0)	*37.5*	7	(7 0)	*43.8*	3	(3 0)	*18.7*	0	*0.0*

PERIODS: WITH ENCLITIC AND SPONDAIC

	V+P+T+S	*%*	*% of Increase*	*Planus (P^3)*		*%*	*Tardus (T^3 T^4)*		*%*	*Spondaic (S^1 S^2 S^3 S^4 S^5)*		*%*	*Nonrhythmical*	*%*
Dedication	17	*94.4*	*0.0*	7	(0)	*38.9*	4	(0 0)	*22.0*	0	(0 0 0 0 0)	*0.0*	1	*5.6*
Without par. 4	16	*100.0*	*0.0*	7	(0)	*43.8*	3	(0 0)	*18.7*	0	(0 0 0 0 0)	*0.0*	0	*0.0*

TABLE 8 *Epistle to Cangrande*, Dedication: Clauses

CLAUSES: REGULAR AND PROCLITIC

	Total	*V+P+T*	*%*	*Velox (V^1 V^2 V^3 V^4)*	*%*	*Planus (P^1P^2)*	*%*	*Tardus (T^1T^2)*	*%*	*Nonrhythmical*	*%*
Dedication	71	57	*80.2*	19 (15 3 1 0)	*26.8*	22 (21 1)	*31.0*	16 (14 2)	*22.5*	14	*19.7*
Without par. 4	64	55	*85.9*	19 (15 3 1 0)	*29.7*	21 (20 1)	*32.8*	15 (13 2)	*23.4*	9	*14.1*

CLAUSES: WITH ENCLITIC AND SPONDAIC

	V+P+T+S	*%*	*% of Increase*	*Planus (P^3)*	*%*	*Tardus (T^3 T^4)*	*%*	*Spondaic (S^1 S^2 S^3 S^4 S^5)*	*%*	*Nonrhythmical*	*%*
Dedication	65	*91.5*	*14.0*	24 (2)	*33.8*	20 (3 1)	*28.2*	2 (2 0 0 0 0)	*2.8*	6	*8.4*
Without par. 4	60	*93.8*	*9.4*	22 (1)	*34.4*	19 (3 1)	*29.7*	0 (0 0 0 0 0)	*0.0*	4	*6.2*

Tables 9 and 10 first give the totals of the Accessus and Exposition together, then the Accessus by itself; next, they show the figures for the Accessus without the material assigned to the Compiler, and finally, for the Accessus without the Compiler and without the cadences quoted verbatim from Guido da Pisa.

TABLE 9 *Epistle to Cangrande*, Accessus: Periods

PERIODS: REGULAR AND PROCLITIC

	Total	*V+P+T*	*%*	*Velox (V^1 V^2 V^3 V^4)*	*%*	*Planus (P^1P^2)*	*%*	*Tardus (T^1T^2)*	*%*	*Nonrhythmical*	*%*
Accessus with Exposition	102	37 /41	*36.3* *40.2*	12 (8 1 2 1) /13 (9 1 2 1)	*11.8* *12.7*	17 (11 6)	*16.7*	8 (6 2) /11 (9 2)	*7.8* *10.8*	65 /61	*63.7* *59.8*
Accessus	37	13 /16	*35.1* *43.2*	5 (3 0 1 1) /6 (4 0 1 1)	*13.5* *16.2*	6 (5 1)	*16.2*	2 (2 0) /4 (4 0)	*5.4* *10.8*	24 /21	*64.9* *56.8*
Without Compiler	20	5 /7	*25.0* *35.0*	2 (1 0 1 0)	*10.0*	3 (3 0)	*15.0*	0 (0 0) /2 (2 0)	*0.0* *10.0*	15 /13	*75.0* *65.0*
Without Compiler and Guido	11	4	*36.4*	2 (1 0 1 0)	*18.2*	2 (2 0)	*18.2*	0 (0 0)	*0.0*	7	*63.6*

PERIODS: WITH ENCLITIC AND SPONDAIC

	V+P+T+S	*%*	*% of Increase*	*Planus (P^3)*	*%*	*Tardus (T^3 T^4)*	*%*	*Spondaic (S^1 S^2 S^3 S^4 S^5)*	*%*	*Nonrhythmical*	*%*
Accessus with Exposition	54 /57	*52.9* *55.9*	*45.9* */39.0*	20 (3) /21 (4)	*19.6* *20.6*	10 (2 0) 13 (2 0)	*9.8* *12.7*	12 (5 1 3 2 1) /10 (2 1 3 2 2)	*11.2* *9.8*	48 /45	*47.1* *44.1*
Accessus	18 /20	*48.6* *54.0*	*38.5* */25.0*	6 (0)	*16.2*	3 (1 0) /5 (1 0)	*8.1* *13.5*	4 (3 0 0 0 1) /3 (1 0 0 0 2)	*10.8* *8.1*	19 /17	*51.4* *45.9*
Without Compiler	10 /11	*50.0* *55.0*	*100.0* */57.1*	3 (0)	*15.0*	1 (1 0) /3 (1 0)	*5.0* *15.0*	4 (3 0 0 0 1) /3 (1 0 0 0 2)	*20.0* *15.0*	10 /9	*50.0* *45.0*
Without Compiler and Guido	5	*45.5*	*25.0*	2 (0)	*18.2*	1 (1 0)	*9.1*	0 (0 0 0 0 0)	*0.0*	6	*54.5*

TABLE 10 *Epistle to Cangrande*, Accessus: Clauses

CLAUSES: REGULAR AND PROCLITIC

	Total	V+P+T	%	Velox (V^1 V^2 V^3 V^4)	%	Planus (P^1P^2)	%	Tardus (T^1T^2)	%	Nonrhythmical	%
Accessus with Exposition	394	149	37.8	40 (26 3 8 3)	10.2	68 (40 28)	17.3	41 (28 13)	10.4	245	62.2
		/155	39.3					/47 (34 13)	11.9	/239	60.7
Accessus	130	52	40.0	11 (8 1 1 1)	8.5	23 (13 10)	17.7	18 (11 7)	13.8	78	60.0
		/58	44.6	/12 (9 1 1 1)	9.2			/23 (16 7)	17.7	/72	55.4
Without Compiler	72	26	36.1	6 (4 1 1 0)	8.3	14 (10 4)	19.4	6 (3 3)	8.3	46	63.9
		/31	43.1					/11 (8 3)	15.3	/41	56.9
Without Compiler and Guido	49	17	34.7	4 (2 1 1 0)	8.2	9 (7 2)	18.4	4 (1 3)	8.2	32	65.3
		/20	40.8					/7 (4 3)	14.3	/29	59.2

CLAUSES: WITH ENCLITIC AND SPONDAIC

	V+P+T+S	%	% of Increase	Planus (P^3)	%	Tardus (T^3 T^4)	%	Spondaic (S^1 S^2 S^3 S^4 S^5)	%	Nonrhythmical	%
Accessus with Exposition	227	57.6	52.3	85 (17)	21.6	51 (9 1)	12.9	51 (20 8 8 10 5)	12.9	167	42.4
	/229	58.1	/47.7	/86 (18)	21.8	/57 (9 1)	14.5	/46 (14 8 8 10 6)	11.7	/165	41.9
Accessus	77	59.2	48.1	26 (3)	20.0	23 (5 0)	17.7	17 (9 4 0 2 2)	13.1	53	40.8
	/79	60.8	/36.2			/28 (5 0)	21.5	/13 (4 4 0 2 3)	10.0	/51	39.2
Without Compiler	44	61.1	69.2	15 (1)	20.8	10 (4 0)	13.9	13 (9 1 0 1 2)	18.1	28	38.9
	/45	62.5	/45.2			/15 (4 0)	20.8	/9 (4 1 0 1 3)	12.5	/27	37.5
Without Compiler and Guido	29	59.2	70.6	9 (0)	18.4	8 (4 0)	16.3	8 (5 1 0 1 1)	16.3	20	40.8
			/45.0			/11 (4 0)	22.4	/5 (2 1 0 1 0)	10.2		

Tables 11 and 12 show the figures for the Exposition as a whole and then without the material assigned to the Compiler—all appearing, except for the introductory clause, at the end, in paragraphs 32 and 33. Also given are the figures for the Exposition without the Expositor's translations of Dante's Italian verse into Latin.

TABLE 11 *Epistle to Cangrande*, Exposition: Periods

PERIODS: REGULAR AND PROCLITIC

	Total	*V+P+T*	%	*Velox (V^1 V^2 V^3 V^4)*	%	*Planus (P^1P^2)*	%	*Tardus (T^1T^2)*	%	*Nonrhythmical*	%
Exposition	65	24 /25	*36.9* *38.5*	7 (5 1 1 0)	*10.8*	11 (6 5)	*16.9*	6 (4 2) /7 (5 2)	*9.2* *10.8*	41 /40	*63.1* *61.5*
Without Compiler	60	22 /23	*36.7* *38.3*	6 (4 1 1 0)	*10.0*	10 (5 5)	*16.7*	6 (4 2) /7 (5 2)	*10.0* *11.7*	38 /39	*63.3* *61.7*
Without Compiler and *Paradiso* translations	53	20 /21	*37.7* *39.6*	6 (4 1 1 0)	*11.3*	9 (5 4)	*17.0*	5 (4 1) /6 (5 1)	*9.4* *11.3*	33 /32	*62.3* *60.4*

PERIODS: WITH ENCLITIC AND SPONDAIC

	V+P+T+S	%	*% of Increase*	*Planus (P^3)*	%	*Tardus (T^3 T^4)*	%	*Spondaic (S^1 S^2 S^3 S^4 S^5)*	%	*Nonrhythmical*	%
Exposition	36 /37	*55.4* *56.9*	*50.0* *48.0*	14 (3) /15 (4)	*21.5* *23.1*	7 (1 0) /8 (1 0)	*10.8* *12.3*	8 (2 1 3 2 0) /7 (1 1 3 2 0)	*12.3* *10.8*	29 /28	*44.6* *43.1*
Without Compiler	34 /35	*56.7* *58.3*	*54.5* */52.2*	13 (3) /14 (4)	*21.7* *23.3*	7 (1 0) /8 (1 0)	*11.7* *13.3*	8 (2 1 3 2 0) /7 (1 1 3 2 0)	*13.3* *11.7*	26 /25	*43.3* *41.7*
Without Compiler and *Paradiso* translations	30 /31	*56.6* *58.6*	*50.0* */47.6*	10 (1) /11 (2)	*18.9* *20.8*	6 (1 0) /7 (1 0)	*11.3* *13.2*	8 (2 1 3 2 0) /7 (1 1 3 2 0)	*15.1* *13.2*	23 /22	*43.4* *41.5*

TABLE 12 *Epistle to Cangrande*, Exposition: Clauses

CLAUSES: REGULAR AND PROCLITIC

	Total	*V + P + T*	*%*	*Velox (V^1 V^2 V^3 V^4)*		*%*	*Planus (P^1P^2)*		*%*	*Tardus (T^1T^2)*		*%*	*Nonrhythmical*	*%*
Exposition	264	96	*36.4*	28	(16 3 7 2)	*10.6*	45	(26 19)	*17.0*	23	(18 5)	*8.7*	168	*63.6*
				/27	(15 3 7 2)	*10.2*				/24	(19 5)	*9.1*		
Without Compiler	240	87	*36.3*	27	(15 3 7 2)	*11.3*	38	(22 16)	*15.8*	22	(17 5)	*9.2*	153	*63.7*
				/26	(14 3 7 2)	*10.8*				/23	(18 5)	*9.6*		
Without Compiler and *Paradiso* translations	226	80	*35.4*	26	(15 2 7 2)	*11.5*	34	(20 13)	*15.0*	20	(17 3)	*8.8*	146	*64.6*
				/25	(14 2 7 2)	*11.1*				/21	(18 3)	*9.3*		

CLAUSES: WITH ENCLITIC AND SPONDAIC

	V + P + T + S	*%*	*% of Increase*	*Planus (P^3)*		*%*	*Tardus (T^3 T^4)*		*%*	*Spondaic (S^1 S^2 S^3 S^4 S^5)*		*%*	*Nonrhythmical*	*%*
Exposition	149	*56.4*	*55.2*	59	(14)	*22.3*	28	(4 1)	*10.6*	34	(11 5 6 9 3)	*12.9*	115	*43.6*
				/60	(15)	*22.7*	/29	(4 1)	*11.0*	/33	(10 5 6 9 3)	*12.5*		
Without Compiler	130	*54.2*	*49.4*	49	(11)	*20.4*	27	(4 1)	*11.3*	27	(10 4 6 6 1)	*11.3*	110	*45.8*
				/50	(12)	*20.8*	/28	(4 1)	*11.7*	/26	(9 4 6 6 1)	*10.8*		
Without Compiler and *Paradiso* translations	120	*53.1*	*50.0*	43	(9)	*19.0*	25	(4 1)	*11.1*	26	(10 4 6 5 1)	*11.5*	106	*46.9*
				/44	(10)	*19.5*	/26	(4 1)	*11.5*	/25	(9 4 6 5 1)	*11.1*		

Tables 13 and 14 give the data for the periods and clauses assigned to the Compiler, first in the obvious sections, and then counting all of paragraph 4. As explained above (pp. 65, 67–68, 92), this paragraph is very different from the rest of the Dedication, but quite consonant with the style of the Compiler.

TABLE 13 *Epistle to Cangrande*, Compiler: Periods

PERIODS: REGULAR AND PROCLITIC

	Total	*V+P+T*	*%*	*Velox* (V^1 V^2 V^3 V^4)	*%*	*Planus* (P^1P^2)	*%*	*Tardus* (T^1T^2)	*%*	*Nonrhythmical*	*%*
Compiler	22	10 /11	*45.4* *50.0*	4 (3 0 0 1) /5 (4 0 0 1)	*18.2* *22.7*	4 (3 1)	*18.2*	2 (2 0)	*9.1*	12 /11	*54.5* *50.0*
With par. 4	24	11 /12	*45.8* *50.0*	4 (3 0 0 1) /5 (4 0 0 1)	*16.7* *20.8*	4 (3 1)	*16.7*	3 (3 0)	*12.5*	13 /12	*54.2* *50.0*

PERIODS: WITH ENCLITIC AND SPONDAIC

	V+P+T+S	*%*	*% of Increase*	*Planus* (P^3)	*%*	*Tardus* (T^3 T^4)	*%*	*Spondaic* (S^1 S^2 S^3 S^4 S^5)	*%*	*Nonrhythmical*	*%*
Compiler	10 /11	*45.4* *50.0*	*0.0*	4 (0)	*18.2*	2 (0 0)	*9.1*	0 (0 0 0 0 0)	*0.0*	12 /11	*54.5* *50.0*
With par. 4	11 /12	*45.8* *50.0*	*0.0*	4 (0)	*16.7*	3 (0 0)	*12.5*	0 (0 0 0 0 0)	*0.0*	13 /12	*54.2* *50.0*

TABLE 14 *Epistle to Cangrande*, Compiler: Clauses

CLAUSES: REGULAR AND PROCLITIC

	Total	*V+P+T*	*%*	*Velox (V^1 V^2 V^3 V^4)*	*%*	*Planus (P^1P^2)*	*%*	*Tardus (T^1T^2)*	*%*	*Nonrhythmical*	*%*
Compiler	84	37 /38	*44.0* *45.2*	6 (5 0 0 1) /7 (6 0 0 1)	*7.1* *8.3*	16 (7 9)	*19.0*	15 (10 5)	*17.9*	47 /46	*55.9* *54.8*
With par. 4	91	39 /40	*42.9* *44.0*	6 (5 0 0 1) /7 (6 0 0 1)	*6.6* *7.7*	17 (8 9)	*18.7*	16 (11 5)	*17.6*	52 /51	*57.1* *56.0*

CLAUSES: WITH ENCLITIC AND SPONDAIC

	V+P+T+S	*%*	*% of Increase*	*Planus (P^3)*	*%*	*Tardus (T^3 T^4)*	*%*	*Spondaic (S^1 S^2 S^3 S^4 S^5)*	*%*	*Nonrhythmical*	*%*
Compiler	54 /55	*64.3* *65.5*	*45.9* */44.7*	21 (5)	*25.0*	16 (1 0)	*19.0*	11 (1 4 0 4 2)	*13.1*	30 /29	*35.7* *34.5*
With par. 4	59 /60	*64.8* *65.9*	*51.3* */50.0*	23 (6)	*25.3*	17 (1 0)	*18.7*	13 (3 4 0 4 2)	*14.3*	32 /31	*35.2* *34.1*

Appendix 3

Cadence Analysis of the *Epistle to Cangrande*

The text is based on the edition of Giorgio Brugnoli, with only a few alterations—for instance, changing *Poetria* to *poetria*, recognizing editorial emendation in *rithimos* by putting *rith(i)mos*, and expanding *O* to *O*[*mega*]. I also change *Metaphysicorum* to *Metaphysice*.

The various types of *cursus* or cadences are identified according to the system explained in Appendix 2. The portions assigned to the Accessor are those that I take to belong to the Proto-Accessus. The passages assigned to the Compiler are those most clearly attributable to the final assember of the work, who may or may not be the same person as the Dedicator and the Expositor. Italicized cadences are those directly quoted from Guido da Pisa.

Part One: Dedication

Dedicator:

1 [0]. Magnifico atque victorioso domino domino Cani Grandi de la Scala
sacratissimi Cesarei Principatus in urbe Verona et civitate Vicentie Vicario
generali,V[1] devotissimus suus Dantes Alagherii florentinus natione non moribus,T[2] vitam orat per tempora diuturna felicem et gloriosi nominis per-
petuum incrementum.V[1]

2 [1]. Inclita vestre Magnificentie laus, quam fama vigil volitando dissemi-
nat,T[1] sic distrahit in diversa diversos,P[1] ut hos in spem sue prosperitatis at-
tollat,P[1] hos exterminii deiciat in terrorem.V[2] Huius quidem preconium, facta
modernorum exsuperans,T[1] tanquam veri existentia latius arbitrabar ali-
3 quando superfluum.T[1] Verum ne diuturna me nimis incertitudo suspen-
deret,T[1] velut Austri regina Ierusalem petiit,T[3] velut Pallas petiit Elicona,V[1]
Veronam petii fidis oculis discursurus audita,P[1] ibique magnalia vestra
vidi,V[3] vidi beneficia simul et tetigi;T[2] et quemadmodum prius dictorum ex
parte suspicabar excessum,P[1] sic posterius ipsa facta excessiva cognovi.P[1]
Quo factum ut ex auditu solo cum quadam animi subiectione benivolus prius
exstiterim,T[1] sed ex visu postmodum devotissimus et amicus.V[2]
4 [2]. Nec reor amici nomen assumens,P[1] ut nonnulli forsitan obiectarent,V[1]
reatum presumptionis incurrere,T[1] cum non minus dispares connectanturV[1]
quam pares amicitie sacramento.V[1] Nam si delectabiles et utiles amicitias
inspicere libeat,T[3] illis persepius inspicienti patebitP[1] preheminentes inferiori-
5 bus coniugari personas.P[1] Et si ad veram ac per se amicitiam torqueatur in-
tuitus,T[1] nonne summorum illustriumque principum plerunque viros fortuna
obscuros,P[1] honestate preclaros,P[1] amicos fuisse constabit?P[1] Quidni, cum
6 etiam Dei et hominis amicitia nequaquam impediatur excessu?P[1] Quod si cui-
quam quod asseritur nunc videretur indignum,P[1] Spiritum Sanctum audiat,N
amicitie sue participes quosdam homines profitentem;V[1] nam in Sapientia de
sapientia legitur "quoniam infinitus thesaurus est hominibus, quo qui usi
7 sunt, participes facti sunt amicitie Dei." Sed habet imperitia vulgi sine dis-
cretione iudicium;T[1] et quemadmodum solem pedalis magnitudinis ar-
bitratur,V[1] sic et circa mores vana credulitate decipitur.T[1] Nos autem quibus
optimum quod est in nobis noscere datum est,T[4] gregum vestigia sectari non
decet,P[2] quin ymo suis erroribus obviare tenemur.P[1] Nam intellectu ac ratione vigentes,P[1] divina quadam libertate dotati,P[1] nullis consuetudinibus as-
tringuntur;V[1] nec mirum, cum non ipsi legibus, sed ipsis leges potius
8 dirigantur.V[1] Liquet igitur quod superius dixi,P[3] me scilicet esse devotissi-
mum et amicum,V[2] nullatenus esse presumptum.P[1]

9 [3]. Preferens ergo amicitiam vestram quasi thesaurum carissimum,T[1]
10 providentia diligenti et accurata solicitudine illam servare desidero.T[1] Itaque,
cum in dogmatibus moralis negotii amicitiam adequari et salvari analogo

doceatur,[V1] ad retribuendum pro collatis beneficiis plus quam semel
analogiam sequi mihi votivum est;[N] et propter hoc munuscula mea sepe multum conspexi[P1] et ab invicem segregavi[V1] nec non segregata percensui,[T1] dig-
11 niusque gratiusque vobis inquirens.[P1] Neque ipsi preheminentie vestre
congruum comperi[T3] magis quam *Comedie* sublimem canticam[N] que
decoratur titulo *Paradisi*;[V1] et illam sub presenti epistola,[T1] tanquam sub
epigrammate proprio dedicatam,[V1] vobis ascribo,[P1] vobis offero,[N] vobis de-
nique recommendo.[V1]

(Compiler:)

12 [4]. Illud quoque preterire silentio simpliciter inardescens non sinit affectus,[P1] quod in hac donatione pius dono quam domino et honoris et fame
conferri videri potest;[N] quin ymo cum eius titulo iam presagium de gloria
vestri nominis amplianda satis attentis videbar expressisse;[S1] quod de
13a proposito.[N] Sed zelus gratie vestre,[P3] quam sitio vitam parvipendens,[S1] a
primordio metam prefixam urgebit ulterius.[T1]

Part Two: Accessus

Compiler:

13b Itaque, formula consumata epistole,[T1] ad introductionem oblati operis aliquid sub lectoris officio compendiose aggrediar.[T1]

14 [5]. Sicut dicit Phylosophus in secundo *Metaphysice*, "sicut res se habet
ad esse, sic se habet ad veritatem"; cuius ratio est, quia veritas de re, que in
veritate consistit tanquam in subiecto,[S2] est similitudo perfecta rei
15 sicut est.[N] Eorum vero que sunt, quedam sic sunt ut habeant esse absolutum
in se;[N] quedam sunt ita ut habeant esse dependens ab alio per relationem
quandam,[N] ut eodem tempore esse et ad aliud se habere ut relativa;[N] sicut
pater et filius, dominus et servus, duplum et dimidium, totum et pars, et
16 huiusmodi, in quantum talia.[N] Propterea quod esse talium dependet ab
alio,[T2] consequens est quod eorum veritas ab alio dependeat;[N] ignorato enim
dimidio,[T1] nunquam cognoscitur duplum,[P3] et sic de aliis.[N]

17 [6]. Volentes igitur aliqualem introductionem tradere de parte operis alicuius,[V1] oportet aliquam notitiam tradere de toto cuius est pars.[N] Quapropter et ego, volens de parte supra nominata totius *Comedie* aliquid tradere per modum introductionis,[N] aliquid de toto opere premittendium existimavi,[N] ut facilior et perfectior sit ad partem introitus.[T1]

Accessor:

18 Sex [**Compiler**: igitur] sunt que in principio cuiusque doctrinalis operis inquirenda sunt,[N] videlicet subiectum, agens, forma, finis, libri titulus, et genus phylosophie.[N]

Compiler:

De istis tria sunt in quibus pars ista quam vobis destinare proposui variatur
a toto,[P2] scilicet subiectum, forma, et titulus;[T2] in aliis vero non variatur,[N]
sicut apparet inspicienti;[N] et ideo circa considerationem de toto ista tria inquirenda seorsum sunt:[N] quo facto, satis patebit ad introductionem partis.[N]
19 Deinde inquiremus alia tria non solum per respectum ad totum,[P2] sed etiam
per respectum ad ipsam partem oblatam.[P1]

Accessor:

20 [7]. Ad evidentiam itaque dicendorum sciendum est quod istius operis
non est simplex sensus,[N] ymo dici potest polisemos,[S1] hoc est plurium sen-
suum;[T3] nam primus sensus est qui habetur per litteram,[T2] alius est qui
habetur per significata per litteram.[T2] Et primus dicitur litteralis.[V1] secundus
21 vero allegoricus sive moralis sive anagogicus.[N] Qui modus tractandi, ut
melius pateat,[T3] potest considerari in hiis versibus: "In exitu Israel de
Egipto, domus Iacob de populo barbaro, facta est Iudea sanctificatio eius,

Israel potestas eius." Nam si ad litteram solam inspiciamus,[N] significatur nobis exitus filiorum Israel de Egipto, tempore Moysis;[T3] si ad allegoriam, nobis significatur nostra redemptio facta per Christum;[P2] si ad moralem sensum, significatur nobis conversio anime de luctu et miseria peccati ad statum gratie;[N] si ad anagogicum, significatur exitus anime sancte ab huius corrup-
22 tionis servitute ad eterne glorie libertatem.[V1] Et quanquam isti sensus mistici variis appellentur nominibus,[T1] generaliter omnes dici possunt allegorici,[N] cum sint a litterali sive historiali diversi.[P1] Nam allegoria dicitur ab "alleon" grece, quod in latinum dicitur "alienum," sive "diversum."[P1]

23 [8]. Hiis visis, manifestum est quod duplex oportet esse subiectum,[P1] circa quod currant alterni sensus.[N] Et ideo videndum est de subiecto huius operis,[N] prout ad litteram accipitur;[N] deinde de subiecto,[S2] prout allegorice
24 sententiatur.[N] Est ergo subiectum totius operis, litteraliter tantum accepti,[P1] status *animarum post mortem*[P2] *simpliciter sumptus*;[P3] nam de illo et circa
25 illum totius operis *versatur processus*.[P1] Si vero accipiatur *opus allegorice*,[N] subiectum est homo prout merendo et demerendo per *arbitrii libertatem*[V1] iustitie premiandi et *puniendi obnoxius est*.[N]

26 [9]. Forma vero est duplex:[P2] forma tractatus et *forma tractandi*.[P1] Forma *tractatus est triplex*,[P2] secundum *triplicem divisionem*.[N] Prima divisio est, qua totum opus dividitur in tres canticas.[N] Secunda, qua quelibet cantica *dividitur in cantus*.[S5] Tertia, qua quilibet cantus *dividitur in rith(i)mos*.[N/S5]
27 Forma sive modus tractandi est poeticus, fictivus, descriptivus, *digressivus, transumptivus*,[N] et cum hoc diffinitivus, divisivus, probativus, improbativus, et *exemplorum positivus*.[S1]

28 [10]. Libri titulus est: *Incipit Comedia Dantis Alagherii, florentini natione, non moribus*. Ad cuius notitiam sciendum est quod comedia dicitur a "comos" villa et "oda" quod est cantus, unde comedia quasi "villanus
29 cantus."[N] Et est comedia genus quoddam poetice narrationis ab omnibus aliis differens.[T3] Differt ergo a tragedia in materia per hoc, quod tragedia in principio est admirabilis et quieta,[V2] in fine seu exitu est *fetida et horribilis*;[N] et dicitur propter hoc a "tragos" quod est hircus et "oda" quasi "*cantus hircinus*,"[P1] id est fetidus *ad modum hirci*,[N] ut patet per Senecam in *suis tragediis*.[S1/T1] Comedia vero inchoat asperitatem alicuius rei,[N] sed eius materia *prospere terminatur*,[V1] ut patet per Terentium in *suis comediis*.[S1/T1] Et hinc consueverunt dictatores quidam in suis salutationibus dicere loco sa-
30 lutis "tragicum principium et comicum finem." Similiter differunt in modo loquendi:[P1] elate et sublime tragedia;[S1/T1] comedia vero remisse et humiliter,[N] sicut vult Oratius in sua poetria,[S1/T1] ubi licentiat aliquando comicos ut tragedos loqui,[N] et sic e converso:

> Interdum tamen et vocem comedia tollit,
> iratusque Chremes tumido delitigat ore;
> et tragicus plerunque dolet sermone pedestri
> Telephus et Peleus, etc.

31 Et per hoc patet quod *Comedia* dicitur presens opus.[V3] Nam si ad materiam
respiciamus,[N] a principio horribilis et fetida est,[N] quia Infernus,[P1] in fine
prospera, desiderabilis, et grata,[S5] quia Paradisus;[S1] ad modum loquendi,[P1]
remissus est modus et humilis,[T2] quia locutio vulgaris in qua et muliercule
32 comunicant.[N] Sunt et alia genera narrationum poeticarum,[N] scilicet carmen
bucolicum, elegia, satira, et sententia votiva,[S4] ut etiam per Oratium patere
potest in sua poetria;[S1/T1] sed de istis ad presens nichil dicendum est.[N]

Compiler:

33 [11]. Potest amodo patere quomodo assignandum sit subiectum partis
oblate.[P1] Nam si totius operis litteraliter sumpti sic est subiectum, status
animarum post mortem[P2] non contractus sed simpliciter acceptus,[S4]
manifestum est quod hac in parte talis status est subiectum,[S2] sed contractus,
34 scilicet status animarum beatarum post mortem.[P2] Et si totius operis allegorice sumpti subiectum est homo prout merendo et demerendo per arbitrii
libertatem[V1] est iustitie premiandi et puniendi obnoxius,[T1] manifestum est in
hac parte hoc subiectum contrahi,[N] et est homo prout merendo obnoxius est
iustitie premiandi.[V1]

35 [12]. Et sic patet de forma partis per formam assignatam totius;[P1] nam
si forma tractatus in toto est triplex,[P2] in hac parte tantum est duplex,[P2]
36 scilicet divisio cantuum et rith(i)morum.[N/V2] Non eius potest esse propria
forma divisio prima,[P3] cum ista pars sit prime divisionis.[N]

37 [13]. Patet etiam de libri titulo;[N] nam titulus totius libri est *Incipit*
Comedia, etc., ut supra; titulus autem huius partis est *Incipit cantica tertia*
Comedia Dantis, etc., *que dicitur Paradisus*.[V1]

38 [14]. Inquisitis hiis tribus in quibus variatur pars a toto,[N] videndum est
de aliis tribus in quibus nulla variatio est a toto.[V4] Agens igitur totius et partis est ille qui dictus est,[N] et totaliter videtur esse.[N]

39 [15]. Finis totius et partis esse posset et multiplex,[T2] scilicet propinquus
et remotus;[S2] sed,

Accessor:

omissa subtili investigatione,[N] dicendum est breviter[T2] quod finis [**Compiler**:
totius et partis] est removere viventes in hac vita de *statu miserie*[T1] et perdu-
cere ad statum felicitatis.[N]

40 [16]. Genus vero phylosophie sub quo hic [**Compiler**: in toto et parte]
proceditur,[T1] est *morale negotium*,[T1] *sive ethica*;[N] quia non ad speculandum,
sed ad opus inventum est *totum et pars*.[N] Nam si in aliquo loco vel passu
41 pertractatur ad modum speculativi negotii,[T1] hoc non est gratia speculativi
negotii,[T1] sed gratia operis;[T3] quia, ut ait Phylosophus in secundo
Metaphysice, "ad aliquid et nunc speculantur practici," aliquando.

Part Three: Exposition

Compiler:

42 [17]. Hiis itaque premissis,[S4]

Expositor:

ad expositionem littere secundum quandam prelibationem accedendum est,[N] et illud prenuntiandum quod expositio littere nichil aliud est quam forme
43 operis manifestatio.[N] Dividitur ergo ista pars,[N] seu tertia cantica que *Paradisus* dicitur,[N] principaliter in duas partes,[N] scilicet in prologum et partem executivam.[N] Pars secunda incipit ibi: "Surgit mortalibus per diversas fauces."[N]

44 [18]. De parte prima sciendum est[N] quod, quamvis comuni ratione dici posset exordium,[T1] proprie autem loquendo non debet dici nisi prologus;[N] quod Phylosophus in tertio *Rethoricorum* videtur innuere,[T1] ubi dicit quod "proemium est principium in oratione rethorica sicut prologus in poetica et
45 preludium in fistulatione." Est etiam prenotandum[V1] quod prenuntiatio ista, que comuniter exordium dici potest,[V3] aliter fit a poetis,[N] aliter fit a rethori-
46 bus.[N] Rethores enim concessere prelibare dicenda[P1] ut animum comparent auditoris,[V1] sed poete non solum hoc faciunt,[T2] quin ymo post hec invoca-
47 tionem quandam emittunt.[P1] Et hoc est eis conveniens,[T1] quia multa invocatione opus est eis,[P2] cum aliquid contra comunem modum hominum a superioribus substantiis petendum est,[N] quasi divinum quoddam munus.[S3]
48 Ergo presens prologus dividitur in partes duas,[N] quia in prima premittitur[T1] quid dicendum sit,[N] in secunda invocatur Apollo;[P1] et incipit secunda pars ibi:[P2] "O bone Apollo, ad ultimum laborem."[S4]

49 [19]. Propter primam partem notandum[P1] quod ad bene exordiendum tria requiruntur,[S1] ut dicit Tullius in *Nova rethorica*, scilicet ut benivolum et attentum et docilem reddat aliquis auditorem;[V1] et hoc maxime in ad-
50 mirabili genere cause,[P3] ut ipsemet Tullius dicit.[P3] Cum ergo materia circa quam versatur presens tractatus sit admirabilis,[N] et propterea ad admirabile reducenda,[V1] ista tria intenduntur in principio exordii sive prologi.[N] Nam
51 dicit se dicturum ea que vidit in primo celo[N] et retinere mente potuit.[N] In quo dicto omnia illa tria comprehenduntur;[N] nam in utilitate dicendorum benivolentia paratur;[S4] in admirabilitate attentio;[T1] in possibilitate docilitas.[T1] Utilitatem innuit,[N] cum recitaturum se dicit[P2] ea que maxime allectiva sunt desiderii humani,[S4] scilicet gaudia Paradisi;[V1] admirabilitatem tangit,[N] cum promittit se tam ardua tam sublimia dicere,[T3] scilicet conditiones regni celestis;[P1] possibilitatem ostendit,[P1] cum dicit se dicturum que
52 mente retinere potuit;[N] si enim ipse, et alii poterunt.[T3] Hec omnia tanguntur in verbis illis[N] ubi dicit se fuisse in primo celo,[N] et quod dicere vult de regno celesti[P1] quicquid in mente sua,[N] quasi thesaurum,[P1] potuit retinere.[V1]

Viso igitur de bonitate ac perfectione prime partis prologi,[N] ad litteram accedatur.[V1]

53 [20]. Dicit ergo quod "gloria primi Motoris," qui Deus est, "in omnibus partibus universi resplendet";[P1] sed ita ut "in aliqua parte magis, et in
54 aliqua minus."[P3] Quod autem ubique resplendeat,[T1] ratio et auctoritas
manifestat.[V1] Ratio sic: Omne quod est, aut habet esse a se, aut ab alio:[N] sed
constat quod habere esse a se non convenit nisi uni,[V3] scilicet primo seu principio, qui Deus est,[N] cum habere esse non arguat per se necesse esse,[N] et per
se necesse esse non competat nisi uni,[V3] scilicet primo seu principio,[N] quod
est causa omnium;[N] ergo omnia que sunt, preter unum ipsum,[S3] habent esse
55 ab alio.[T2] Si ergo accipiatur ultimum in universo,[N] non quodcunque,[N]
manifestum est quod id habet esse ab aliquo;[T2] et illud a quo habet,[N] a se
vel ab aliquo habet.[P3] Si a se, sic est primum;[N] si ab aliquo, et illud similiter
vel a se vel ab aliquo.[N] Et cum esset sic procedere in infinitum in causis agentibus,[T1] ut probatur in secundo *Metaphysice*, erit devenire ad primum,[P2]
56 qui Deus est.[N] Et sic, mediate vel inmediate,[N] omne quod habet esse habet
esse ab eo;[P2] quia ex eo quod causa secunda recipit a prima,[S5] influit super
causatum ad modum recipientis et reddentis radium,[N] propter quod causa
57 prima est magis causa.[N] Et hoc dicitur in libro *De causis* quod "omnis causa
primaria plus influit super suum causatum quam causa universalis secunda."
Sed hoc quantum ad esse.[P2]

58 [21]. Quantum vero ad essentiam, probo sic:[T4] Omnis essentia, preter
primam, est causata,[S2] aliter essent plura[V3] que essent per se necesse esse,[N]
quod est impossible:[N] quod causatum, vel a natura est vel ab intellectu,[N] et
quod a natura, per consequens causatum est ab intellectu,[N] cum natura sit
opus intelligentie;[N] omne ergo quod est causatum,[N] est causatum ab aliquo
59 intellectu vel mediate vel inmediate.[N] Cum ergo virtus sequatur essentiam
cuius est virtus,[P2] si essentia intellectiva,[N] est tota et unius que causat.[P2] Et
sic quemadmodum prius devenire erat ad primam causam ipsius esse,[N] sic
60 nunc essentie et virtutis.[V2] Propter quod patet quod omnis essentia et virtus
procedat a prima,[P2] et intelligentie inferiores recipiant quasi a radiante,[N] et
reddant radios superioris ad suum inferius ad modum speculorum.[S1] Quod
61 satis aperte tangere videtur Dionysius de celesti hierarchia loquens.[N/P3] Et
propter hoc dicitur in libro *De causis* quod "omnis intelligentia est plena
formis." Patet ergo quomodo ratio manifestat[V1] divinum lumen, id est divinam bonitatem, sapientiam, et virtutem,[V2] resplendere ubique.[P1]

62 [22]. Similiter etiam et scientius facit auctoritas.[T1] Dicit enim Spiritus
Sanctus per Hieremiam: "Celum et terram ego impleo"; et in Psalmo: "Quo
ibo a spiritu tuo? et quo a facie tua fugiam? Si ascendero in celum, tu illic
es; si descendero in infernum, ades. Si sumpsero pennas meas," etc. Et
Sapientia dicit quod "Spiritus Domini replevit orbem terrarum." Et Ec-
63 clesiasticus in quadragesimo secundo: "Gloria Domini plenum est opus eius."

Quod etiam scriptura paganorum contestatur;[S1] unde Lucanus in nono:
"Iuppiter est quodcunque vides, quocunque moveris."

64 [23]. Bene ergo dictum est cum dicit quod divinus radius sive divina
gloria, "per universum penetrat et resplendet":[V2] penetrat, quantum ad es-
65 sentiam;[N] resplendet, quantum ad esse.[P2] Quod autem subicit de "magis et
minus,"[P2] habet veritatem in manifesto;[N] quoniam videmus in aliquo ex-
cellentiori gradu essentiam aliquam,[T3] aliquam vero in inferiori;[N] ut patet
de celo et elementis,[N] quorum quidem illud incorruptibile,[N] illa vero corrup-
tibilia sunt.[N]

66 [24]. Et postquam premisit hanc veritatem,[N] prosequitur ab ea circum-
loquens Paradisum;[V1] et dicit quod fuit in celo illo quod de gloria Dei,[P3] sive
67 de luce,[P2] recipit affluentius.[N] Propter quod sciendum quod illud celum est
celum supremum,[P1] continens corpora universa et a nullo contentum,[P1] intra quod omnia corpora moventur,[S4] ipso in sempiterna quiete permanente[S1]
[virtute sua omnia sua contenta recipiens][T1] et a nulla corporali substantia
68 virtutem recipiens.[T1] Et dicitur empyreum,[V1/N] quod est idem quod celum
igne sui ardoris flagrans;[N] non quod in eo sit ignis vel ardor materialis,[N] sed
spiritualis,[N] quod est amor sanctus sive caritas.[N]

69 [25]. Quod autem de divina luce plus recipiat,[N] potest probari per
duo:[P2] primo, per suum omnia continere et a nullo contineri;[S1] secundo, per
70 sempiternam suam quietem sive pacem.[S3] Quantum ad primum probatur
sic:[N] Continens se habet ad contentum in naturali situ sicut formativum ad
formabile,[N] ut habetur in quarto *Physicorum*: sed in naturali situ totius
universi primum celum est omnia continens;[T3] ergo se habet ad omnia sicut
formativum ad formabile,[N] quod est se habere per modum cause.[N] Et cum
omnis vis causandi sit radius quidam influens a prima causa que Deus est,[N]
manifestum est quod illud celum quod magis habet rationem cause,[N] magis
de luce divina recipit.[N]

71 [26]. Quantum ad secundum, probatur sic:[N] Omne quod movetur,[S2]
movetur propter aliquid quod non habet,[V4] quod est terminus sui motus;[V3]
sicut celum lune movetur propter aliquam partem sui,[V3] que non habet illud
ubi ad quod movetur;[N] et quia sui pars quelibet non adepto quolibet ubi,[P3]
quod est impossibile,[N] movetur ad aliud,[T2] inde est quod semper movetur[P1]
et nunquam quiescit,[P1] et est eius appetitus.[S4] Et quod dico de celo lune,[N]
72 intelligendum est de omnibus, preter primum.[V3] Omne quod movetur est in
aliquo defectu,[S4] et non habet totum suum esse simul.[S3] Illud igitur celum
quod a nullo movetur,[P1] in se in qualibet sui parte habet[S3] quicquid potest
modo perfecto,[P1] ita quod motu non indiget ad suam perfectionem.[N] Et cum
omnis perfectio sit radius primi,[P3] quod est in summo gradu perfectionis,[N]
manifestum est quod celum primum magis recipit de luce primi, qui est
73 Deus.[N] Ista tamen ratio videtur arguere ad destructionem antecedentis,[N] ita

quod simpliciter et secundum formam arguendi non probat.[P2] Sed si con-
sideremus materiam eius,[P3] bene probat,[N] quia de quodam sempiterno,[S1] in
quo potest defectus sempiternari:[N] ita quod, si Deus non dedit sibi motum,[S3]
74 patet quod non dedit sibi materiam in aliquo egentem.[S4] Et per hanc sup-
positionem tenet argumentum ratione materie;[T1] et est similis modus
arguendi ac si dicerem:[N] Si homo est,[N] est risibile;[N] nam in omnibus con-
vertibilibus tenet similis ratio gratia materie.[N] Sic ergo patet:[N] cum dicit "in
illo celo, quod plus de luce Dei recipit,"[N] intelligit circumloqui Paradisum,[V1]
sive celum empyreum.[S1/T1]

75 [27]. Premissis quoque rationibus consonanter dicit Phylosophus in
primo *De celo* quod celum "tanto habet honorabiliorem materiam istis in-
76 ferioribus, quanto magis elongatum est ab hiis que hic." Ad hoc etiam posset adduci[P1] quod dicit Apostolus ad Ephesios de Christo: "Qui ascendit super omnes celos, ut adimpleret omnia." Hoc est celum delitiarum Domini;[N]
de quibus delitiis dicitur contra Luciferum per Ezechielem: "Tu signaculum
similitudinis, sapientia plenus et perfectione decorus in deliciis Paradisi Dei
fuisti."

77 [28]. Et postquam dixit quod fuit in loco illo Paradisi per suam circum-
locutionem,[N] prosequitur dicens se vidisse aliqua que recitare non potest qui
descendit.[S2] Et reddit causam dicens "quod intellectus in tantum profundat
se" in ipsum "desiderium suum,"[P3] quod est Deus, "quod memoria sequi
78 non potest."[P2] Ad que intelligenda sciendum est[N] quod intellectus humanus
in hac vita,[N] propter connaturalitatem et affinitatem quam habet ad substan-
tiam intellectualem separatum,[S1] quando elevatur, in tantum elevatur,[S1] ut
79 memoria post reditum deficiat propter transcendisse humanum modum.[N] Et
hoc insinuatur nobis per Apostolum ad Corinthios loquentem, ubi dicit:
"Scio hominem, sive in corpore sive extra corpus nescio, Deus scit, raptum
usque ad tertium celum, et vidit arcana Dei, que non licet homini loqui."
Ecce, postquam humanam rationem intellectus ascensione transierat,[T1] quid
80 extra se ageretur non recordabatur.[N] Et hoc est insinuatum nobis in
Matheo,[S2] ubi tres discipuli ceciderunt in faciem suam,[P3] nichil postea
recitantes,[V1] quasi obliti.[P1] Et in Ezechiele scribitur: "Vidi, et cedidi in
faciem meam." Et ubi ista invidis non sufficiant,[N] legant Richardum de
Sancto Victore in libro *De contemplatione*, legant Bernardum in libro *De con-
sideratione*, legant Augustinum in libro *De quantitate anime*, et non in-
81 videbunt.[N] Si vero in dispositionem elevationis tante propter peccatum lo-
quentis oblatrarent,[S1] legant Danielem, ubi et Nabuchodonosor invenient
82 contra peccatores aliqua vidisse divinitus,[T1] oblivionique mandasse.[P1] Nam
"qui oriri solem suum facit super bonos et malos, et pluit super iustos et in-
iustos," aliquando misericorditer ad conversionem,[N] aliquando severe ad
punitionem,[N] plus et minus, ut vult, gloriam suam quantumcunque male
viventibus manifestat.[V1]

83 [29]. Vidit ergo, ut dicit, aliqua "que referre nescit et nequit rediens."[N]
Diligenter quippe notandum est quod dicit "nescit et nequit":[P2] nescit quia
oblitus,[P1] nequit quia, si recordatur et contentum tenet,[N] sermo tamen
84 deficit.[N] Multa namque per intellectum videmus[P1] quibus signa vocalia
desunt:[P3] quod satis Plato insinuat in suis libris per assumptionem
metaphorismorum;[N] multa enim per lumen intellectuale vidit[N] que sermone
proprio nequivit exprimere.[T1]

85 [30]. Postea dicit se dicturum illa que de regno celesti retinere potuit,[N] et hoc dicit esse "materiam" sui operis;[N] que qualia sint et quanta,[V4] in parte executiva patebit.[P1]

86 [31]. Deinde cum dicit: "O bone Apollo," et cetera,[T2] facit invocatio-
nem suam.[N] Et dividitur ista pars in partes duas:[N] in prima invocando
petit;[N] in secunda suadet Apollini petitionem factam,[N] remunerationem
quandam prenuntians;[T1] et incipit secunda pars ibi: "O divina virtus."[N]
87 Prima pars dividitur in partes duas:[N] in prima petit divinum auxilium,[T1] in
secunda tangit necessitatem sue petitionis,[N] quod est iustificare ipsam,[N] ibi:
"Hucusque alterum iugum Parnassi," et cetera.[T2]

Compiler:

88 [32]. Hec est sententia secunde partis prologi in generali.[N] In speciali vero non exponam ad presens;[P2] urget enim me rei familiaris angustia,[T1] ut hec et alia utilia reipublice derelinquere oporteat.[N] Sed spero de Magnificentia vestra[P3] ita ut alias habeatur procedendi ad utilem expositionem facultas.[P1]

89 [33]. In parte vero executiva,[N] que fuit divisa contra prologum,[N] nec
dividendo nec sententiando quicquam dicetur ad presens,[P2] nisi hoc, quod
ubique procedetur ascendendo de celo in celum,[P2] et recitabitur de animabus beatis inventis in quolibet orbe,[P3] et quod vera illa beatitudo in sentiendo
veritatis principium consistit;[S4] ut patet per Iohannem ibi: "Hec est vita
eterna, ut cognoscant te Deum verum," etc.; et per Boetium in tertio *De consolatione* ibi: "Te cernere finis." Inde est quod ad ostendendum gloriam
beatitudinis in illis animabus,[S1] ab eis tanquam videntibus omnem veritatem
90 multa querentur[P1] que magnam habent utilitatem et delectationem.[N] Et
quia, invento principio seu primo,[S5] videlicet Deo,[P3] nichil est quod ulterius
queratur,[S4] cum sit A[lfa] et O[mega],[S2] idest principium et finis,[S5] ut visio
Iohannis designat,[P1] in ipso Deo terminatur tractatus,[P1] qui est benedictus
in secula seculorum.[T1]

Bibliographical Index to the Footnotes

N.B. NUMBERS IN BOLD PRINT INDICATE WHERE EACH WORK IS CITED IN THE FOOTNOTES: E.G., **4.21** MEANS "CITED ABOVE, CHAP. 4 N. 21."

Accessus Horatii. Ed. R. C. B. Huygens, *Accessus ad auctores*, 2d ed. (Leiden 1970), pp. 49–53: **4.21**

Accursius. *Glossa ordinaria ad Digestum* (*see Digestum*): **4.35**

Agamben, Giorgio. "Comedìa: La svolta comica di Dante e la concezione della colpa." *Paragone* 29, no. 346 (December 1978) 3–27: **1.38**

Alessio, G. V. "Hec Franciscus de Buiti." *IMU* 24 (1981) 64–122: **1.2; 4.23; 6.62, 64–65**

Alighieri: *See* Dante; Jacopo; Pietro

Anecdoton lugdunense. Ed. Friedrich Leo, *Commentationes in honorem Francisci Buecherleri, Hermanni Useneri* (Bonn 1873): **3.10**

Anonymous of Florence. *Commento alla Divina commedia d'Anonimo Fiorentino del secolo xiv*. Ed. Pietro Fanfani, 3 vols. (Bologna 1866–74): **6.56, 58–59**

Aquinas, Thomas. *In duodecim libros Metaphysicorum Aristotelis expositio*. Ed. Raimondo M. Spiazzi (Turin: Marietti, 1950): **2.20, 23**

Aristotle. *Metaphysics*: **2.18–21, 23; 7.29**

Balbus, Iohannes. *Catholicon* (Mainz 1460, repr. Farnborough 1971): **1.34, 39; 4.13, 21; 5.13**

———. ——— (Lyons 1491): **1.34**

Basile, Bruno. "Villani, Filippo." *ED* 5:1011–13: **7.36**

Baysio, Guido de. *Rosarium super Decreto* (Strassburg ca. 1473): **5.19**

Bede the Venerable, Saint. *De schematibus et tropis*. Ed. C. B. Kendall, *Bedae opera*. Corpus Christianorum series latina 123A (Turnhout 1975): **5.13**

Beleth, John. *Summa de ecclesiasticis officiis*. Ed. Herbert Douteil. Corpus Christianorum continuatio medievalis 41–41A (Turnhout 1976): **5.13**

N.B. Numbers in bold print indicate where each work is cited in the footnotes: e.g., **4.1-2, 9** means "cited above, Chap. 4 nn. 1-2, 9."

Bellomo, Saverio. "Primi appunti sull'*Ottimo commento* dantesco." *GSLI* 157 (1980) 368-82; 532-40: **4.1-2,9**

———. "Tradizione manoscritta e tradizione culturale delle *Expositiones* di Guido da Pisa (prime note e appunti)." *Lettere italiane* 31 (1979) 153-75: **3.10**

Benvenuto da Imola. 1 Benvenuto: Bologna notes. Ed. Vincenzo Promis and Carlo Negroni, *La Commedia di Dante Alighieri col commento inedito di Stefano Talice da Ricaldone*, 2d ed., 3 vols. (Milan 1888): **6.17, 30-32**

———. 2 Benvenuto: Ferrara redaction. Florence: Biblioteca Laurenziana MS Ashburn. 839: **6.17, 20, 23-25, 29**

———. 3 Benvenuto: Final version. Ed. James Philip Lacaita, *Comentum super Dantis Aldigherij Comoediam*, 5 vols. (Florence 1887): **6.17, 21, 23-25, 27-28, 34, 47-48**

Billanovich, Giuseppe. "La leggenda dantesca del Boccaccio: Dalla lettera di Ilaro al *Trattatello in laude di Dante*." *SD* 28 (1949) 45-144: **6.42, 44-46; 7.34, 40**

Boccaccio, Giovanni. *Esposizioni sopra la Commedia di Dante*. Ed. Padoan (q.v.): **2.4, 9, 13, 15; 6.6-7, 9-10, 12-14, 16, 41**

———. *Trattatello in laude di Dante*. Ed. Ricci (q.v.): **2.24-25, 28-29; 6.10, 39-40, 43; 7.13, 34**

Boffito, Giuseppe. *L'Epistola di Dante Alighieri a Cangrande della Scala* (Turin 1907): **2.1, 16; 7.12**

Bowden, John Paul. *An Analysis of Pietro Alighieri's Commentary on the Divine Comedy* (New York 1951): **5.4**

Brixiensis, Bartholomaeus. *Glossa ordinaria in Gratiani Decretum. Corpus iuris canonici*, vol. 1 (Rome 1582, repr. Lyons 1606): **5.18**

Brugnoli, Giorgio. "Dante *Inf.* 30.13 sgg." *L'Alighieri* 7 (1966) 98-99: **1.3**

———. "Orazio." *ED* 4:173-77: **1.34; 5.6**

———. *Per suo richiamo* (Pisa 1981): **1.3**

———. "La tradizione manoscritta di Seneca tragico alla luce delle testimonianze medioevali" (1957). *Atti della Academia Nazionale dei Lincei: Memorie, classe di scienze morali, storiche, e filologiche* 8.8 (Rome 1959): **3.10**

———. "Ut patet per Senecam in suis tragediis." *Rivista di cultura classica e medioevale* 5 (1963) 146-63: **1.3**

———, ed. *Epistle to Cangrade*. Dante, *Opere minori*, vol. 2, ed. P. V. Mengaldo et al. (Florence 1979): **1.2-3, 22; 2.3-4, 18-19, 27; 7.30**

———, ed., with Riccardo Scarcia. Dante, *Le egloghe* (Milan 1980): **1.21**

Buti, Francesco da. *Accessus ad Terentium*. Ed. Alessio (q.v.): **6.64-65**

N.B. Numbers in bold print indicate where each work is cited in the footnotes: e.g., **6.50–52, 55, 60** means "cited above, Chap. 6 nn. 50–52, 55, 60."

———. *Commento sopra la Divina comedia*. Ed. Crescentino Giannini, 3 vols. (Pisa 1858–62): **6.50–52, 55, 60**

Caglio, Anna Maria. "Materiali enciclopedici nelle *Expositiones* di Guido da Pisa," *IMU* 24 (1981) 213–56: **3.10, 12**

Canal, Antonio. *Il mondo morale di Guido da Pisa, interprete di Dante*. Il mondo medievale 8 (Bologna 1981): **3.2, 4; 5.9**

Cangrande, see Epistle to Cangrande

Caplan, Harry. *Of Eloquence*. Ed. Anne King and Helen North (Ithaca N.Y. 1970), pp. 247–70: "A Mediaeval Commentary on the *Rhetorica ad Herennium*": **1.4**

Caricato, Luigi. "Il *Commentarium* all'*Inferno* di Pietro Alighieri: Indagine sulle fonti." *IMU* 26 (1983) 125–50: **4.34; 5.14**

Cassian, John. *Collationes*. PL 49: **5.13**

Coluccia, Rosario. "Due nuove canzoni di Guglielmo Maramauro, rimatore napolitano del sec. xiv." *GSLI* 60 (1983) 161–202: **6.1**

Dante Alighieri. *Comedia*.
—*Inferno*: **1.1, 18–19; 3.33; Appendix 2.4**
—*Purgatorio*: **3.33; Appendix 2.4**
—*Paradiso*: **1.20; 3.33; Appendix 2.4**

———. *Convivio*. Ed G. Busnelli and G. Vandelli, new edition by Antonio Enzo Qualio, 2 vols. (Florence 1964): **1.1; 2.22**

———. *De monarchia*. Ed. Pier Giorgio Ricci (Milan 1965): **2.22–23; 7.30**

———. *De vulgari eloquentia*. Ed. Mengaldo, 1979 (q.v.): **1.7–16; 7.23–25; Appendix 2.5**

———. *Donne ch'avete*: **1.11–12**

———. *Eclogues*. Ed. Giorgio Brugnoli and Riccardo Scarcia (Milan 1980): **1.21**

———. *Vita nova*: **1.11**

De Angelis, Violetta. "Indagine sulle fonte dell'*Elementarium* di Papias, lettera A." *Scripta philologica* 1 (Milan 1977) 117–34: **1.28**

———, ed. Papias, *Elementarium doctrinae rudimentum*, vols. 1-3: *Littera A*. Testi e documenti per lo studio dell'antichità 58.1-3 (Milan 1977–80): **1.28; 5.13**

De Medici, Guiliana. "Le fonti dell'*Ottimo commento* alla *Divina commedia*." *IMU* 26 (1983) 71–123: **4.1**

Della Vedova, Roberto, and Maria Teresa Silvotti (= DVS), transcribers; Egidio Guidubaldi, intro. *Il "Commentarium" di Pietro Alighieri nelle redazioni ashburnhamiana e ottoboniana* (Florence 1978): **4.12, 25–26, 29–30, 33; 5.5, 12, 14**

N.B. Numbers in bold print indicate where each work is cited in the footnotes: e.g., **4.35** means "cited above, Chap. 4 n. 35."

Digestum Iustiniani. Corpus iuris civilis, vol. 1 (Lyons 1550): **4.35**

Donatus, Aelius. *Commentum Terentii.* Ed. Paulus Wessner, vol. 1 (Leipzig 1902, repr. Stuttgart 1962): **1.2, 31; 4.23**

Dronke, Peter. *Dante and Medieval Latin Traditions* (Cambridge 1986): **7.15, 18–19; Appendix 2.1–2**

Encyclopedia dantesca (*ED*), 6 vols. (Rome 1970–78): **1.32, 35; 4.36; 5.6; 6.49, 57; 7.36**

Epistle of Brother Ilaro. Ed. Billanovich (q.v.), pp. 141–44: **6.42, 44–46**

Epistle to Cangrande. Editions: *see* Boffito; Brugnoli; Mancini; Schneider; Toynbee
—Citations:
Cangrande 3.11: **7.33**
Cangrande 4.12–3: **7.21**
Cangrande 5.14: **7.22**
Cangrande 6.17: **2.4**
Cangrande 8.24: **2.8**
Cangrande 8.25: **2.26; 7.4**
Cangrande 9.26: **2.27; 7.8, 13**
Cangrande 10.29: **1.1; 5.1; 7.7, 9, 32**
Cangrande 10.30: **4.19; 5.3; 6.11; 7.11**
Cangrande 10.31: **1.22; 5.7; 7.6**
Cangrande 10.32: **5.8; 7.11**
Cangrande 11.34: **7.5**
Cangrande 12.35: **7.14**
Cangrande 15.39: **2.12**
Cangrande 16.40: **2.14**
Cangrande 16.41: **2.15**
Cangrande 17.42: **2.2**
Cangrande 19.49: **7.30**
Cangrande 19.50: **7.31**
Cangrande 20.54–57: **5.10**
Cangrande 20.56: **7.29**
Cangrande 21.61: **5.10**
Cangrande 22.64–65: **5.10**
Cangrande 28.77: **5.10**
Cangrande 30.85: **5.10**
—For other citations in the text, see pp. 65–68.

Evanthius. *De fabula.* Ed. Giovanni Cupaiuolo (Naples 1979): **1.31; 4.23**

Faral, Edmond. *Les arts poétiques du xii*^{e} *et du xiii*^{e} *siècles* (Paris 1924): **1.6; 4.15**

Fenzi, Enrico. "Boezio e Jean de Meun, Filosofia e Ragione nelle rime allegoriche di Dante." *Studi di filologia e letteratura* 2-3 (Genoa 1975) 9–69: **1.17, 23**

N.B. Numbers in bold print indicate where each work is cited in the footnotes: e.g., **6.2** means "cited above, Chap. 6 n. 2."

Festa, Nicola. *Saggio sull'Africa del Petrarca* (Palermo 1926): **6.2**

Fiammazzo, Antonio, ed. *Il commento dantesco di Graziolo de' Bambaglioli dal "Colombino" di Siviglia con altri codici raffrontato* (Savona 1915): **4.36**

Frasso, Giuseppe. Review of Della Vedova-Silvotti (q.v.). *Aevum* 54 (1980) 381-83: **5.5**

Gallick, Susan. "Medieval Rhetorical Arts in England and the Manuscript Traditions." *Manuscripta* 18 (1974) 67-95: **1.25**

Garland, John of. *Parisiana poetria*. Ed. Lawler (q.v.): **1.23**

Gilbert, Allan H. "Did Dante Dedicate the *Paradiso* to Can Grande della Scala?" *Italica* 43 (1966) 100-24: **2.3**

Goetz, Georg. *Corpus glossariorum latinorum*, vols. 5-6 (Leipzig 1894-99): **1.30**

Gratian. *Decretum*. Ed. Emil Friedberg, *Corpus iuris canonici*, vol. 1 (Leipzig 1879, repr. Graz 1959): **5.14-15, 18-19**

Guido da Pisa. *Expositiones et glose super Comediam Dantis; or, Commentary on Dante's Inferno*. Ed. Vincenzo Cioffari (Albany N.Y. 1974): **1.1; 2.7, 9, 11, 14-15, 18; 3.4-5, 7-10, 13, 15, 17-21; 5.1, 8; 7.4, 6-9, 38**

———. Prologue in the Laurentian MS, ed. Vandelli, 1900-01 (q.v.); pp. 150-57: **2.9, 15; 3.3, 7**

Guizzardo da Bologna. *Recollecte super Poetria magistri Gualfredi* (Vatican MS Ottob. lat. 3291): **1.5**

Haas, Renate. "Chaucer's *Monk's Tale*: An Ingenious Criticism of Early Humanist Conceptions of Tragedy." *Humanistica lovaniensia* 36 (1987) 44-70: **1.38**

Hardie, Colin G. "The *Epistle to Cangrande* Again." *Deutsches Dante-Jahrbuch* 38 (1960) 51-74: **7.2**

———. Preface and bibliographical supplement. Reprint of Paget Toynbee, ed., *Dantis Alagherii Epistolae*, 1920 (Oxford 1966): **2.1**

Herent, Jean de. Gloss to *Laborynthus*. Ed. Faral (q.v.): **1.6**

Hispanus, Laurentius. *Glossa palatina in Gratiani Decretum* (Vatican MS Regin. lat. 977): **5.18**

Hollander, Robert. "Tragedia nella *Commedia*." Hollander, *Il Virgilio dantesco* (Florence 1983), pp. 117-54: **1.22; 3.25; 6.53**

———. "Tragedy in Dante's *Comedy*. *Sewanee Review* 91 (1983) 240-60: **1.22; 3.25; 6.53**

———. "The Tragedy of Divination in *Inferno* 20." Hollander, *Studies in Dante* (Ravenna 1980), pp. 131-218: **1.22; 3.25; 6.53**

N.B. Numbers in bold print indicate where each work is cited in the footnotes: e.g., **1.36–37; 3.11** means "cited above, Chap. 1 nn. 36–37, and Chap. 3 n. 11."

Horace. *Ars poetica*: **1.36–37; 3.11; 4.15–16, 29; 5.3–5, 8**

———. ———, variants: ed. Otto Keller, *Opera Horatii* (Leipzig 1869): **5.4**

———. *Epistle 1*: **3.13**

Hugh of St. Victor (attributed). *Miscellanea*. PL 177: **5.13**

Huguccio of Pisa. *Magne derivationes*. Oxford Bodleian MS Laud Misc. 626: **1.1, 27, 33; 4.13, 21, 32; 5.2, 17**

———. *Summa super Gratiani Decreto*. Vatican MS lat. 2280 and Admont MS 7: **5.16**

Ianucci, Amilcare A. "Dante's Theory of Genres and the *Divina commedia*." *Dante Studies* 91 (1973) 1–25: **1.22**

Isidore of Seville. *Etymologiae*: **1.29, 31–32; 3.6; 4.15, 30; 5.19; 6.25**

Jacopo Alighieri. *Chiose alla cantica dell'Inferno*. Ed. Jarro, i.e., G. Picini (Florence 1915): **3.28**

James the Greek of Venice. Translation of Aristotle's *Metaphysics*. Ed. Vuillemin-Diem (q.v.): **2.21, 23**

Janson, Tore. *Prose Rhythm in Medieval Latin from the Ninth to the Thirteenth Century*. Studia latina stockholmiensia 20 (Stockholm 1975): **Appendix 2.2**

Jenaro-MacLennan, Luis. "'Remissus est modus et humilis' (*Epistle to Cangrande*, § 10)." *Lettere italiane* 31 (1979) 406–18: **1.4; 4.21**

———. *The Trecento Commentaries on the Divina commedia and the Epistle to Cangrande* (Oxford 1974): **2.4–5, 10; 3.1, 6, 22, 26; 4.4, 12–13, 15, 20–22, 24; 6.27**

Jerome, Saint. *Commentary on Zechariah*: **5.15**

Kelly, Henry Ansgar. "Aristotle-Averroes-Alemannus on Tragedy: The Influence of the *Poetics* on the Latin Middle Ages." *Viator* 10 (1979) 161–209: **1.5, 29, 38; 3.16, 27; 4.6; 6.18–19, 22**

———. "Chaucer and Shakespeare on Tragedy." *Leeds Studies in English* 20 (1989): **6.8**

———. Review of Woods (q.v.). *Manuscripta* 32 (1988) 54–58: **7.12**

———. "Tragedy and the Performance of Tragedy in Late Roman Antiquity." *Traditio* 35 (1979) 21–44: **1.29**

Lactantius. *Divinae institutiones*: **1.29**

Lana, Jacopo della. *Commento alla Comedia di Dante*, Ed. Luciano Scarabelli, 2d. ed. (Bologna 1866): **3.23–24**

Lancia, Andrea. *0 Ottimo commento*. Described by Bellomo, "Primi appunti" (q.v.): **4.1–2**

N.B. Numbers in bold print indicate where each work is cited in the footnotes: e.g., **4.3** means "cited above, Chap. 4 n.3."

———. *1 Ottimo commento: L'Ottimo commento della Divina commedia*. Ed. A. Torri, 3 vols. (Pisa 1827–29): **4.3**

———. *2 Ottimo commento*, Prologue. Ed. Scarabelli in his edition of Lana (q.v.): **4.4–5, 7; 6.27**

———. *3 Ottimo commento*, Proem. Ed. Giuseppe Vandelli, "Una nuova redazione dell'*Ottimo*." *SD* 14 (1930) 93–174: **4.8, 10–11**

Lawler, Traugott, ed. *The Parisiana poetria of John of Garland*. Yale Studies in English 182 (New Haven 1974): **1.23–25**

Liber glossarum, Ed. Georg Goetz, *Corpus glossarum*, vol. 5 (Leipzig 1894): **1.30**

Lindholm, Gudrun. *Studien zum mittellateinischen Prosarhythmus: Seine Entwicklung und sein Abklingen in der Briefliteratur Italiens*. Studia latina stockholmiensia 10 (Stockholm 1963): **Appendix 2.3**

Mancini, Augusto. "Un nuovo codice dell'*Epistola a Can Grande*." *SD* 24 (1939) 111–22: **2.1**

Manuscripts:

Admont (Austria). Monastic Library. MS 7 (Huguccio, *Summa super Decreto*): **5.16**

Florence. Biblioteca Laurenziana. Ashburn. 839 (2 Benvenuto): **6.17, 20, 23–25, 29**

———. ———. Ashburn. 841 (2 Pietro): **4.12, 25–29; 5.5, 21**

———. ———. Plut. 40.38 (1 Pietro): **5.4**

———. ———. Plut. 90 sup. 118 (1 Pietro): **5.4**

———. Biblioteca Nazionale Centrale. Panciatichiano 4 (1 Pietro): **5.4**

———. Biblioteca Riccardiana. MS 1075 (1 Pietro): **5.4**

Isola Bella. Archivio e Biblioteca di Palazzo Borromeo. Borromeo L.ii 54 (Maramauro, *Commentario all'Inferno*): **6.1–5**

Oxford. Bodleian Library. Laud Misc. 626 (Huguccio, *Magne derivationes*): **1.27, 33; 5.17**

Vatican City. Biblioteca Apostolica. Barb. lat. 4007 (1 Pietro): **5.4**

———. ———. Barb. lat. 4029 (2 Pietro): **4.25–29; 5.5, 21**

———. ———. Barb. lat. 4098 (1 Pietro): **5.4**

———. ———. Capponi 176 (1 Pietro): **5.4**

———. ———. Lat. 1367 (Iohannes Teutonicus, *Glossa in Decretum*): **5.18**

———. ———. Lat. 2280 (Huguccio, *Summa super Decreto*): **5.16**

———. ———. Lat. 4782 (1 Pietro): **5.4**

———. ———. Ottob. lat. 2231 (Papias): **1.28–32**

———. ———. Ottob. lat. 2867 (3 Pietro): **4.12, 30–33**

———. ———. Ottob. lat. 3291 (Guizzardo, *Super Poetria nova*): **1.5**

———. ———. Regin. lat. 977 (Laurentius Hispanus, *Glossa palatina in Decretum*): **5.18**

Maramauro, Guglielmo. *Commentario all'Inferno*. Isola Bella: Archivio e Biblioteca di Palazzo Borromeo, MS Borromeo L.ii 54: **6.1–5; 7.38**

N.B. Numbers in bold print indicate where each work is cited in the footnotes: e.g., **4.15** means "cited above, Chap. 4 n. 15."

Matthew of Vendôme. *Ars versificatoria*. Ed. Faral (q.v.): **4.15**

Mazzoni, Francesco. "Anonimo Fiorentino." *ED* 1:291-92: **6.57**

———. "Francesco di Bartolo da Buti." *ED* 3:23–27: **6.49**

———. "Per l'*Epistola a Cangrande*." *Studi in onore di Angelo Monteverdi* (Modena 1959): **5.10**

Mengaldo, Pier Vincenzo. "L'elegia 'umile' (*DVE* 2, 4, 5–6)" (1966), revised in his *Linguistica e retorica di Dante* (Pisa 1978), pp. 200–22: **1.4, 11, 23, 32; 3.27**

———. "Stili." *ED* 5:435–38: **1.32**

———, ed. Dante, *De vulgari eloquentia* (1968): Introduction, as revised in *Linguistica e retorica di Dante* (Pisa 1978), pp. 11-123: **1.40**

———, ed. *De vulgari eloquentia*. Dante, *Opere minori*, vol. 2, ed. Mengaldo et al. (Milan 1979), pp. 1-237: **1.7, 23**

Metricam siquidem artem. Ed. Thurot (q.v.): **1.39**

Minio-Paluello, Lorenzo. "Dante's Reading of Aristotle." *The World of Dante*, ed. Cecil Grayson (Oxford 1980), pp. 61-80: **2.22**

Minnis, Alastair. "Aspects of the Medieval French and English Traditions of the *De consolatione Philosophiae*." *Boethius*, ed. Margaret Gibson (Oxford 1981), pp. 312–61: **3.14**

Moerbeke, William of. Translation of Aristotle, *Metaphysica*. Ed. Spiazzi (*see* Aquinas): **2.20, 23**

Mombrizio, Bonino, ed. *Papias vocabulista* (Venice 1496, repr. Turin 1966, with later supplement from edition of Milan 1476): **1.28, 30–31**

Montano, Rocco. *Lo spirito e le lettere: Disegno storico della letteratura italiana*, vol. 1 (Milan 1970): **1.22**

Mussato, Albertino. *Lucii Annei Senece cordubensis vita et mores*. Ed. Anastasios Megas, Ὁ προουμανιστικὸς κύκλος τῆς πάδουας (Lovato Lovati—Albertino Mussato) καὶ οἱ τραγῳδίες τοῦ *L. S. Seneca* (Salonica 1967), pp. 154–61: **4.6**

Nannucci, Vincenzo, ed. *Petri Allegherii super Dantis ipsius genitoris Comoediam commentarium* (Florence 1845 and 1846): **4.12–18; 5.4–5, 14, 20**

Nardi, Bruno. "Osservazioni sul medievale *accessus ad auctores* in rapporto all'*Epistola a Cangrande*" (1961), reprinted in his *Saggi e note di critica dantesca* (Milan 1966), pp. 268–305: **5.11**

———. *Il punto sull'Epistola a Cangrande* (Florence 1960): **5.11**

Novem requiruntur. Ed. Alessio (q.v.), pp. 94–101: **1.2; 4.23; 6.62**

Opusculum de accentibus. Cit. Thurot (q.v.): **1.39**

N.B. NUMBERS IN BOLD PRINT INDICATE WHERE EACH WORK IS CITED IN THE FOOTNOTES: E.G., **Appendix 2.2** MEANS "CITED ABOVE, APPENDIX 2 N. 2."

Orlandi, Giovanni. Review of Janson (q.v.). *Studi medievali* 3.19 (1978) 701–18: **Appendix 2.2**

Osbern of Gloucester. *Derivationes*. Ed. Angelo Mai, *Thesaurus novus latinitatis*. Classici auctores e vaticanis codicibus editi 8 (Rome 1836): **6.26**

Ottimo commento. *See* Lancia, Andrea

Ovid. *Amores*: **1.38**

Oxford English Dictionary: **2.17**

Padoan, Giorgio, ed. Boccaccio, *Esposizioni sopra la comedia di Dante. Tutte le opere*, vol. 6 (Milan 1965): **2.4**

Paolazzi, Carlo. "Le letture dantesche di Benvenuto da Imola a Bologna e a Ferrara e le redazioni del suo *Comentum*." *IMU* 22 (1979) 319-66: **6.17, 29, 33**

———. "Petrarca, Boccaccio, e il *Trattatello in laude di Dante*." *SD* 55 (1983) 165-249: **6.37-38**

Papias. *Elementarium doctrinae rudimentum*. Vatican MS Ottob. lat. 2231: **1.28-32: 4.13, 21; 5.13**

———. ———. Editions: *see* De Angelis; Mombrizio

Paratore, Ettore. "L'eredità classica in Dante" (1965), revised in his *Tradizione e struttura in Dante* (Florence 1968), pp. 55–121: **7.1**

Petrarch, Francis. *Africa*: **6.2**

———. *Familiares res*. Ed. Umberto Bosco, *Le familiari*, vol. 4 (Florence 1942): **6.35–36**

———. *Invective contra medicum*, book 3. Ed. and trans. Pier Giorgio Ricci. Petrarch, *Prose*. Ed. Guido Martellotti et al. (Milan 1955), pp. 648–693: **1.38**

Pietro Alighieri. 1 Pietro. Ed. Nannucci (q.v.): **4.12–17; 5.4–5, 14, 20; 6.7**

———. ———. Manuscripts cited: *see* Manuscripts

———. 2 Pietro. Florence, Bibl. Laur. MS Ashburn. 841; Vatican MS Barb. lat. 4029: **4.12, 25–29; 5.5, 21**

———. 3 Pietro. Vatican MS Ottob. lat. 2867: **4.12, 30–33; 5.2, 4–5, 12, 21**

Pisoni, Pier Giacomo. "Guglielmo Maramauro, commentatore di Dante e amico del Petrarca." *Studi petrarcheschi* n.s. 1 (1984) 253–55: **6.1–2**

———. Transcription of Maramauro, *Commentario* (q.v.): **6.3–5**

Placidus. *Glossae*. Ed. J. W. Pirie and W. M. Lindsay, *Glossaria latina*, vol. 4 (Paris 1930, repr. 1965): **1.31; 6.54**

Quadlbauer, Franz. *Die antike Theorie der Genera dicendi im lateinischen Mittelalter* (Vienna 1962): **1.4**

N.B. Numbers in bold print indicate where each work is cited in the footnotes: e.g., **6.61** means "cited above, Chap. 6 n. 61."

Reeve, M. D., and R. H. Rouse. "New Light on the Transmission of Donatus's *Commentum Terentii.*" *Viator* 9 (1978) 235–49: **6.61**

Rhetorica ad Herennium: **4.21**

Ricci, Pier Giorgio, ed. Boccaccio, *Trattatello in laude di Dante. Tutte le opere*, vol. 3 (Milan 1974): **2.24; 7.13**

Rosciate, Alberigo da. *Commentarii in Digestum*, 2 vols. (Venice 1585, repr. Bologna 1974–77): **4.35**

———. Introduction to his Latin translation of Lana. Ed. Antonio Fiammazzo, *Il commento dantesca di Graziolo de' Bambaglioli* (Savona 1915): **4.36**

Sandkühler, Bruno. *Die frühen Dantekommentare und ihr Verhältnis zur mittelalterlichen Kommentartraditionen* (Munich 1967): **4.36**

Sapegno, Natalino. *Storia letteraria del Trecento* (Milan 1963): **1.22**

Schneider, Friedrich. *Die Handschriften des Briefes Dantes an Can Grande della Scala* (Zwickau 1933): **2.1**

Scott, J. A. Review of Jenaro-Maclennan, *Trecento* (q.v.). *Modern Language Review* 71 (1976) 932–34: **4.21**

Teutonicus, Iohannes. *Glossa in Gratiani Decretum*. Vatican MS lat. 1367: **5.18**

Thurot, Charles. *Notices et extraits de divers manuscrits latins pour servir à l'histoire des doctrines grammaticales au moyen âge*. Notices et extraits des manuscrits de la Bibliothèque Impériale et autres bibliothèques 22.2 (Paris 1868): **1.39**

Toynbee, Paget. "The Bearing of the *Cursus* on the Text of Dante's *De vulgari eloquentia*" (14 March 1923). *Proceedings of the British Academy* 10 (1921–23) 359–77: **7.17, 19**

———. "Dante and the *Cursus*: A New Argument in Favor of the Authenticity of the *Quaestio de aqua et terra*," *Modern Language Review* 13 (1918) 420–30. Expanded as Appendix C: "Dante and the *Cursus*" in his edition, *Dantis Alagherii Epistolae* (Oxford 1920), pp. 224–47: **7.16**

———. "Dante's Latin Dictionary," Toynbee, *Dante Studies and Researches* (London 1902), pp. 97–114: **1.26–27**

———, ed. *Epistle to Cangrande. Dantis Alagherii Epistolae*, ed. Toynbee (Oxford 1920, repr. with additions by Colin Hardie, Oxford 1966), pp. 166–211: **2.1; 7.21**

Vallone, Aldo. "Buti nella critica dantesca del Trecento." *Accademie e biblioteche d'Italia* 45 (1977) 422–37: **6.49, 60**

Vandelli, Giuseppe. Review article. *Bullettino della Società Dantesca Italiana* n.s. 8 (1900–01) 137–64: **2.4, 9, 15; 3.3, 7**

N.B. NUMBERS IN BOLD PRINT INDICATE WHERE EACH WORK IS CITED IN THE FOOTNOTES: E.G., **4.8, 10** MEANS "CITED ABOVE, CHAP. 4 NN. 8, 10."

———. "Una nuova redazione dell'*Ottimo*." *SD* 14 (1930) 93–174: **4.8, 10**

Villa, Claudia. *La lectura Terentii*, vol. 1: *Da Ildemaro a Francesco Petrarca*. Studi sul Petrarca 17 (Padua 1984): **1.2; 6.7**

———. "Un'ipotesi per l'*Epistola a Cangrande*." *IMU* 24 (1981) 18–63: **1.2**

Villani, Filippo. *Il commento al primo canto dell'Inferno*. Ed. Giuseppe Cugnoni (Città di Castella 1896): **7.35, 37–41**

———. *De vita et moribus Dantis poete comici insignis*. Ed. Angelo Solerti, *Le vite di Dante, Petrarca, e Boccaccio* (Milan [1904–5]), pp. 82–90: **7.42–43**

Vincent of Beauvais. *Speculum historiale*: **3.10**

Vuillemin-Diem, Gudrun. "Untersuchungen zu Wilhelm von Moerbekes Metaphysikübersetzung." *Studien zur mittelalterlichen Geistesgeschichte und ihren Quellen*, ed. Albert Zimmermann and G. Vuillemin-Diem. Miscellanea mediaevalia 15 (Berlin 1982), pp. 102–208: **2.20**

———, ed. Aristotle, *Metaphysica: Translatio Anonyma sive "Media."* Aristoteles latinus 25.2 (Leiden 1976): **2.20**

———, ed. Aristotle, *Metaphysica: Translatio Iacobi*. Aristoteles latinus 25.1 (Brussels 1970): **2.21**

Woods, Marjorie Curry, ed. *An Early Commentary on the Poetria nova of Geoffrey of Vinsauf* (New York 1985): **7.12**

Zaccaria, Vittorio. Introduction to Boccaccio, *De casibus virorum illustrium*, ed. Pier Giorgio Ricci and V. Zaccaria. *Tutte le opere*, vol. 9 (Milan 1983): **6.8**

General Index

N.B. Modern scholars are only selectively indexed here. FOR A COMPLETE INDEXING OF SECONDARY SOURCES, SEE THE BIBLIOGRAPHICAL INDEX TO THE FOOTNOTES.